ENGLISH MEDIAEVAL LAPIDARIES

EARLY ENGLISH TEXT SOCIETY

Original Series, No. 190

1933 (for 1932 ; reprinted 1960)

Price 20s.

ENGLISH MEDIAEVAL LAPIDARIES

by

JOAN EVANS, D.Litt., D.Lit.

and

MARY S. SERJEANTSON, M.A., D.Phil.

Published for

THE EARLY ENGLISH TEXT SOCIETY

by the

OXFORD UNIVERSITY PRESS

LONDON   NEW YORK   TORONTO

OXFORD
UNIVERSITY PRESS

Great Clarendon Street, Oxford OX2 6DP
United Kingdom

Oxford University Press is a department of the University of Oxford.
It furthers the University's objective of excellence in research, scholarship,
and education by publishing worldwide. Oxford is a registered trade mark of
Oxford University Press in the UK and in certain other countries

First Edition published in 1933 (for 1932)
Reprinted 1960

Published in the United States of America by Oxford University Press
198 Madison Avenue, New York, NY 10016, United States of America

British Library Cataloguing in Publication Data
Data available

Library of Congress Cataloging in Publication Data
Data available

Original Series, 190

ISBN 978-0-85-991925-8

TO THE MEMORY OF
PAUL STUDER
Sometime Taylorian Professor of Romance Languages
in the University of Oxford

PREFACE

OUR thanks are due to the Chapter of Peterborough Cathedral for the communication of a manuscript in their possession and the permission to publish it; and to the officials of the Manuscript Room of the British Museum and of the Bodleian Library.

Miss E. A. Francis and Dr. and Mrs. Charles Singer have been so kind as to help us on points of detail.

J. E.
M. S. S.

CONTENTS

INTRODUCTION

PRECIOUS stones have figured much in literature, because of their beauty, their symbolic significance, and their supposed virtues. In this book we are concerned only with treatises that deal with the last of these aspects.

The ascription of such virtues to precious stones is older than written history; and treatises on them were composed by classical authors alike in Greece and Rome. This tradition was summed up for the Middle Ages in the writings of St. Isidore, Bishop of Seville, in the early seventh century, and of Marbode, Bishop of Rennes between 1067 and 1081. Isidore describes the stones in detail and distinguishes many varieties of them, but lays little stress on their magical virtues; Marbode describes only some sixty stones, but gives a full account of the virtues ascribed to them in preceding lapidaries. From these two sources the main stream of the mediaeval tradition of the virtues of stones is derived.

The remarkable popularity of lapidaries in England during the Middle Ages remains one of the curiosities of mediaeval literature. The earliest known vernacular lapidary of Western Europe is the Old English example which comes first in our collection; thirteen Anglo-Norman lapidaries have come down to us in a complete or fragmentary state, of which three at least go back to the first half of the twelfth century; and we have found six lapidaries of the fifteenth century and one of the sixteenth written in English. Further, a considerable number of the surviving manuscripts of the Latin lapidaries of the Middle Ages appear to have been written in England.[1] Wonder-working stones, too, play a part in literature of English origin; they figure alike in the *De Laudibus Divinae Sapientiae*, in the *De Naturis Rerum* of Alexander Neckam, and in

[1] See Joan Evans, *Magical Jewels*, Oxford, 1922, p. 21; p. 33, note 2; pp. 64, 70, 81, 83, 92.

the *De Proprietatibus Rerum* of Bartholomaeus Anglicus.[1] Interest in them survived into the seventeenth century, in which manuscript lapidaries were still compiled,[2] and literary allusions to the virtues of stones were still not infrequent.

The lapidaries we publish here are derived from such sources as might be expected. The Old English Lapidary draws its account of gems from Isidore and from Bede's glosses on the apocalyptic stones, and has little to say of their virtues. The fifteenth and sixteenth century lapidaries are all derived from French or Anglo-Norman sources, enriched, in the case of the Peterborough Lapidary, with considerable borrowings from Bartholomaeus Anglicus and other contemporary English lapidaries. We have not found the exact source of the Ashmole Lapidary, but it is in the same stream of tradition as the rest.

We cannot, therefore, claim any originality of thought for the texts which we publish here; but they have a certain linguistic interest, and in any case represent a literary genre remarkably characteristic of Mediaeval England.[3]

---

[1] The lapidary attributed to Sir John Mandeville is not by him. See Pannier, *Les lapidaires français*, p. 201; Evans, op. cit., p. 66.

[2] See ibid., pp. 147-150.

[3] We have included Richardoune's verses as illustrating the influence of the lapidaries upon literature of another kind.

ENGLISH MEDIAEVAL LAPIDARIES

MS.

A. Eleventh century. B. M. Cott. Tiberius A III.
B. Early fifteenth century. Bodleian Douce 291.
C. Fifteenth century. Bodleian Add. A 106.
D. Late fifteenth century. Bodleian Ashmole 1447.
E. Late fifteenth century. B. M. Add. 34360.
F. Late fifteenth century. Peterborough Cathedral 33.
G. Late sixteenth century. B. M. Sloane 2628.

THE MANUSCRIPTS

A. MS. COTTON TIBERIUS A III

THE eleventh century quarto volume which contains the earliest English Lapidary is described in Wanley's Catalogue, and a detailed list of the contents, Latin and English, is given by Dr. Logeman in his edition of the Rule of St. Benet from this MS. (E.E.T.S. 90.) The MS. is made up of 178 folios in various hands, and includes the interlinear Old English version of Ælfric's Colloquy. The Lapidary itself has been published by R. V. Fleischhacker (*Ein altenglischer Lapidar*, in *Zeitschrift für deutsches Altertum*, xxxiv, 1890, p. 229). We have collated his transcription with the text.

The hand in which the Lapidary is written is fairly large, and for the most part very distinct. The heading is in red, as are also the initial capitals. These initials have evidently been added after the completion of the text; each stands strikingly far from the rest of the word; in two instances the capital has been omitted.

The language is late West Saxon, with few divergencies from the normal. Smoothing appears in *ehtoþa, lece, wexseð, wexsendan*, but the diphthong remains in *gefeohtan*. OE. *ȳ* is unrounded in *gildene, dri(cræftum)*. The form *derwyrðan* (<*dēor-*) seems to be an early example of the monophthongization of *ēo* to *ē*, rare in the eleventh century, particularly in a southern text (see Luick, *Histor. Gram.*, §357, Anm. 1). Confusion between *e* and *æ* is seen only in the unstressed syllable of *oþær*.

B   I

B. DOUCE 291

First half of fifteenth century. Parchment. 146 leaves. 10⅝" × 7½". The lapidary is contained in ff. 121-135. Preceding it in the volume is a translation of the *Epitome* *rei militaris* of Vegetius, made, as stated in the colophon, 'at þe ordenaunce & biddynge of þe worþi & worschipfull Lord Sire Thomas of Berkeley. . . . Ðe turnynge of þis book into Englische was writen & ended in þe vigile of alle halewes the ʒeer of oure lord mcccc & viij.' The lapidary is in a different but contemporary hand, very clear and legible. A few capitals are illuminated; others, usually at the beginning of paragraphs, are touched in with red.

The dialect is that of London in the fifteenth century, and there are few remarkable features. (In the following notes, references are to folios.)

Vowels

OE. *æ* is regularly *a*: *after* 123; *what* 121; *water(e)* 122v, 124; etc.

OE. *an* appears as *an* (when unlengthened): *man* 123v; *many* 121; *name* 123; etc., etc.

OE. *y̆* is usually *i*, *y*; *u* occurs once, *e* in a few forms only: *muchel* 132v; *berstille*, 'bristle,' 128v; *euel* 135v²; *whech* 121; *swech* 132; *fire* 129v, 133v, 134, 135; *hide* 122v; *hyde* 127; *kynde* 133²; *first(e)* 121v, 122, etc.; *kysse* 132v; *synne* 122v; *synner* 121; *thriste* 127v; etc.

OE. *ĕah* (L. Saxon *eh*) appears in one form as *eih*: *feighten*, '(they) fight,' 124v². (See Jordan, *M.E. Gram.* §63.)

OE. *ēag*, *ēah* appear as *ey*, *igh*: *eye* 124, 124v, 135; *eyen* 125v, 127, 129v, 130v, 134²; *high* 123, 125v; *highnesse* 128.

OE. *ēa-i* is *e* in *herde* 122.

OE. *ĕo* is regularly *e*: *breest* 123; *breste* 121v; *preest* 122v; *thefe* 133; *thre* 126v; *hert*, 'heart,' 124v; *ben* 124v.

Vowel-lengthening (before -*st*?) is shown in *geestis*, 'guests,' 122v; vowel-shortening (in comparatives) in *grettir* 124v; *sonner* 126, 133v; *whitter* 131; also in *grettist* 124.   A form with apparent monophthongization and shortening is *solle*, 'soul,' 124.

Unstressed *-e* usually remains *e*, but *i* (*y*) is fairly common: *clepid* 121; *gladith* 127; *colith* 123; *clerkis* 121; *rotis* 121; *geestis* 122v; *werkys* 124.

CONSONANTS

The only forms of interest seem to be (*a*) the spelling *whoole*, 'whole,' with development of *w* before *hō-*. (See Wyld, *Hist. Coll. Eng.*, p. 307). (*b*) The form *shewith*, 'follows,' 127v (M.E. *sewen*) with *sh* from initial [sj] (ibid., p. 293).

ACCIDENCE

a. PRONOUNS

The feminine singular pronoun is *she*, Poss. and Acc. *her*. The plural pronoun of the third person is as follows: Nom. *thei, þei;* Acc. *hem;* Poss. *þeir(e)*.

b. NOUNS

An interesting strong plural in place of the usual weak form is seen in *oxes* 127.

c. VERBS

The verbal inflexions are South Midland in character.

The Present Participle always ends in *-yng(e)*: *fleynge* 124; *growyng* 123v; *lastynge* 123; *rennyng* 124, etc.

The Past Participle has the prefix *y-* rarely in Weak Verbs (*y-armed* 124; *y-honored* 130; *ytouched* 125v), but never in Strong Verbs. The latter (in the P.P.) end in -(*e*)*n* more frequently than in *-e*: *bounden* 126v; *borne* 128v, 133v; *founden* 124v, 125, 126; *knowen* 132v; *leyn* 129v, 132v; *spoken* 131v, 132; etc. Cf. *corue* 123; *founde* 125, 126v; *shape* 126, 129v; *sowe* 133v; *take* 135; etc.

Present Indicative Third Singular. The usnal ending is *-th*: *hath* 121; *beleueth* 121; *maketh* 122; *telleth* 122v, etc. Two examples of contracted forms occur: *fynt*, 'finds,' 131v; *withholte* 127.

The Plural Present usually ends in *-n*; both *-eth* and *-e* occur rarely: *comforteþ* 125; *preyeth* 122v; *putteth* 125; *seith*

129; *fynde* 125, 127v; *haue* 124²; *helpe* 125; *take* 125. Cf. *beholden* 123v; *beren* 124v; *commen* 124; *kepen* 124; *lyven* 123; *taken* 124.

The only -*es* ending occurs in the Imperative Plural *wittes* 124.

The Plural of the verb *be* is *arne* or *ben*, rarely *be*.

C.   BODLEY ADD. A 106

Fifteenth century. 295 leaves. 8½″×6½″. Paper, except for three parchment leaves at the beginning and two at the end. The binding is contemporary, and consists of brown leather on boards, fastened with a leather thong. The volume contains six MSS., mostly medical recipes and religious poems. The lapidary, which begins on f. 44 and covers seventeen folios, has been wrongly bound up; the MS. breaks off at the end of f. 47v, another MS., in a different hand, follows, beginning on f. 48, and the lapidary is continued on ff. 126-136.

The dialect is that of the North Midlands, possibly the southern border of Yorkshire. There are no distinctively Eastern or Western features. It is noticeable that OE. *ō* appears regularly as *u*, but OE. *ā* as *o*, with only one certain example of *a* (*stanes* 129v); OE. *āw* is represented by both *aw* and *ow*. OE. *an*, *am* (without lengthening) has remained, except in *mony* by the side of *many*. OE. *ȳ* appears as *i*, *y*, except in *euyl*[1]; OE. *ēo* as *e*. The inflexions are Northern; the P. P. very rarely has the *i*- prefix; the Pres. Part. has usually -*yng*, but sometimes -*and*. The ending of the third Sing. Pres. is -*es*; the same ending is used in the Plural, together with -*e*, and rarely -*eth*, -*yn*. The Fem. Pron. Nom. is *scho*; the Plural Pron. (third pers.) is *yai*, *yar*, *yer*; *yam*,[2] and once *ham*.

The following summary includes all the important features of the language of the text.

---

[1] A curious mistake occurs on f. 129v, where the MS. has *boghte*, 'bought,' instead of *beys*, 'are.' Does this imply a South-eastern original, with *beyþ*, 'buys'?

[2] *þ* is indistinguishable from *y* in this text.

Vowels

a. STRESSED

E.M.E. *a* is usually *a*, but *e* appears in several instances, possibly indicating L.M.E. fronting to *æ* (see Wyld, *Hist. Coll. Eng.*, p. 198): *efter* 129v, 130, 131v², 134v, 136; *efterward* 45v; *gederers* 44; (*thonder*)*clepe* 134; *wesch*(*e*) 124, 135, 136. An inverted spelling (*a* for *e*) is seen in *wader*, 'weather,' 130.

E.M.E. *a* + nasal (final or before vowel): *an, am*, except in *mony* (44v, 45v², 126, 126v, 128; but also *many* 44³, 126, 126v); cf. *man* 44v, 45v, 46, etc.; *name*(*s*) 45², 126; *namly* 46, 127.

O.E. *ā*: Once *a*, *stanes* 129v; otherwise *o*: *stones* 44⁴, 44v⁶, etc.; *lond* 146, 147v; *hole* 129v; *one* 46v, 47; *behold* 47; etc. Cf. also *halsom*, with early shortening.

O.E. *āw* appears as *aw, au*, and as *ow*: *awn* 134v; *knaw* 46, 46v, 135v; *saule* 46v; cf. *know* 126, 128v.

O.E. *ǣ*¹ (W. Gmc. *ā*) appears as *e*, except in *war*(*e*), vb., which is probably from O.N., without rounding of *ā*.

M.E. *ĕ*. There are several instances in which *e* is raised to *i* before a point consonant: *bytter*, 'better,' 125; *forgytt*, 133; *syttes*, 'sets,' 126v; *defyneʒ*, 'defence,' 131.

M.E. *er*. A change from *er* to *ar* appears in the following forms: *hard* (P.P.) 45v, 129; *warkes* 46v, 130v; *warld* 45v, 47v, 125, 127, 127v, 133.

M.E. *wo*. The northern unrounding of *o* in the group *wol-* is seen in *wald*, 'would,' 46², 124v.

M.E. *ō* is very commonly *u*, especially before *k*. This probably represents the northern fronting and raising of *ō*. Forms with *o* occur also. Cf. *buk*(*e*) 44³, 44v, 46³, 47, 124v; *bukes* 44; *luk*(*e*) 46, 135v; *lukes* 125, 125v; *gud* 46³, 46v, 47³, etc.; *blod* 125, 126, 127, 128v, 133; *blody* 134; *fote* 124; *god* 46; *lokes* 125; *most* 127v; *mot* 47, 127; *mone* 133v, *sothly* 134; *þe toþer* 44v, 130v, 131, etc.; *oþer* 124, 131, 131v, etc.

O.E. *ȳ* appears as *i, y*, except in *euyl*(*e*), in which the E.M.E. vowel (*i*) was lengthened, lowered and made tense in an open syllable: *euyl* 126, 130v; *euyl* 124v, 130v; cf.

byinge, 'buying,' 131; *dirk(e),* 'dark,' 124, 133 (see Jordan: *M.E. Gram.* §66, Anm. 2); *dirknes* 47v²; *fyr(e)* 129, 136²; *first* 126, 128v; *fyrst* 45³, 45v, 47, etc.; *hydes* 125v; *hyd* 126; *hydyd* 126; *lift* 127v; *mynd* 125, 127, 128; *syn* 127v; *synn* 44v², 128; *synes* 127; *thrist,* 'thirst,' 132.

O.E. *ēag, ēah* appears in three forms: (i) without diph-thongization: *ee,* 'eye,' 46v, 47; (ii) with diphthongization in inflected form: *eyn* 135; (iii) with raising to *ī: yen* 135v³.

O.E. *ēo* is invariably *e: dep* 125v; *erth* 126²; *heuen,* pas-sim. The western *u* never appears.

Shortening of long vowels is exemplified by a number of forms, and is particularly common before a point con-sonant; it also occurs before *p, f: oppyn* 'open' 44v; *theffes* 'thieves' 135v; *theffeʒ* 132v²; *byttyng* 'biting' 126v; *colleʒ* 'coals' 132v; *ett* 'eat' 133v³; *fruttes* 134v; *helles* 'heals' 46v, 132v, 135; *kell* 'to cool' 124v; *kelles* 126; *laddes* 'ladies' 126; *lesse* 'lose' 130; *smyttes* 128v²; *spreddes* 47v; *stell* 'steal' 124v, 130v; *watter* 46v, 124. In some of these cases shor-tening is due to inflectional forms containing consonant groups; in others probably to the influence of the following consonant.

b. UNSTRESSED VOWELS

Unstressed *e* is usually so written, but *y* is fairly common: *louyd* 45; *schapyd* 46v; *betokynnes* 46v; *deuyll* 128; *stepys* 128; *dolyuerys* 126; etc., etc. The ending *-us* is used once only: *purpusus* 131v.

Unstressed *u* in *upon* is always *a: apon* 45, 46v, 124v, etc.; *appon* 45v, 46v, 124, 125, etc.

The spelling *awnges* 'anguish' probably illustrates the development of Fr. *oi* (AN. *ui*) in an unstressed syllable.

a. SUBSTITUTION   CONSONANTS

The Northern change of [sχ] to [s] in an unstressed word is seen in *suld* 'should' 44v⁵; *sal* 'shall' 45v³, by the side of *shuld,* etc. (see Jordan, *M.E. Gram.* §183).

The development of a lip-cons. for a back open cons. appears only in *þof* 'though' 133.

b. LOSS

The only form which, if genuine, shows a definite consonantal loss is *hodes* 'holds' 127.

c. ADDITION

Addition of final cons. is rare: *þand* 'than' 124; *thurght* 'through' 45, 45v, 47v, 124, 124v; *thrught* 135.

ACCIDENCE

a. PRONOUNS

The Feminine Pronoun is the Northern *scho*, 125, 132², 132v.

The Plural Pronoun of the Third Person is as follows: Nom. *þai* 44v, 45, 46v, etc.; Poss. *þar* 45v, 47, 132; *þer* 46v², 130v²; Acc. *þam* 47², 47v⁴, 125, 126, *etc.*; *ham* 129v. The stressed form of the Acc. occurs in *þaimself*.

The Definite Article is *þe* throughout, except in the forms *þe toþer* 44v, *þe toder* 132, in which the O.E. Neuter form survives. The Plural of the Demonstrative 'those' is *tho* 44v², 45, 47.

Occasional irregularities occur in the use of the Indefinite Article *a* before a vowel: *a Aungell* 45; *a emeraud* 46v. Note also, with wrong syllable division: *a nost* 45v; *a nox* 126; *a neuyl woman* 132v.

b. NOUNS

There is little to remark with regard to the declension of Nouns in this text. Weak Plurals are very rare, the only examples being *eyn* 46, 47v, 132v; *oxen* 126. The Possessive form *is* occurs three times: *a man is eyn* 46; *a man is nayle* 128; *a man is gudnes* 136. The word *man* has also an uninflected Possessive: *a man ryches* 46; *a man defyneȝ* 131; cf. also *þe swallow wombe* 132.

c. ADJECTIVES

One example of an inflected (plural) adjective occurs: *stones natureles* 44v.

d. VERBS

The verbal Inflexions are for the most part distinctively Northern in character.

Infinitive: usually *-e* or no ending: *devyse* 45v; *make* 45v; *forgyte* 45v; *loue* 46v; *seche* 46; etc.; *wytt* 44; *dwell* 45v; *spek* 46; *tak* 47; *forgytt* 47v; etc.

-n is rare: *alyghtyn* 47v; *seen* 126v; *comen* 127; *overcomen* 130; *plesen* 132.

Present Participle: usually *-yng*: *helpyng* 125v; *slepynge* 127; *spekyng* 132; *brynyng* 132v. Also *-and*: *flyand* 46v; *boyland* 134v; *re[n]aund* 46v.

Present Indicative: 3. Sing. The ending is almost always *-es*, *-ys*, *-s*: *spekes* 44v; *beleues* 44v; *has* 45v, 46v; *dose* 44v; *gyfys* 45v; *sekes* 46; *helpys* 46; etc. The only exception is the form *comforth* 127, without ending.

Plural Present: the most frequent ending is *-s*, but *-e*, *-n*, and even *-th* are used also: *wexyn* 46; *goth* 46; *leueth* 130, *beleueth* 130; *haue* 45v, 46v, 131v, *kepe* 46v, *signefye* 45v; *has* 44v, 45v, 41, 132, *beholdes* 124, *fyndes* 132v, *comfortte3* 124, *dystrowes* 124, *drynkes* 47, *seches* 47.

The verb 'to be': the forms of the Plural Present vary considerably, the most common being *ben* and *bes*: *ben* 46v[2], 47, 47v, 126v, 128, 130, 131v[2]; *bene* 46v; *be* 125v[2]; *bey* 124[4]; *bes* 124[2], 125[2], 125v, 135v; *beys* 124[3], 125v; *ar* 47, 124, 128; *er* 125, 125v; *ere* 135v.

Past Participle: the *i-* prefix occurs very rarely: *ygurde* 126v; *I-wryte* 131; *I-graue* 131v. The P. P. of Strong Verbs varies between *-n*, *-e*, and no suffix: *born* 125, 132v; *drawen* 132; *gyfyn* 129v, 130[2]; *ouercomen* 131v; *lyen* 128v[2]; *slayn* 132; *waxen* 128; *I-wryte* 131; *I-grave* 131v; *shape* 125; *wesche* 132v; *fund* 47v, 125; *fond* 125v; *hold* 46; *wax* 130v; *wond* 132.

D. ASHMOLE 1447

ASHMOLE 1447. Late fifteenth century. Quarto, paper, $8\frac{1}{2}'' \times 6''$. The volume consists of two parts: (*a*) five MSS. in different hands of the fifteenth century: (*b*) three later

MSS. and odd papers in different hands. The second MS. in the first part contains charms and medical recipes; the lapidary occupies pages 37-8.[1]

The text is too short for the dialect to be determined with any exactitude. It is probably Central East Midland.

VOWELS

An Eastern dialect is indicated for this text by the *e*-spellings for O.E. *ў*: *mechelnys*, *kend*, *therste*; *i*-forms are found also (*lyfte arme*, *kyndely*), and one apparent blend of the two types: *kyend*.

Lowering of *i* to *e* appears in *crestall*; raising of *e* to *i* in *quinche*, *wyxyth* 'grows.' (See Wyld: *Hist. Coll. Eng.*, p. 222.)

The form *yleke* 'like' may be an inverted spelling, suggesting the raising of *ē* to *ī*.

Rounding of *a* after *w* is seen in *swolwe* (N.); *swalwe* occurs also in this text. The rounded form, which is found as early as the fourteenth century, is probably partly due to the influence of *l*. (See Wyld: *Hist. Coll. Eng.*, p. 202.)

Unstressed *e* is usually *y*: *feuerys*, *kockys*, *hennyes*, *stounys*, *theffyȝ*, *loryll*, *wrappyd*, etc.; but *e* is also used: *elles*, *beter*.

GRAMMAR

The unstressed form, *a*, of the pronoun *he* is used three times, of an inanimate object.

Verbs: The ending of the Third Sing. Pres. is *-t*, *-th*: *wan(n)yt*, *tellyt*, *makyt*; *callyth*, *grovyth*, *hath*, *remevyth*, *wyxyth*; but *-s* is used once, in the title: *begynys*.

The Plural Present has *-th* in *byth*, but *-n* in *ben*, *sayn(e)*. The latter ending is used also for the Imperative Plural: *lyen*, *wrappyn*.

The Present Participle ends in *-ynge*: *abryngynge*, *plesynge*, but in one instance in *-ent* (*bovllyent*), apparently representing the S.E. Midland *-end*.

The Past Participle has the *i*-prefix in *y-founde*, *y-wrappyd*, *y-hellyd*; but forms without *y-* occur also: *wrappyd*, *hold*, *drave*, *drawe*.

---

[1] The pages are numbered consecutively, not lr., lv., etc.

E.   B.M. ADDIT. 34360

B. M. Addit. 34360.   Late fifteenth century.   Paper,
116 leaves, $10\frac{1}{2}'' \times 7\frac{5}{8}''$.   The MS., which contains chiefly
poems by Lydgate, is described by Miss E. P. Hammond
in *Anglia* xxviii, 1-28.   The second hand begins with the
verse lapidary which occupies ff. 58-59v, and which consists of eight seven-lined stanzas, rhymning *ababbcc*.   The
title given in the 'Catalogue' (fol. 3) is, *An Hymne vpon
Christs being ye true stone vpon ye cross by Richardoune*.   A
colophon reads:

> Columbina apparuisti Eleyson
> Verba Auctoris *quod* Richardown.

The language is typical of the London dialect of the
fifteenth century.   The most noticeable feature is the use
of the ending *-s* in the Pres. Plural (*swagis, refourmes*), in
addition to *-th* (*holdith, hath*), *-e* (*meane*), and *-n* (*ben*).   The
The Accusative of the Plural Pronoun (Third Pers.)
appears both as *theym* and as *them*, the latter being the
unstressed form.

F.   PETERBOROUGH CATHEDRAL

PETERBOROUGH CATHEDRAL 33.   Late fifteenth century.
124 leaves, of which four are parchment, the rest paper.
$11\frac{1}{4}'' \times 8''$.   The volume has no binding; many of the leaves
are faded, and some badly stained.   The Lapidary occupies
the first sixteen folios, and is written in double columns.
    The language seems to be that of London of the fifteenth
century, with few remarkable features.   The verb endings
are *-eþ* (occasionally *-it*) for the Third Sing., *-en* for the
Plural Pres. (once *com*, without ending); the P. P. occasionally has the *i*-prefix.   The Third Person Plural Pronoun is *þey*, *her(e)*, *hem*; an unstressed *a* (Masc. Sing.
Nom.) occurs twice (v, lxxxii). (References are to sections.)

Vowels

Raising of *ē* to *ī* appears in *brist*, 'breast,' ii; *lyk*, 'leek,' lviii; diphthongization of *ī* in *beyble*, lxviii. Forms with vowel-shortening are: *ett* (inf.) iv; *mett*, 'meat,' iv; *taddestoles*, xxxix.

Consonants

Inverted spellings showing the loss of [j] before *t: biȝting*, 'biting' ii; *wiȝt, whiȝt, wyȝth*, 'white,' vii, viii, xxi.   Metathesis: *wordell, wordil*, 'world,' ii, iv; *bredis*, 'birds,' lxxi; *þerde*, 'thread,' lxxxvi.   Development of initial ȝ: *ȝerly*, 'early,' cxli.   Confusion of initial *w* and *v: verld*, cx; *vaxeþ*, cxiii; *weynes*, i; *w[e]nym*, ii; *wenem*, vii; *wery*, 'very,' xxxi; *walew* lix; *wictor*, cviii; *wessel*, cxxxiii.

G.   SLOANE 2628

Late sixteenth century.   Paper, 65 ff., 4¾" × 3".   The volume contains charms, medicinal recipes and astrological notes in two or more hands.   The lapidary, ff. 14v–29v, is written in a straggling, untidy but usually legible hand.

The spelling is for the most part conventional, and there is little or no trace of regional influence.

Vowels: M.E. *er* has become *ar* in *hart* 15v, 17. Lowering of *i* to *e* is seen in *deleuerance* 17v, perhaps also in *geueth* 15v, 22, *geveth* 17, unless these latter forms represent the Northern (and Eastern ?) lowering and lengthening of *ī* in an open syllable.   The spellings *edders* 26, *adders* 27v, 28v, seem to show respectively the Midland and Southern development of O.E. *ǣ¹* (shortened).

Unstressed Vowels: Reduction of a back vowel in a final syllable is seen in *vertues*-'virtuous' 17v.   The form *nemath* 'takes' 27 may indicate retraction of a front vowel, as in *appull* 23.

Consonants: The form *verchue* 21v, 27v, is a clear example of the Modern development of [-tj-]. (See Wyld, *Hist. Coll. Eng.*, p. 293.)

Grammar: The Possessive Case of the Plural Pronoun (Third Pers.) appears once in its unstressed form *ther* 22. An uninflected Genitive is seen in *man hart* 15v; *man witt* i; *capon shin* xiii; an uninflected Plural in *beaste* 20.

The Third Sing. Pres. ends in -*s* or -*th: comes* 14v, *keep(e)s* 15v, 18, *makes* 22, etc.; *cometh* 14v, *findeth* 14v, *helpeth* 14v, etc. The Plural Present has -*en* or no ending: *streng(t)hen* 14v, 27; *support* 14v. The Past Participle has no *i*-prefix: *bore* 15, 15v, 17, etc.; *washen* 22. With the latter form, cf. the Weak P. P. *washed* 24v.

THE OLD ENGLISH LAPIDARY (MS. A.)

This short account of the twelve apocalyptic stones is interesting as the earliest known vernacular lapidary of Western Europe.[1] It is about a century older than the first French version of Marbode, written in England probably in the first half of the twelfth century, and serves to show how early an interest in the lore of precious stones was felt in this country. It is derived from Isidore and Bede, with a few additions from Pliny. A notable feature is the absence of any account of magical properties, save that of the *mocritum;* in this it offers a marked contrast with the Anglo-Norman Apocalyptic Lapidary of the next century.[2] Like this, however, it includes a list of the twelve gems of the heavenly Jerusalem (one being accidentally omitted) followed by a few other stones.

The lapidary has been previously published by R. Fleischhacker.[3]

MS. COTTON TIBERIUS A III (MS. A.)

Eleventh Century

f. 101v　Her onginþ embe twelf derwyrðan stanas 7 gimmas þe we leornudan in pocalipsis þære bec.[4]

Ðæt æreste gim-cynn is *þæt* is blac 7 grene, 7 þa hiw syndon buto togædere gemenegede, 7 sindon on naman geaspis haten. Oþær is saphyrus, se is sunnan gelic, 7 on him sta[n]da ð[5] swilce gildene steorran. Ðridde is calcedonius haten, se ys byrnendum blacerne gelic. Feorþa smaragdus, se ys swiðe grene. Fyfta sardonix is haten, se is blode licost. Syxta onichinus is haten, se is ge brun 7 hæwen. Seofoða sardius haten, se is luttran blode gelic.

---

[1] See Garrett, *Precious Stones in Old English Literature*, Dissertation zur Erlangung der philosophischen Doctorwürde ... der ... Universität München, 1909, p. 31; Joan Evans, *Magical Jewels*, 1922, p. 51.
[2] Ibid., p. 260.
[3] Ein altenglischer Lapidar, in *Zeitschrift für deutsches Altertum* XXXIV, 1880, p. 229.
[4] *Title in red.*
[5] *MS.* stadað.

13

Ehtoþa is berillus haten, se is luttran wætere gelic. Nigoþa is criso-prassus haten, se is grenum lece gelic, 7 swilce him grene steorran of scinan. Andlyfta is topazius haten, se is golde ge-lic. [T] welfta[1] is carbunculus haten, se is byrnende glede ge-lic.

Sum stan is þe adamans hatte; nele hine isern ne style ne awiht heardes gretan, ac ælc bi$ þe forcu$ra þe hine greteþ. Sum stan hatte magneten; gif *þæt* isern bi$ bufan þæm stane, hit wyle feallan on þane stan; gyf se stan bi$ bufan, hit wil spirngan up on-gean þæne stan.

f. 102r Abestus hatte sum .stan-cynn on claudea rice. Gif/he wyr$ onbyrnede, ne mæg hine wæter ne wind adwæscan. [S]um[2] stan is on persa rice; gif þu hine mid handa ahrinest, he birne$ sona. Se stan is haten piriten. Seleten hatte sum stan þæs gecyndu sind *þæt* he mid wexsendan monan wexse$ 7 mid waniendan wana$. Se stan bi$ gemet[3] on persa rice. Sum stan h[a]tte[4] alexandrius. Se bi$ hwit 7 cristallum ge-lic.

Sum stan is þe stircites hatte, in lucania man finde$, se is in sealfe se betsta. Sum stan is cathotices haten, þone man finde$ on corsia lande, se wile cleofian on wihta ge-wilcere þe him hrine$. Sum stan is þe mocritum hatte; ne bi$ næfre niht to þæs þystre *þæt* twegen heras ne magun gefeohtan heom be-twinan; 7 he is eac wi$ dricræftum god. An stan is in Sicilia,[5] [acates][6] haten, se wæs on Pires hyrnesse persea cyninges; þæs ansine is swilce an man pipige mid nigon pipan 7 an man hearpige. Se mæg wi$ æghwylcum attre 7 duste.

TRANSLATION

HERE begins concerning twelve precious stones and gems, of which we have learned in the book Apocalypse.

The first kind of stone is one that is black and green, and the colours are mingled both together, and they are ⸺

---

[1] *Capital omitted.*
[2] *Capital omitted.*
[3] *MS.* gement.
[4] *MS.* htte.
[5] *MS.* insicilia.
[6] *MS. omits.*

called Hyacinthus by name. The second is Sapphire, which is like the sun, and in it stand as it were golden stars. The third is called Chalcedony, which is like a burning lantern. The fourth, Emerald, which is very green. The fifth is called Sardonix, which is most like blood. The sixth is called Onyx, which is both brown and blue. The seventh, called Sard, which is like clear blood. The eighth is called Beryl, which is like pure water. The ninth is called Chrysoprase, which is like a green herb, and there shine from it as it were green stars. The eleventh is called Topaz, which is like gold. The twelfth is called Carbuncle, which is like a burning coal.

There is a certain stone called Diamond; neither iron nor steel nor anything hard will cut it, but each is the worse for touching it. One stone is called Magnet; if iron is above the stone it will fall on the stone; if the stone is above, it will spring up against the stone. Asbestos is the name of a kind of stone in the kingdom of Arcadia. If it is set on fire, neither water nor wind can extinguish it. There is one stone in the kingdom of the Persians; if you touch it with your hand, it burns. The stone is called Pyrites. One stone is called Selenite, the nature of which is that it grows with the crescent moon, and diminishes with the waning moon. The stone is found in the kingdom of Persia. One stone is called Alexandrius. It is white and like crystal.

There is one stone called Stircites, one finds it in Lucania, which is the best in salve. One stone is called Cathotices, which one finds in the country of Corsica, that will cleave to anything that touches it. There is one stone called Mocritum; there is never so dark a night that two armies cannot see to fight each other. And it has power against sorcery. There is one stone in Sicily called [Agate] which was in the possession of Pirrus, king of the Persians, the appearance of which is like a man piping with nine pipes, and a man harping. It avails against every poison and exhalation.

THE LONDON LAPIDARY OF KING PHILIP
(MS. B)

THIS is a translation of a French lapidary of the second quarter of the fourteenth century,[1] that is in its turn a translation from a Latin original.[2] The French lapidary exists in a considerable number of MSS.[3] in almost all of which the description of the stones of the Apocalypse is followed by that of a series of other stones; the gems thus added vary from manuscript to manuscript. That which most closely approximates to the English text is Bibliothèque Nationale MS. fonds français 2008[4], in which the order and description of the stones is identical with that in our text except for the omission in the English version of the article on Chelonitis and the inclusion of articles on Hexacontalithos, Prasius, Hyaenia, Liparea, Enhygros, Androdamas, Corneolus, and Alabandica, that do not occur in the French manuscript. These are derived from the 'First Anglo-Norman Prose Lapidary'[5] by way of a lapidary of the type of Bibliothèque Nationale MS. Latin 11210.[6]

The slight differences between the French texts and the English version are due to slips, mistakes and small omissions on the part of the translator, when they are not additions of his own that expand the text a little without changing its meaning. Sometimes he is ignorant of a single word, sometimes the meaning of a whole phrase escapes him. He regularly translates *tire* as *corner*, and *fantosme* as *temptacion*. If he cannot understand a phrase, he sometimes omits it and sometimes substitutes a harmless phrase of his own. Occasionally, however, he attempts too much: in his description of *Chelidonius*, for example, he translates 'ung drap taint en safren' as 'a lynnen clothe þat þe sacrement is in.'

The lapidary has already been described,[7] but has not been published.

---

[1] Selections in L. Pannier, *Les lapidaires français*, Paris, 1882, p. 286.
[2] Evans, *Magical Jewels*, p. 78 and Appendix B.
[3] For a list see ibid., loc. cit.
[4] Pannier, p. 289; MS. B.
[5] Studer & Evans, p. 97.
[6] fol. 80 et seqq. The MS. is of the late fifteenth century.
[7] Evans, op. cit., p. 79.

DOUCE 291 (MS. B)

f. 121 For the loue of Philippe Kyng of Fraunce, þat God hath
in his kepyng, was made this boke þat is clepid the boke of
stones. He þat this boke purchaced sought many Abbeyes
& clerkis, & spake to many perireres & to many wyse
dyuinours, for to witte þe auctorite of stones and what þe
boke seyde, & did translate hit oute of latyn in-to Frenshe,
& in playne counseil be accorde of wyse clerkis. This boke
deuised was of kyndelich stones, & þe bible seith þat god
hymself yaue vertu in hem. And Salamon & Moyses þe
prophete & seint Iohn þe euangelist, þat knewe þe vertues
of stones & wordes, & Eracles seith also that mochel more
thei were worth in vertues & miracles yef þe mysbeleue
of men ne were, and in many places shulde haue myghte
where mirre ne herbe ne rotis may not auaile ne helpe.

And wyse men shulde not doute þat god ne hath put
vertu in stones & herbes & wordes; & who so beleueth
hit not but ayeinseith hit, he is but a synner.

The Bible witnesseth hit þat god commaunded be his
mouth to moyses þe prophete, þat he shulde put þe twelue
stones, þe whech he hade made many maneirs, in a moos
f. 121v clene & fine, / quarre of four handbrede of lench & brede
in foure corners, in euery corner thre stones.

And god commanded to moyses þat he shulde take of
iche kyndely, & do shaape þe twelue stones be crafte of
perrere, & commaunded þat in that moos where þe twelue
stones shulde be sette in castrons of golde, oon vppon þe
ryght side, þe oþre vppon þe lefte side; & þat the seid
moos with þe twelue stones shulde be put be þe com-
maundement of oure lord & hanged vppon þe breste of
aaron, þat was þe first preest of the Iewys.

The names of þe twelue stones þat god hath named to
moyses þe prophete be his mouth ben thise: the firste
stone is cleped *sare*[1], þe second *topase*, þe thridde *emeraude*,
þe fourthe *rubis*, the fifte *saphire*, þe sixte *jaspe*, þe seuenth
ligure, þe eighte *Accate*, þe nynthe *aumatiste*, þe tenthe

---

[1] *Names of stones in italics are underlined in red in MS.*

c

crisolide, þe eleuenthe *onicle*, þe twelfe *beril*. This ben þe
names of twelue stones þat god named.

The appocalipse witnesseth vs þat god loued so moche
my lord seint Iohn þe eua*n*gelist þat he did lede him be
his aungel to se þe priuites of paradys; and also be a uision
he sigh þe grete paradys as a Cite. There he sigh þe twelue
f. 122 stones that God named, and the xj stones þ*t* hymselfe /
named be the wille of God þ*t* were þe fou*n*deme*n*t of þe
heuenly kyngdome.

The names of þe elleuen stones þat seint Iohn named
were thise: the first is named *Iaspe*, þe second *saphre*, þe
thridde *calcedoyne*, þe fourthe *emeraude*, þe fifte *sardoyne*,
þe sixte *sarde*, þe seuenthe *crisolide*, þe eighte *berill*, þe
nynthe *topace*, þe tenthe *crisopas*, þe elleuenth *Iagounce*.
Now haue ye herde þe names of the twelue stones þat God
named, & þe names of þe elleuen stones þat seint Iohn
named, the euangeliste. God yaue grete vertues & many
strencthes to thise stones & to many othre, but þe vertu
of thise þat we haue named to yow we shulle reherce, &
deuise þe vertu of othre stones þat we have named to yow.
First of tho þat God hath named be his mouthe, & after of
thoo þat seynt Iohn hath named, and the significacions,
what thei signifieden atte aarons necke, & what thei signifieden as to þe grete kyngdome.

I   *Sardes*, grenas, elamaundines. Sardes & Iagonces ben
wexyng to-gedre, but þe Iagou*n*ce hath þe vertues of all
thise stones and is þe moste fyne thyng of þe Worlde.
He yeueth colour gentil & reed, & maketh men glad &
f. 122v to / dwelle in youthe & trouthe, & maketh a man to
foryete his contrariouste & his mysbeyng, & doute nought
touchinge ne styngynge of worme ne of wylde beeste; and
men may passe þe rather the water perilous; & who-so
hath hit on his fynger, mochel the leuer he shal resceiue
geestis to harbourgh; and when he sheweth hit, of that
men resonably preyeth hym he shal not hide hit, as þe boke
telleth vs. The verray boke telleth vs þat god named first
this stone, & was of þe colour of þe reed[1] erthe wherof

---

[1] *Nine letters erased before* reed.

God made þe first man, Adam, in þe felde of Damas, wherof we be all of þe same begetynge and þerfore named god this stone first; and in that hit is of þe same colour, hit signifieth the synne of Adam, wherof all we be in peyne & traueile.

Seint Iohn seith in þe apocalipce þat he sawe this stone in þe sixte foundament of the verray Kyngdome. And þe sixte signifieth þat Adam was fourmed þe sixte daye. The reednes of this stone signifieth þe blode of Ihesu criste þat was shadde for man on þe sixte day, þat was at þat tyme; and for þat signe was first named this stone of god & of seynt Iohn.

f. 123 II   TOPACE

Topace is of yelowe colour & ben moo þen of oon manere; of þe Este & of arabie cometh þe best. Topace colith & heleth of maladie þat is cleped þe fis; & þe fis þt is with[1] topace corue shal neuer wexe after. The boke seith vs þat topace draweth hym to the semblaunce of þe mone. When þe mone is foule, þenne is he more foule; & when þe mone is feire, then is hit of more gentil colour. He that bereth þis stone shal þe more loue to leede his body in chastite, & þe more loue to loke to the heuenly Ryal weye. The bible seith vs and þe diuinitees þat topace was þe second stone vppon þe breest of aaron, which hath colour of golde & ayre & signifieth þe second life of þe high heuenly Kyngdome. Seynt Iohn seith vs in þe appoca-lipce, þat he sigh þis stone in the nynth foundament of þe lastynge cite, & signifieth the nyne ordres of angeles þat lyven in þat joye þat noon hath enuye of othre, þat is þe life corouned, in þe which shal noon entre but he be kyng corouned or quene, for all be corouned be name. Kynges shulde blithely beholde topaces, for he yeueth hem gode remembraunce to loke to þe Ryal life corounede of heuen þat shal neuer faile.

f. 123v   All þei / þat beholden my stones with sobrete more turne her sight vp to topace, þat signifieth þat we alle

[1] W^t *above the line.*

shulde beholde þat life wherby a man myght se god in þe
face. Holy writte seith þat topace suche as he wexeth is
beste, but hit is not so plesyng, ne no heete may be polisshide of hym, but þerfore ne leste nought his strencthis;
but seint Iohn seith for þe honeste weye þat he hath no
nede to be polisshide of þe tatches of this worlde, & seith
þat more is worth þe leest joye of þat lyfe of the heuenly
Kyngdome then all þe bryghtnes of honeurs þat bene in
this worlde, & þerfore shulde euery man telle þe lesse be
hym-self. For dauid þe prophete seith þat we be dene men.

III   Emeraude

Emeraude passeth all þe grenesses of grenehed, & þe
bokes seyn vs þat þe emeraude & þe prames ben growyng to-gedre, & þat þe fine emeraudes comen oute of þe
londe of syre & of a water of paradys. Emeraudes a-
menden the sight to beholde vppon. Nero hade a[1] myrrour
where he loked in, and he wyste be vertu of þis stone al
þat he wolde seche or witte. Hit encreseth richesse, & hit
maketh worde of man dredeful, & is moche worth for þe
goute & ayeins tempeste & /lecherye. & wittes wele þat he
þat bereth emeraude aboute hym, þe more he shal loue his
body in clennesse, & þe lesse wille to seye vilanies & þe
more loue to thenke on his solle, & to be of better berynge
& to loue gode werkys, for god to this stone yave suche
vertues. The bible seith þat emeraude was þe first stone
named of god vppon the brest of aaron, & þerfore hit
signifieth þe grettist grenehede of hym þat is þe grete
grenehede of the feith of þe Trinite. Seynt Iohn seith in
þe appocalipce þat emeraude is þe first stone vnder þe
veray kyngdome, & þerfore hit signifieth feith of þe iiij
euangelistes, & also seith vs seynt Iohn þat bestes þat be
named gryffons þat kepen þe emeraude vppon the flom of
paradys in þe land of syre; & þat beest hath iiij fete, the
body before & ij wynges in maner of an egle, & behynde
in maner of a lyon; & a peple þat arne named aropiles, þat
haue but on eye in myddes of þe forhede, comen to seche

f. 124

---

[1] *MS.* hade in a.

þe emeraude all y-armed on þe water, and taken hem, &
þe bestes aforeseid co*m*men rennyng & fleynge & wolden
take þe aropiles to þeire powere, & much anguysshen
hem, & harde is to take hem. The fyne emeraude [is]¹
clene & gentile. Þe grenes signifieth þe grete grenehed
þ*t* may not flitten, þ*t* þe gode pa*t*riarches & pr*o*phetes haden
so grete blisse of heuene all þei þ*t* ben in þis grenehede in
þe feith as seynt Iohn was, þ*t* seith þat þei þat haue not but

f. 124v oon / eye, þat is Ihe*s*u Xrist. The aropiles þat comen to
seche the emeraudes armed þat feighten with þe gryffons,
þei ben veray cristen men; the gryffons signifien þe deueles
to whom thei feighten ayeins. All thise thynges shulde þei
haue in my*n*nde þat beren emeraudes.

IV RUBIE

Rubye is reed & steyneth all þe reed stones. Þe
boke telleth vs the gentil rubie fyne & clene is lorde of
stones & is also of water of waters. Hit hath þe vertue of
precious stones & aboue all othre. He is of suche lordeshippe þ*t* when he þat bereth hym cometh amonge men,
all thei shul bere hym honeur & grace & all shul bere hym
joye of his p*r*esence. Þe bokes seyn vs þat þe beestes þat
drynken of² þe wat*er* where þe rubie hath ben wette inne
shul be hoole of þeir sekenes; & he þat is discomforted þat
in gode beleue beholdeth þis stone, hit shal co*m*forte &
make hym to foryete his contrariousete be vertue þat god
hath yeuen þerto. Hit fedeth þe man & co*m*forteth þe hert
& þe body, & wynneth to a man lordeshippe aboue othre
stones. Þer ben gretter rubies & ben founden in lande of
rubie in a flode of paradis. The bokes of moyses seyn vs
what god co*m*maunded þat þe rubie shulde be put first in
þe second corner of the mouce, for he signifieth þe second
lawe, & to liȝte þe werkis be nyght & day. And þough we
take non hede to the signifiance of the rubie & of his

f. 125 blesful colour, yet / Moyses seith þat hit signifieth Jhe*s*u
Xrist þat come in-to this worlde for to lighten oure

¹ *MS. omits.*
² of *above the line.*

derkenes. The boke seith þat seint Iohn seith of þe commyng of Ihesu Xrist þat is veray lighte þat lighteth all
men & all þe worlde. Ysaie þe prophete seith of this lyghte
þt þe peple þat was in derkenes sawe a greet lighte. Seint
Iohn seith þat he sawe not þe rubie in the fundament of þe
heuenly kyngdome of Iherusalem, & þerfore was not þe
rubie there. Al thei þat þe rubie & the veray bryghtnes of
þe rubie beholden shulde beholde þe veray lighte of Ihesu
Xrist, whoso beholdeth þe rubie of þe lymmes of Ihesu
Xrist he shal loue þe more thoo þat ben þe clene livyng
peple of this worlde.

V   SAFIRE

Safire is a ful comly stone vppon a Kynges fynger
& is gracious & gode, & men take hym in graueill of
limbe in a flode of þe Eest beside a rocke of þe see. Þere
þei be so founden, som ben more gentil þen othre. Thei
þat ben moste gentil of colour & moste ynde thei semblen
to þe clene colour of heuen, & in the depe water be founde
þe saphires þt arne derke & ful of vertues & better then
the clene. Other men fynde þat ben lesse worth, & all ben
vertuouse & ful of grace. Thise maner saphires putteth
awey enuie,[1] & comforteþ þe body & þe membres, & helpe
men fro enprisonyng; & yef a man be enprisoned, & he
may touche þe þe iiij corners of þe prisone & his bondes
f. 125v yef / he haue any, & be in gode beleue, with þe saphire,
he shall, by þe vertu þat god hath yeuen & graunted
þerto, be deliuered. The boke seith þt[2] saphire is ful gode
to bryng men to accorde þat ben in discencoun, & ful gode
to voide wicche-craftes & to heele biles & swellinges when
þei ben þerwyth y-touched. Also yef[3] men yeue hit to
drynke to hym þat hath þe bile or swellyng with-inne þe
body, anon shal he be hoole be vertue þat god hath put
þerto; & hit shal cole þe body of þe hoote sekenes, & do
awey þe sorowe fro the heed & heleth þe sekenes of þe

---

[1] *One letter erased before* enuie.
[2] þ^t *above the line.*
[3] *One letter erased before* yef.

gomes, & chaseth oute þe greuaunce of þe eyen, & þe boke
seith þat god counseileth hym þat cleneliche bereth hit,
maketh hym to haue witte, & þei þat this stone bere
shulden lyve clenely. The veray bokes .tellen vs þat
saphire is of þe colour of heuen, for þe strencth of þe high
sight semeth þat hit is gode, þat signifieth þat gode hope
þat a gode man is touched with þe sonne þat is Ihesu Xrist;
& the more strongely he secheth the kyngdome of heuen
right as þe sighte maketh vs to knowe þe syghte of heuen,
ryght so þe vnderstandyng maketh vs to vnderstande þe
blisful blysse of heuen. Seynt Iohn seith in þe appoca-
f. 126 lipce þat he sawe in the/seconde fundament of þe Cite a
blisful saphire, & þerfore signifieth þe saphire þe seconde
vertue þat is hope, & þerfore hit was put in þe seconde
corner vppon þe breste of aaron; & who þat saphire beholdeth he shulde be in memoire of þe blisse of heuen, &
in gode memoire of hym-selfe.

VI   IASPES

Iaspes ben of nyne maners & of diuers colours, & ben
founden in ful depe parties of the worlde. But he þt is
grene ayeins þe day, he is godely; & he þt[1] hath blake
dropes, he is lesse worth; & when he is droped with reed
& is grene, yef he be shape of þe olde shappe, he is lorde
Iaspe. This is þe moste preciouse Iaspe. He is gode
ayeins all manner wormes; & yef þer be any stonggen or
enuenymed with any maner poyson brought in place þere
as Iaspe is, he shal sone be amended of his maladie &
colours. & hit shall staunche blod be reson in hym þat
hath gode beleue, & helpe a man of þe menyson, of þe
ffeuere, of dropesye. & who-so beholdeth the Iaspe ayeins
day, he shal descriue metynge. & hit is moche worth to a
woman þat traueilleth of childe, for þe sonner she shall be
deliured. Iaspe kepeth a man fro his aduersaire. Who-so
f. 126v bereth hit he shal lede clene life. The/veray bokes tellen
vs þat þe gode Iaspe is grene & of grete grenehed, &
signifieth þe trewe peple of men þat ben of þe lesse vnder-

_____
[1] þt _above the line._

standyng in þe ffader & þe sonne & the holy gost; þei be
lewde men, þat yef a gode clerc opposed hem þei couth
not answere hym, for thei ben bounden, and signifien
Iaspe.   Moyses seith þat this stone is ful gode ayeins
temptacion of fendes, of Iewes, & sarazins.   Seint Iohn
seith vs in þe Appocalipce þat [in][1] þe fundement of þe
heuenly kyngdome of Ierusalem þe Iaspe is first, and þerfore hit signifieth thre vertues þt shulde be in euery gode
man. Iaspe is þat stone þat is cleped feith, the second hope,
& þe thridde charite, & he þat grene Iaspe beholdeth
ayeins day, of þe feith of Ihesu Xrist he shulde haue
mynde.

VII   Ligure

Ligure is a stone þat is founde in þe lande of Inde vpon
a flode ful of Ouenes þat a best þt hight [lin]x[2] kepeth, &
hit holdeth in his throote ful depe, þat þe vertues þerof
shulde not be helpyng to vs. The bokes tellen vs þat ligures
ben of many maneres, but the best is þe colour of golde, &
swiche þer ben of colour of mirre, & som þer ben of colour
of encens, and swiche þer ben þat he yeueth þe yolow
f. 127 grenehed, & som þer ben/of colour of mylke, as a maistre
deuised þat hade a name Teopatus.   Moyses seith vs þat
þer ben som of þe colour of Iagounces.   Oure lorde yaue
þis stone many vertues.   He heleth þe Iaundys of man, &
voideth vices, & is gode ayenis many maner goutes, &
clenseth a man of all sorowes þat nourisshed ben with-inne
þe stommak.   Ligure pleseth a man þat is wrathful &
gladith hym, & stauncheth menyson & bledyng woundes.
The boke telleth vs þat this stone is ful gode for ladyes, for
the more thei shul be plesyng & lovyng. Þis stone colith
a man of grete heete yef he put it in his mouth, & who-so
wole touche his eyen þerwith hit dryueth awey þe greuaunce & þe blode. & þis stone hath ben named of many
othre names, but oure lord cleped hit ligure. Moyses seith
þat þe beest þat kepith þis stone diggeth þe erthe & parteth

[1] *MS. om ts.*
[2] *MS.* six.

hit & with-holte hym with-inne þe graueile, & so kepeth
þe ligure. Moyses clepeth þis beest oxe, & þe vertue of
this stone is in his lymmes & his strencthe in his nauel.
The vertue of his lymmes, telleth vs Iob, this lecherous
men ayeins their vices shulde haue þe vertue þerof, þat is
chastite. The forseid beest þat diggeth þe erthe to hyde
his stone signifieth the oxes of Ihesu Xrist þat his lande
kepen & eryen & wynnen be holy predicacoun. The bible
f. 127v seith þat this/stone was first put in the thridde corner
vppon the breste of aaron, & signifieth þe gode precheurs
of Ihesu Xrist that shulden come at thre tymes, þat were
þe tymes of the gospell.

VIII   ACCATE

e Agate
his na-
e.1
Accate is an stone founden in a flode named accate;
ther ben founden of many maneres. There arne whyte
& blacke colours, & som þer ben þat haue not but oon
maner of colour, & som þat haue whyte crosces, & som
þat haue braunches figured as trees, leuys, & as hedes;
som þer ben þt be grene as Iaspe droped with reed dropis,
& this accate is cleped of muche peple dyodropie, þat hath
muche vertue, and muche in deuyse of þe lapidarie. &
som accates þer ben þat haue golden veynes. The scripture telleth vs þat þer ben of colours of golde, of myrre, of
encens, &² of coraulys droped. The veray accate comforteth & saueth an olde man, and stauncheth thriste, &
holdeþ hym yongely³ and in strencthe, & kepeth hym fro
venym & bitynge of serpentes, & techeth a man to speke
gode. We fynde in redynge þat ther is an acchate þat
who-so putteth hit in an herbe þat is cleped þe goulde, &
putteth hit in his fyst cloos, no man may se hym as þe boke
seithe. Þis maner herbe shewith þe sonne. This accate is
grene dropid with reede. Moyses seith þat this accate
was vppon þe breste of aaron his brother, & was blacke
f. 128 & whyte braunched; þe blak/nesse signifieth the sorowe

---

¹ *Different hand and ink.*
²*& above the line.*
³ly *above the line.*

of this worlde, þat we haue for oure synne; þe whitnes
signifieth þe highnesse of the Trinite & þe braunches þat
bare þe pardurable fruyte. Be this two significacions was
þe ston, as þe bokes tellen, in the thridde corner, & was
signified oure cristendome þat Ihesu Xrist & seynt Iohn[1]
þe baptist precheden to þe peple.

IX   AMATIST

Amatist is of purpure colour & draweth to colour of
blode newe shedde. The boke telleth vs þat this stone is
comfortable to hym that bereth hit when wylde beestis
commen to hym, & hit is comfortable in all sorowes, &
holdeth man in gode beleue & stronge. & as þe boke of
Moyses seith vs, he þat bereth Amatist shal be welcome
before kyng & prince, & deliuerly shal wirke in all crafte
þat he entermeth of, & holdeth man lowely. Who-so
bereth this stone shal haue in hym þe more mynde of God,
& is ful graciouse. The scripture of diuinite seith vs þat
amatist is of purpure colour þt þe Iewys clothed inne oure
lorde Ihesu Xrist in despite for he made hym kyng. Of
þat colour & for þat cause kynges shulde clothe hem when
thei holden high courtes. For Salamon seith vs þat þe
clothyng of þe colour of Amatist shulde remembre vs of
þe clothynge of purpure þat god was clothed inne atte his
deethe, where-inne þe Iewys clothed hym in scornyng, &
f. 128v the lordeshippe of / angeles & þe deethe of martyres.

X   CRISOLIDE

Crisolide ressembleth water of þe see, & casteth flaume
as hit were of golde. The boke seithe þat hit is ful gode to
bere amonges kyndely stones; & who-so be oute of synne
may entre in-to many contrees with-oute any ayein-saying,
&[2] all men shul bere grace to hym. And as þe boke telleth
vs, þat who-so hath crisolide perced and put thorough a
berstille of an asse, he shulde goo amonges deueles &
chace hem with myght. & as the boke seith, þat who þat

---

[1] Iohn *above the line.*
[2] & *above the line.*

blisful stone berith he shulde lyue trewly, & hit shulde
be borne vppon þe lefte side. Crisolide cometh of cyop.
Holy writte seith vs þat he bereþ þe colour of þe see water
& of golde, & signifieth þe sauour of hem þat wisely lyuen
here in erthe. The glose of the appocalipce seith þat
Crisolide of þe Este signifieth þe holy predicacions &
miracles of Ihesu Xrist; & casteth flame as golde in all
sides, & where-so hit tourneth hit signifieth gode amonestyng þat þe gode precheurs don to þe peple. Seynt Iohn
seith in þe appocalipce þat the same crisolide is þe sixte
stone in foundement of þe veray kyngdome, & signifieth
þe holy yefte of þe holy goost.

The bible wytnessyth vs þat god ordeined crisolide þe
tenthe stone in signifiyng þe ten commaundementes of þe
lawe of God.

XI   ONICLES

f. 129 Onicles & sardoynes ben wexyng to-gedre & founden
in þe lande of ynde & Arabie, & ben of diuers colours
& vertues, & eueryche is a stone be hymselfe kyndely.
Onicle is blacke, & when he hath whyte sydes or veines or
Russetes, or parscour, the best onycle is blak & ploncket.
Any onicle maketh a man bolde, hardy & courageful,
& maketh hym to haue plente of spotel, & gederith
plente of gode, & holdeth hym in heele þat bereth hit.
& as the boke telleth vs, hit maketh man to speke to
his deede frend be nyght in metynge; & yef he falle to
mete be the morow then þe dede is in traueile. He þt bereth
hit shul haue many graces. The gloses of moyses seith
þat the onycle wexith blak, þat signifieth the synne of man
and also þe tendrenesse of þe tendrenesse of þe flesshe þat
is alwey freele to falle; and betokeneth the holy men of
this worlde þat be gode lyvyng ouercommen the temptacions of the deuel; the which ressembleth to the vertue of
þe onycle þt god yafe þerto. Also þe glose of moyses seith
þat the onicle kyndely, þere as he hath blak & ploncket
colours, signifieth þe fauour þat commeth fro god & þe
charite þat is þe vertue of Ihesu Xrist. The bible seith þat

onicle was in þe fourth corner of the moce þat was vppon
þe breste of aaron, in signifying þe iiij euangelistis þat haue
f. 129v þe figures of man, of egle, of lyon & of Oxe, & signi/fien
the onicles of diuers colours.

XII   BERILL

Berille is a stone þat is a colour like to water when
þe sonne shyneth, & cometh of þe lande of Inde. The
riall berill casteth fire ayein þe sonne. The boke seith þat
berill norissheth loue betwene man and woman; & þe
water þat hit hath leyn inne is much worth to sore eyen;
& who þat drynketh þat water hit wole kepe hym fro
yixyng, & dothe awey þe heete & þe chaufyng of þe liure;
& who þat berith hit shall be muche worshipped. The
bokes of diuinite seyn þat berill shulde not be shape, but
hit behoueth to be plain & polisshed. When the sonne
shyneth þervppon, hit takeþ feruent heete; hit signifieth þe
first precheurs of holy chirche þat precheden the cristendome of Ihesu Xrist, where þe deueles mowe not fynde
her enfourmynges ne her temptacions. The bible witnesseth þat oure lorde commaunded twelue stones of berill
to þe likenes & significacoun of þe twelue apostles þat
first precheden þe cristendome. Seynt Iohn seith þat in þe
appocalipce he sawe þe berill þe eyght stone in the foundement of þe lastyng Cite; þat signifieth þe holy age of þe
Resurreccion. And also þe auctorites seyn þat who-so
berith berill nere his flesche ayeins þe sonne, þt þe fire þat
cometh oute cacheth þe flesche; þat signifieth thoo þat
f. 130 arne assembled & speken with holy men þt ben fired/with
charite & bren of hemself.

XIII   THE NATURE OF BALEYS

Nowe haue ye herde þe vertues & þe significacouns of
þe twelue stones þat god named to moyses þe prophete;
& þe elleuen stones þat seynt Iohn euangelist named.

First the Baleys is a stone þat seynt Iohn named
Iagounce, & drawith hym to þe colour of a rubie, & is

founden in an ile þat men clepe oracle betwene two sees.
Iagonces yeueth colour gentil & reede & maketh a man
glad, & to dwelle in youthe & trouthe, & hym thare not
doute pestilence ne puson, ne to passe the water perilouse.
And who-so berith hym on his fynger, much the leuer he
shall receive gestys, & þe more y-honored. Yet is þe Rubie
lorde of Iagounce; after þe rubie, Iagounce baleys, iagounce
saphire, iagounce garnade, Iagounce cetryn. Thise maner
of stones may men clepe iagounces. Þe stone of baleys is a[1]
ful gode stone. Our lord yaue þerto many feire vertues.
The bokes tellen vs þat who-so berith veray baleys, hit shal
put fro man idel thoughtes & sorow, & kepeth a man fro
grete lecherie. The bokes tellen vs þat who-so berith veray
baleys, & he shewe hit to his ennemy, he shal sone be
accorded with hym; & who þat berith hit amonges his
ennemys he shall go safe fro hem. & who þat touchith
þerwith þe iiij corners of his chambre or of his halle or of
f. 130v his gardynn/worme ne tempeste shal not do þere harme
ne greuaunce. Seynt Iohn seith in þe glose vppon þe appocalipce þt þis stone chaungeth ayein the feire tyme; &
signifieth othre wyse clerkes & maistres þe whech preched
& speke to men after þat thei were, as seint poule spake to
clerkes & to lewde men after þat thei were, & chaunged
hem as the gentil baleys þat chaungeth hym ayein þe feire
tyme & amendeth his colour. That ile where þis stone is
founden inne is in þe contree of cyop.

XIV   CRISOPHAS

Crisophas is a stone & is brought oute of þe lande of
ynde. The bokes tellen vs þat his colour is of grenes, &
ben like swynes eyen, & casteth oute as golde on all sides.
Who-so berith hit, men shul be glad and joyful of his
commynge. The glose of þe appocalipce seith þat this
stone & his colour signifien hem lyving in traueille.

XV   CALCEDOYNE

Calcedoyne is a stone of a troubles whitnes, & is of
þe Eest. Our lord yaue swiche vertue to this stone þat

[1] a *above the line.*

he þat berith hit shal be wele spekyng of gode; & yef he
speke & shewe hit to his aduersaire, hym behoueth to
wynne his cause; & yef he be enpleted with wronge, hit
kepeth hym his ryghte.   He þat sardoyne, onicle & calcedoyne berith, he shal be wel entatched, but yef he lose it[1]
be his synne.

Calcedoyne berith grace; this stone & his colour signi-
f. 131 fien / tho þat gedren her godenese. Þe glose of þe appocalipce seith vs þat this ston drawith þe worde of man, þat
signifien þe gode men þat drawen þe synful men blisfully
to her gode werkys.

XVI   Sardoynes

Sardoynes is a stone of a redisshe Reedness & black-
ysshe. Þis ston be hym-self swagith wrathe of a man &
makith him reste wele be nyghte, & voideth much drechyng & noying tatches, & dothe awey noying vices fro
man, & kepith chaste & shamefast & graciouse.   The
glose of þe appocalipce seith þat sardoyne signifieth hem
þat suffren grete peines in her body for þe loue of our lord
god & dispisen her flesche as þei were synful men.

XVII   Diamaunde

Diamaunde is a stone þat is named & deuised in þe
lapidarie. Euax, þat was Kynge of Arabie, seith þat þe
diamaundes þat commen oute of ynde ben cleped þe males,
& arne broun of colour & of violet; & tho þat commen
oute of arabie be cleped þe femmales & ben whitter. No
diamaunde is no more then a litel note, & is moste harde
of all þe stones. What man that bereth the dyamaunde of
yefte withouten desir, he shal neuer be amenused of his
riches.   The lapidarie seith þt muche vertue yaue god to
þe diamaunde & many graces. Hit yeuyth to a man þat
berith hym strencthe & vertue, and kepith hym fro greu-
f. 131v ouse metynge & temptacions & fro / venym. Also hit
kepeth þe boones & þe membres whoole. In so fer forth
þat thou shalte not falle fro thine hors ne oþer beest, but

---

[1] it *above the line.*

þat thi bones shullen be hoole, who-so be welbelevyng.
Also hit voideth þe drede þat commeth be nyght, & doth
awey hatrede & wrathe & lecherie, & kepith a man in
poynt as he fynt hym of pris, of witte, of value, of Richesse,
& encreaseth hym in Richesse, & shal not be made lesse, &
shall be of lyghter dispenses þat berith hit. Diamaunde is
much worth to beholde to a witles man, & is defense ayeins
his ennemys; for he þat berith hit shal þe more loue god.
Also hit saueth þe sede of man within þe¹ wombe of his
wyfe, & þe chylde hit kepith all his membres hoole. The
boke seith vs þt hit shulde be borne on þe lefte syde. And
who-so wole proue his vertues he moste haue hit of trewe
beyng or of yefte & hoole; & holy he shal be þat þis vertuouse ston berith in clennesse.

XVIII ALLECTORIES

Allectories wexen in the wombe of a capon, after he
hath ben iiij yere capon, & wexith alwey til he be of
seuen yere age, but hit is no more then a been. Hit is
clere as cristall & water. He yeueth þe victoire to a man
þat berith hit, & yef he holde hit to his mouthe hit
stauncheth thriste. Many kynges haue wonne her batailles
be helpe of þis stone, & brought hym-self ayein fro the
chaces; & bryngeth to a man gode frendes. & hit maketh
f. 132 a man well spoken / of & loued, & is moche worth to a
woman þat traueillith of chylde, & to a woman þat wole
be loued of her lord; when she touchith hit with her
mouthe then hath hit sweche vertues.

XIX CELIDOYNE

Celidoyne is a stone þat men fynden in the wombe
of a swalewe. She nys not feire, & not-for-þenne she
is more worthi then many of this feire stones in profite.
Thei ben of two maneres & of two colours; þei ben blak
& reede. Þe reede is gode ayein þe maladye þat taketh a
man lunatyk, whereby he failleth & is folisshe & witles

---

¹ þe above the line.

longe tyme. & he þat berith it,[1] hit makith wel spoken of
& beloued of men. He shulde bere hit in lynnen cloth wel
wounden, & hong hit vppon þe lefte syde. But þe blak,
& a man bere hit in swiche a maner, hit shall helpe to do
grete thyng. Hit helpeth ayeinſ manaces of Kynges &
Princes. The water þat hit is wasshe inne is much worth
to an hoote sekenesse. This stone wounden in a lynnen
clothe þat þe sacrement is in[2] with-holdeth þe feuere &
ayein-streyneth wicked humours þat commen aboute in
many maners.

XX   IEET

Ieet is a stone þt growith in a contree þat is cleped lytie,
& ressembleth the ademaunde; hit faillith not muche,
but the beest of the worlde is in bretaigne maior þat nowe
is cleped yngelande. Shynyng & blak hit is, & lyght / &
plain, & when hit is chaufed be frotynge hit drawith to
him the strawe þat is be-syde hym. Hit brenneth in water.
Hit is gode to bere to hym þat hath swellyng in skyn and
in flesche, as a man þat is enfounded. The poudre of hym,
wasshed in a litel water, clenseth a mans teth, & yef thei
waggen, be a stonnde vnderneth, hit yelte his kynde. When
a man brenneth hit, & when a man hath þe goute fallyng,
be þe odeur anon therof he resteth. The smelle of þe bren-
nynge dryueth awey serpentes, & muche is worthe to hem
that haue her wombes tourned, & to hem þat taken
crowes; & hit vndothe & voideth witchecrafte & shames.
& also hit disproueth maynden-hoode; & yef a woman
traueile of chylde, & dryncke of þe water þat hit hath leyn
inne thre dayes & thre nyghtes, sone she shal be deliured.

f. 132v

XXI   MAGNETE

Magnete is a stone þat is founden in a place that hath
the name Tragodice in Inde. Men fynde hem & haue
hem of Iren. Deldour þe enchauntour vsed hit muche, þat
he wyste wele hit was muche helpyng to enchauntement;

---

[1] it *above the line.*
[2] is in *above the line.*

& after hy*m* muchel vsed hit Cyors, the merueilleuse enchauntour þat was a woman. & amonges all other thynges thise exp*erimentes* were founden & knowen is þat hit is soth þat who wole witte yef his wyfe do folie or non, put þe magnete vnder þe bedde of his wyfe when she is on f. 133 slepe, & yef she be chaste she shal kysse þe / stone in slepyng, & yef she be spouse-breker she shall falle doun*n* of þe bedde as a man put her forth with his hande; & þat is by a fauour þat þe stone yeueth be kynde. And yef a thefe entre in-to an house for to stele, & he tak a quyk bronde of fire, & put vppon þe bronde þe poudre of the magnete so þat þe smoke go aboute to þe iiij corners of þe house, then thei þerinne shul fle for drede, wenyng þ*t* þe house shall falle vppon hem; & so may the thefe take al that hym lyste. This stone norissheth loue betwene man & woman, & yeueth a man grace to speke swetely, & witte to dispute; & yef a man yeue hit to drynke in oyle to hym þat hath þe dropesie hit shall spurgen hym; & the poudre of hym is ful gode to brennyng.

XXII   TERAMUS

Teramus is a stone þat fallith with þe thondre; & he that berith hit clenely, þe thondre shal neu*er* smyte hym in house ne in fire; he shal not be loste i*n* debate amonges men; & gode hit is to ouercome batailles, & hit yeueth gode metynges, & hit is of many colours.

XXIII   ELYTROPE

Elyotrope is a stone of swiche kynde, þat yef a man put hit in a vessell ful of water ayeins þe sonne she shal make þe sonne smered, & in a litel tyme shall make þe vessell to boile & caste oute þe water as hit reyned. & he þat berith hit may profite many thynges. She yeueth to f. 133v a man gode loos, / & stauncheth blode; & hit is gode ayein venyms & filthe. & who þat takith þe herbe elyotrope & the charme þat is longyng þerto, & yef he put hit with þe ston, he shall go there as he wolde. This ston com*m*eth of

D

cyope & of cypte & of Aufrike, & is swiche as hit were an
emeraude, & dropes like blode.

XXIV   Aspites

Aspites is reed & shinynge, & is of suche vertue þat
she letteth þe Caudron of his boillyng & coldeth þe
water in shorte tyme. She doth awey the briddes fro þe
land þat is sowe, & for-doth medelynge, & makith a
man hoole; & when a man puttith hit in þe sonne beem
hit yeueth bryghtnes as hit were fire; & yef he wole bere
hit, hit moste be borne vp-on the Ryghte Syde.

XXV   Egiftys

Egiftys is a ston in the contre of archade, & hath
colour of iren; & an-othre swiche þer is, þe femel, when
she conceiueth & bryngeth forth an-othre stone, & þerfore
hit is much worthe to a woman þt traueilleth of chylde, for
she shal þe sonner be deliured.

XXVI   Hadda

Hadda is euel to fynde aboue all þe stones þat arne,
for she shal neuer be founden but men kerue þe bordes
of þe shippe, for she sitteth so strongly þat men mowe
not do hit awey with-oute kervyng of the tree; & hath
þe colour of Reed.

XXVII   Medus

f. 134   Medus is a ston in þe south landes þat yeueth / life
and deeth. For who-so wetith it in a womans mylke,
& afterward puttith to his eyen þat hath lost his sight, hit
yeueth hym sight[1] ayein. And who-so distemprith hit
with mylke that ne hath hade but oon lombe, yef hit be a
male, hit is muche worthe to heele þe potagre, & shall
heele þe lymmes of hym. Men shulde stewe hit in siluer;
when hit is tempred with water hit hath all þe maner of his
kynde; & afterward hit shall be yeuen to wasche his eyen,

[1] sight *above the line.*

and hit shal make hym to se; & yef he drynke hit, hit shal slee hym. This ston is all blacke, but hit is all vertues; &[1] thei[1] arne not blacke, for þei ben white in doyng wel, & blacke when thei noyen.

XXVIII   ARACONTALIDES

Aracontalides is a ston þat men þt hight limatonş bryng in-to ynde. She is purpure & blacke. Yef a man wasche his mouthe & holde hit vnder his tonge, as longe as the mone is wexynge may a man diuine fro þe mornyng to þe mydday, & þe cours afore þe day, & when she primeth then lasteth her pouste all þe day, right as when she is of fiftene dayes of ful age. This ston holdeth no fire.

XXIX   CARCIUS

Carcius is accounted among þe stones, & is not lefe, for she hath no profite but þat she is grene. Also þer ben oþer maner þt haue smale veynes like blode. The thridde maner hath thre maneres & ben figured white.

XXX   CALADISTA

f. 134v   / Caladista hath colour of sendrine. Þt woman þat drynketh hit in oyle hit shal multiplie her mylke, but she shulde vse it afore mete or after bathinge; & yef hit be perced with[2] an heer of wolle of a shepe þat is white lombe, & put thorough & hanged at the norisce necke, hit shal muche auaile her; & yef a woman traueille on chylde, yef she bynd hit to her thee, & yef a man make poudre þerof, & tempre hit with salte & water & anoynte þe thee with-inne & oute, hit shal auayle her muche. This thinge helith þe shepe fro reeme. & þe olde auncestres seyn þat he þat berith þis ston, hit shal auaile as muche os all þe othre stones. Yef a man bere hit in his mouthe & take it oute ayein, hit stedfasteth his witte; & when a man frotith hit vn-to the tyme þt þe stone is hoote, then this ston sauour of mylke.

[1] & thei *above the line.*
[2] wt *above the line.*

XXXI   CORYNTHE

Corynthe is a ston blacke & rounde, & muche is
worthe ayeins envenemyng of bitynge of euel beestis or
eddres & oþre; & yef a man stampe hit with oyle russeth,
& bere hit when he gooth amonges wylde beestis in desert,
& haue with hym þe corinthe þat tourneth in-to grenehede, he thare not retche of hertynge of eddres. The
thridde maner is more preised; hit is vppon on partie
sharpe & on þe oþre partie iren grounden. A woman þat
berith hit vppon her, she thar not retche with whom she
f. 135 goo[1] / with childe, for yef she bere hit vppon her she shal
be for-lore.

XXXII   HYEME

Hyeme is a stone þat a beest þat hight yeme berith in
the Ball of the eye. Þis stone, as olde Auncestres seyn,
makyth a man diuinable yef he holde hit vnder his tonge;
but his mouthe moste be clene wasshe or he put hit inne
& then he hath his strencthe.

XXXIII   DIPPAREA

Dipparea is a stone in libie, & his kynde is suche þat
all huntyng commeth to his likyng that berith hit, & he
may take ynough, þerof suche vertu hath this stone.

XXXIV   ONIDROS

Onidros is a stone þat alwey swetith & is not ful grete,
and is take in arrabie in the reed see, & hath semblaunce
of cristall; and yef a man holde hit to þe sonnebeem, hit
shewith a man all þe coloures of the Reynbowe, & of hym
cometh the Reynbowe.

XXXV   DIADAMA

Diadama is an oþre stone fourmed quarre, & hath
colour of Siluer, & men fynden hit in the graueille in
the reed see, & hit fordoth ire.

[1] with chylde *as catchword at foot of page.*

XXXVI CRISTALLE

Cristalle is frost harde as thise olde Auncestres seyne
& oþre ayein-sey hit; & nought-for-that he with-holdeth
the colour & þe colours of the Froste; & þerfore ayein-
seyn olde Auncestres, & so many contraries ther ben; &
somme þer ben þt arne notte so greete of coldenes. This
stone conceiueth wele the fire atte the sonne-beem, &
f. 135v catcheth & brennyth. & the / olde Auncestres made þerof
poudre & yaue hit to drynke to norisces, & hit helpeth to
haue þe more mylke.

XXXVII CORNEAL

Corneal is a derke stone, & hath grete vertue; she
fordoth ire, & hath þe colour of Coralle, and staunchith
blode of all membres, & specially of a woman that hath
the priue maladye.

XXXVIII ALEMAUNDINE

Alemaundine cometh oute of a lande þat is cleped Daise
þt hight alabrace. She ressembleth to Sardoyne, that euel
is to knowe þe on fro þe oþre.

XXXIX ATHEMAUNDE

Athemaunde is a stone of his name that man may
not ouercome; when he hath hit on an anfeld of iren
and smytith aboue with a grete hamer of iren, more is
empeired the Anfeld & the hamer then is the stone; & so
may a man proue yef the athemaunde be veray or non; &
be-cause a man not breke hit in swiche wise, men put hit
in hoote newe blode of a goote, & þat shal in shorte tyme
breke hit & departe hit in many parties. And who þat
berith hit vppon hym thare not drede of euel blode, ne of
þe feuere, ne of Ague, nor thevys shul not take hym, &
shal kepe hym fro oþre greuance. And þe man þat berith
hit shal not be ouercome in no bataille.

THE NORTH MIDLAND LAPIDARY OF
KING PHILIP (MS. C.)

THIS version of the Lapidary of King Philip appears to be
an independent translation of the French text, and not to be
in any direct relation with the translation preserved in
MS. B. It follows the Lapidary of King Philip, with addi-
tional stones as in B.N. MS. français 2008, as far as the
end of the description of the diamond; a short section
based on the prologue of Marbode's Lapidary is then
inserted, and then the author continues his version of the
French text, with a few omissions, as far as Magnet. It
ends with accounts of Coral, Cornelian, Aetites, Selenitis,
Ceraunius, Heliotrope, Aspetites, Haematite, Galactite,
Pantheros, Ophthalmos, Tecolites, Chryselectrum and
Capuduascum, of which all but the last appear to be from
a version, possibly a Latin one, of the Lapidary of Marbode. The lapidary has been described,[1] but has not
hitherto been published.

BODL. MS. ADD. A 106 (MS. C.)

f. 44 FOR ye loue of kyng phelypp of Fraunce, ye whych god
kepe, is thys buke of precious stones I-begynne. & he yt
purchased yis buke serched ma[n]y[2] Abbay, & wyth many
clerkes spak, & wyth gederers of precyuous stones, &
wyth many ladys, for to wytt ye meysterys & ye value &
ye vertus of precyous stones; & yt ye bukes sayd of stones
he turned of latyn in-to fraunce in full consell for loue of
yes wyse clerkes. Yis buke deuysed vs & schewed vs of
f. 44v ye stones/natureles, of tho yt ye byble spekes of, & of tho
yt god hym-self[3] spake of, & of tho yt Saloman spake of, &
of tho yt saynte Iohn Euangelist spake of, ye whyche knew
ye vertus of stones, & of tho yt clerkes spake of. & moche
more oppyn shuld be ye vertus & ye miracles of ye precyous stones[4] ne ware ye mysbelefe of ye pepyll & ye

---

[1] Evans, op. cit., p. 78.
[2] *MS.* may.
[3] h *crossed through after* self.
[4] *MS.* stonnes.

38

vntreuth & ye synn; & a wyse man suld noȝte mysbelefe yt god has noȝte sett vertus in stones & in herbes & in wordes, & he yt beleues noght yis dose gret synn. Ye buke beres wyttnes yt god hym-self commaundyd of hys mouth to Moyses ye profett yt he suld sett xij stones, ye whiche has of mony dyuers maners, in sum apariall of fyn gold iiij, of four pames of lenght & of bred; & yai suld be sett in foure settynges, in euery tire iij¹ stones & he commaundyd yt ye sam aparayl yer yes xii stones suld be yer suld be two chens of gold, & yes two chens of gold suld be sett to ye aparial vnto ye ryght syd & ye toyer to ye lyft

f. 45 syde; ye wh[i]che²/worke wyth ye xii precyous stones thurght ye commaundment of oure lord was sett apon ye pyse Aaraon yt was ye fyrst priste of Iewes. Ye names of ye xii stones yt our lord named of his mouth to Moyses þe profett: The fyrst named Sarde, ye ij Topace, ye iij Amaraud, ye iiij Ruby, ye v Iaspe, ye vi Saphyre, ye vij lygure, ye viij Acate, ye ix Anymatist, ye x Grisolyt, ye xj Onyche, ye xij Birrus. Yes be ye names of ye xij stones yt god hymself named. Ye Apocolyps beres wyttnes yt god louyd so well saynt Iohn Euangelist yt he was sent by A aungell to se ye priuytes of paradyse, as it ware by a vysyon; & he saw paradys huge as a cyte, & he saw xi stones, ye whyche saynte Iohn named: ye fyrst Iaspe, ye ij Saphire; ye iij Cancydonye, ye iiij Ameraud, ye v Sardane, ye vi Sarde, ye vij Grysolet, ye viij Beryl, ye ix Thopace, ye x Crisopas, ye xi Iagunce. Huge vertus gafe

f. 45v god to yes stones yt ȝe/haue hard named, & mony strenthes & to mony oder; bot ye vertu of ye fornamed stones we suld devyse vs fyrst, & efterward we suld deuyse vs ye vertus of ye stones whiche we haue noȝte namede.

Now we haue deuysed ye stones yt god named of his own mouth, & yar vertus, & of tho yt saynt Iohn named, & ye significacons yt yai signefye appon ye nek of Aaron, & ye significacons of tho yt wer in ye fondiment of paradyse.

¹ MS. iiij.
² MS. whche.

I. Sardes & grenes & Alemandres & Iagunce both grew
to-ged*er*, but y*e* Iagunce has y*e* v*er*tu of all y*es* stones,
& he is y*e* fynest thyng of yis warld, & he gyfys to hym-
self colo*ur* gentil & red, & he sal make a ma*n* glad, &
dwell & in trowth; & he sal do a ma*n* forgyte his dysses &
his myschef, & he suld noght dred enchauntime*nt* ne
stangyng of wormes noy*er* of wyld best*es*, & he may pass
well thurght p*er*lyous places; & he y*t* has hym on his
f. 46 fyng*er* A nost sal gladly resaue hym for to be her/bered, &
when he schew*es* hym y*e* ston he sal noght resonable hele
a thyng fro hym y*t* he sek*es*, as y*e* buk says, y*e* trew buk y*t*
II god [is]¹ to vs tak hed to. Dauid y*e* pro*f*eth telles vs y*t* ye
Thopace is god*es* stere.

III.   Emeraud ou*er*-passes al grennes. Ye buk tell*es* vs
y*t* ye emeraud & y*e* pr*a*umes both wexyn to-ged*er*, bot y*e*
fyn emeraud comes of y*e* lond of Syr & of y*e* flom of p*ar*a-
dyse. Emeraud² helpys a ma*n* is eyn & kep*es* y*e* syght
[wt]out³ apperyng, & namly of hym y*t* is in gud belef, for
myche is y*e* emeraud gud for to be-hold & auyse. Neyrons
had a myrro*ur* on y*e* whyche he wald luke, & he wald
knaw by v*er*tu of y*e* ston what thyng y*t* he wald seche; &
also y*t* ston increses a ma*n* ryches, & sal do a ma*n* spek in
gud tempo*ur*; & also he helles a ma*n* of a sekenes y*t* is cald
ennentesce; & also he is myche worth a-gayns tempest &
a-gayns lyghthinge⁴; & knaw it well y*t* he y*t* ber*es* a
emeraud apon hym y*e* mor he sal loue to kepe his body in
f. 46v chast, & y*e* lesse/he sal loue to spek velany, and gladly he
sal ber hym-self fayr, & y*e* gladlyer he sal thynk on y*e*
saule, &⁵ mor he sal loue dysport chast,⁵ & y*e* mor he sal
loue gud wark*es*, & he y*t* has yis ston he has y*es* v*er*tus.
Y*e* byble telles vs y*t* y*e* emeraud was y*e* iij ston named of
god appon y*e* pyce Aaron, & y*er* for it betokynnes y*e* gret
gre*n*nes of hy*m* & y*e* gre*n*nes of y*e* syght of y*e* t*r*inite.

---

¹ *MS.* god to.
² *First minim of* m *above the line.*
³ *MS.* out.
⁴ i *above the line.*
⁵ 5—5 *repeated in MS, beginning* & ye more.

Saynt Iohn tell*es* vs in y*e* Apokalips y*t* he saw y*e* emeraud be y*e* iiij ston in y*e* fundeme*n*t of y*e* varay kyngdom, & y*er*for it betokenes y*e* feyth of y*e* iiij Euangelistez, & saynt Iohn tell*es* vs y*t* y*er* is a man*er* of best*es* y*t* ben cleped Grifons, & yai kepe y*e* emeraud appon y*e* wat*er* of p*ar*adys in y*e* lond of Syr, & yis man*er* of best*es* ben schapyd as a Egle & behynd as a lyon. & y*er* is a man*er* of pepyll y*t* ben clepyd Arimples, & yai haue bot one ee in y*er* hedd*es* and y*t* is befor in y*e* forhed, & yai go for to sech y*e* emeraud al armed on y*e* watt*er*; and y*e* forsayd best*es* goth re[n]aund[1] and flyand and bene myche y*e* **f. 47** me*n* stones at y*er* / power, bot y*e* me*n* ben armed y*t* yai may noght tak yam away fro y*e* me*n*. Ye fyn emeraud & gentil is ryght gren, & he be-tokenes y*e* gre*n*nes of gud fayth, for y*e* gud patriarkes & y*e* gud p*ro*fettes wer so fynly gretly gre*n*nhed, y*er*for yai haue y*e* gret Ioy of heuen. Al tho y*t* ar in yis gret gre*n*nes of sych[t]e,[2] as saynt Iohn says, has bot one Ee, y*t* is to Ih*es*u crist. And y*t* armes of[3] yam y*t* seches y*e* emeraud; and y*e* grifon betokenes y*e* fend*es*. And al yes thyng*es* mot haue in mynd he y*t* wyll ber ane emeraud.

IV.   Ruby is red, and he is worth al y*e* red stone͡ʒ. Ye buk tell*es* vs y*t* y*e* gentil ruby fyn & red is y*e* lord of all p*re*cyous stones & ge*m*me of ge*m*mes, & he has y*e* v*er*tus of[4] all stones & abowue a[l][5] oy*er*, for he is of suche lordchipp y*t* [when][6] he y*t* ber*es* hym comes emonge me*n* al yai suld do hym worschope & hono*ur*. Ye buk tell*es* vs y*t* best*es* y*t* drynk*es* of y*t* wat*er* y*t* y*e* ruby is wett in, y*er*of yai be heled of yar malody; & y*t* is dyscomforth, & he haue gud belefe & he behold y*e* ston he suld be comforted, & **f. 47ᵛ** he/sal forgytt his awng*es* thurght y*e* v*er*tu of y*t* ston; & comforth y*e* eyn & y*e* herte & y*e* body; & also he conquers a ma*n* lordchype abowue[7] yes two stones y*t* ben

---

[1] *MS.* reaund.
[2] *MS.* syche.
[3] of *above the line.*
[4] of *above the line.*
[5] *MS.* a oyer.
[6] *MS.* yt he.
[7] o *above the line.*

cleped grinonfeȝ. Ruby is fund in ye lond of leby, in ye reuer of paradys. Ye buk of Moyses telles yt god bad ye Ruby suld be ye fyrst in ye secund tir of ye xij stones, for to be-token ye secund law & for to alyghtyn yam by nyght & be day; al he lyghtyd yam & hugely he alyghtyd yam, & makes yam cler; yer is no lyght yt spreddes to his gentil colour. Moyses telles vs yt he be-tokenes Ihesu criste yt gretly has a-lyghtyd vs in dirknes. And saynt Iohn euangelist telles yt Ihesu criste, varay lyght, lyghtyned al tho of yis warld. Elyas telles, ye profett, of yis lyght yt went in-to dirknes & yer gafe gret lyght. Saynte Iohn telles yt he couthe noȝte fynd ye ruby in ye fundement of ye kyngdam of heuen of ierusalem, & yerfor was noȝte ye ruby named emong ye xi stones yt Saynt Iohn named and saw in ye

f. 124 fundement of ye kyng/dom of heuen. All men yt beholdes ye varay Ruby & bryghtenes yer of suld be-hold ye varay lyght & clernes of Ihesu criste. He yt wald be-hold he most thynke on Ihesu criste.

V.   Saphir is a conabil ston appon a kynges fynger, and moche is ye saphir holy and gracious of god. In[1] ye lond of leby, in ye reuer of ye oryent, beys sum I fynd mor gentil yand oyer, tho yt bes mor gentil of colour & mor ynde; bot I fynd yt yar bey sum saphyrs yt bes moche dirk, & tho beys bryght ful of vertus at ye fote of yt watter. I fynd oyer saphyrs yt bes noght so moche worth; & al bes vertus & al of god & all bes naturell and al beys full of vertu of gode & of his grace. Yes iiij maner of Saphyrs dystrowes fully enuy & comforttes ye body and ye lymmeȝ; and it helpes[2] gretly to dolyuer hym & a presoner mote toche ye iiij cornars of ye preson & toche hys bondes, & if he haue gud belefe he suld be dolyueryd thurght ye vertu yt god gafe to ye Saphyrs. The buk telles vs yt ye saphyrs ar moche

f. 124v worth for/to hele al maner of boches & almaner of swellynges, if a man belefe well on ye vertu of yt ston; & if a man wesch ye saphyr in water and gyf ye water to drynke to hym yt has ye boche or ye swellyng within his body, he

---

[1] in *above the line.*
[2] *On erasure.*

suld be hole thurght *ye* vertu *yt* sett in *ye* sapher, & *ye*
saphir sal kell a mans body of *ye*[1] hote euyle; & *ye* saphir
sal do a ma*n* be agast for to stell; & also he sal hele a ma*n*
of seknes in *ye* hed, & he sal do away ache fro a mans teth.
And *ye* buk tell*es yt* god counseld hym *yt* wald a saphir
ber for to ber it in chastite, for gretly most he ber hym-
selfe chast *yt* so *ve*rtuus a ston wald ber; & moche is worth
for to ber a saphir for to accord me*n* & to brek wychecraft.
Ye trew buke tell*es* vs *yt ye* saphir is of suche colo*ur* as
heuen, but *ye* strenge of *ye* gret hyght of syght semes *yt* it
be so; & *yt* betokenes *ye* gret hope of *ye* gud holy me*n*
when he is tuched of *ye* varay son*e yt* is Ihe*s*u cr*i*ste.
Saynte Iohn in *ye* Apocalips says *yt* he saw *ye* saphir in *ye*
secund fundeme*n*t of *ye* Cyte of Ioy, & *ye*rfor he be-
tokenes *ye* secunde *ve*rtu, *yt* is hope, & *ye*rfor he was sett
f. 125 in *ye* secunde tyr apon *ye* pyc[e][2] of Aaron/. He *yt* lokes
appon a saphir, he most haue in mynd *ye* Ioy of heuen an*d*
most be in gret hope.

VI.   Iaspes bes of nyne man*er*s and diu*er*s of colo*ur*s
& diu*er*s of *ve*rtus; |and *ye* Iaspes bes fund in welles in
diu*er*s partt*es* of *ye* warld; bot he *yt* is gren agayns *ye* day
he is *ye* bytt*er* whe*n* he is sleked, & mor is worth blak
precle, & when he is frekled wyth red frekles & he be
gren, [a]nde[3] be shape of *ye* old shape, he is *ye* lord of
Iaspes.   & *ye* p*re*cyous Iaspes is gud agayns almane*r* of
venu*m;* & if he toche or be born in place *ye*r Iaspes er in,
he suld swet & schaunge of his colo*ur*s, and he *yt* belefes
well in yis ston he suld staunche blod, malsen & feue*r* &
ye dropcy. & he *yt* luk*es* on a Iaspe sal mak hym myghty
& halsom. Iaspe help*es* gretly a woma*n yt* trauell*es* w*ith*
child *yt* scho sal be dolyue*re*d. & Iaspe sal kep a ma*n* fro
ydell thoghtt*es;* & he *yt* ber*es* hym most ber a caste lyfe.
& *ye* buk tell*es yt* gud Iaspe is gren of grace & of gre*n*nes,
it betokenes *ye* syght of *ye* trew pepyll *ye* whiche tak*es* hed
to *ye* fader, *ye* son & *ye* holy gost; & if any clerke appose

---

[1] *ye above the line.*
[2] *MS.* pyco.
[3] *MS.* ynde.

yam yai can awnswer no nother, bot yai / er trew pepyll;
& suche maner of pepyll betokenes Iaspe. Moses says
yt he is gud agayns fantisyes, for yis ston betokenes ye
faythe of god ye whiche dystroys ye fantasyes of ye dewyll,
of Iewez, of sarazinz. Saynte Iohn says in ye Apokalips yt
he saw ye Iaspe fyrst sett in ye fundement of ye kyngdom
of heuen, yerfor be-tokenes ye Iaspe yes iij vertuys yt suld
be on euery gud man: fayth, hope and charyte; for he yt
lukes appon a Iaspe agayns ye day, of[1] ye fayth of Ihesu
criste he most remembre hym.

VII.   Lygur is a ston yt is fond in ye land of ynd, apon
ye reuer yt is in ye plan forest; & a best yt is cleped lynx
hydes it within ye grauell dep, yt ye gret vertus of ye ston
suld not[2] be helpyng to vs.   The buk telles vs yt lygur is of
dyueris maneres, bot ye best is of ye colour of gold; & yar
beys of colour of Mirr, & som yer bes of colour of ensens, &
som yer be of ye colour of lettur; & yes deuysed a Master
yt is a-clepyd Mayster Thefatus.   Moyses telles vs yt yer
be som of ye colour of Iagunces.   God gafe to yis ston many
vertus: it sal hele a man of ye Iountes, and he sal dysturbe
a man of / euyl vyces.   Ligur is gud to be born agayn many
maner of gowttes, and he dolyuerys a man of al maner of
sekenes yt is nurresched in ye stomak.   Lygur is gladnes
to a man yt is wr[a]tfull[3] and staunches ye malsen.   The
buk telles yt yis ston is gretly gud [for][4] laddes, for he
makes yam plesaunte & mor[5] to be loued.   Yis ston kelles
ye gret hete yt a man has in hys mouth; and who yt tuches
any sor with hym he sal chace away sekenes & blod.   &
know well yt yis ston has of mony men cleped anoyer
name, but god hym-self cleped hym lygur.   Moyses telles
vs yt ye best yt keped yis ston deluyd in ye erth and
yer within ye grauel hydyd ye ston, & so kepes he ye
lygur.   Moyses cleped yis ston ye maner of a nox, and
ye vertu of yis ston is in his rynes & his strength is in

---

[1] *MS.* of of.
[2] not *above the line.*
[3] *MS.* wrtfull
[4] *MS. omits.*
[5] om *crossed through before* mor.

his navil; for ye vertu of his reynes, says Iop, we most vnderstand[1] yes lycherus men, & ay next ye reynes we most haue ye vertu in vs yt signified chastite; & yis for-sayd best yt deluyd in ye erth for to hyd yis ston be-tokenes ye oxen of Ihesu criste, yt is londes kepes. And so with ye holy predicacon ye byble telles yt yis ston was first sett in [th]r[y]d[2] tir apon Aaron yt be-betokend ye gud prechers

f. 126v of Ihesu criste yt comen / on ye thryd tyme of ye gospell.

VIII.   Acate is fund in a reuer cleped Acate, & he bes fund of many manere3. Yer ben som blake & som whyte, diuers colored, & som ygurde; & yer be som of ye sam stones yt haues a whyt crosse; & ycr be som yt haues fygures as yt wer resonne3 & som as bestes yt naturs has sette; & som yer be as Iaspe3 and sprek[l]ed[3] with red sprekle3; & suche maner of Acate is named of mony & gretly full of vertu, and gretly has devysed yes lapyders; and of such Acates bes on vayne3 as of gold; so says ye scriptur yt yer be som has colour of gold, & of Myrr, & of ensens, and of Coral frekleld, and of wex. Ye veray Acate comforthes an old mans lyfe, & kepes fro venum & of byttyng of a serpent, and he gyfues gud spech & cler. We fynd in redyng yt yer is such an Acate yt he yt syttes it in an herbe yt is cleped Cylyne, & he set it in his hand and close his hand, yer sale no man seen hym for ye strength of ye ston; as bukes telles vs yis maner of herbe folowes ye son.[4] Yt maner of Acate is gretly sprekled with red. Moyses says yt suche maner of Acate was apon ye pyce of Aaron & it was blak & he had a strake of white;

f. 127 blakne3e be-tokenes / ye sorow yt we haue in yis warld for our synes, and ye whyt strake be-tokenes ye hyght of hytere3 yt beres ye frute euer-lastyng. By yes two signifi-couns was þis ston sett secund in ye thred tyr, & yt was for ye significacouns of [th]e[5] baptym of Ihesu criste yt saynte Iohn preched to ye pepyll.

[1] *First* n *above the line.*
[2] *MS.* red.
[3] MS. spreked.
[4] *MS.* ston.
[5] *MS.* be; the *in margin.*

IX.   Amatistes is of purpur colour & he drawes to ye colour
of blod. Ye bukes of Mercur telles yt yis ston is comforth to
hym yt beres hym, namly agayns wild bestes yt comes a-
gayns hym; & gretly he comforth a-gayns drynkenchipe,
& holdes a man in gud belefe & stedfast¹ yt wyl comon befor a kyng & a prinse, & he sal do a man worschop in
ye crafte on ye whyche he entermeth; & also he ho[l]des²
a man mekly; & he yt beres yis ston sall haue on hym-self
mynd of god; & also he sal be ryȝte gracyouse. The
scriptur of holy wrytt telles vs yt Amatist is a purpur
colour, & yt he betokenes ye purpur clothyng yt ye Iewes
dyd appon our lord Ihesu criste in dyspyte for yt he mad
hym-self a kyng, and yer-for mot kynges wer purpur when
yai hold gret courteȝ and gret festes; for Salamon telles
yt [by]³ ye clothyng of ye Amatist colour we most man-
127ᵛ teyn ye clothyng proper yt Ihesu criste we/red at his dyinge,
ye lord of Aungels, & worschop it also for ye deth of ye
marters.⁴

X.   Crisolyte semes water of ye see, & castes to ye egh
as gold on euery syd. Ye buke telles yt he is gud to be born
a-gayns naturell stones. He yt beres a Crisolyte may well
enter in many courteȝ withoutyn lettyng, outher any yain
seynge, & all men sall cun hym gret thanke. & ye
scriptur deuysys ye sam ston, & says he yt beres so glorius
ston he most kepe his body in chastite, & treuly he most
ber it on his lift syde. Crisolyte comes of ye lond of
Ethiope; & ye holy scriptur telles yt ye Crisolyte beres
colour of ye water of ye se & of gold. Yt be-tokenes ye
wytt of yam yt wysely gouer[n]es⁵ yam her in yis warld.
Ye glose of ye Apokalips telles yt ye Crisolyte oryentile be-
tokenes ye holy predicacouns of ye myrakels of Ihesu
criste, & yt is lytted with gold in yt syde yt a man coueres
hym; yt betokenes ye gud forbydyng of syn yt ye gud

¹ stadsta crossed through before stedfast.
² MS. hodes.
³ MS. omits.
⁴ a crossed through before marters.
⁵ MS. goueres.

prechour forbydes ye pepyll. Saynte Iohn says in ye
Apokalips yt he saw ye Crisolyte ye vij ston in ye fundement of ye varay kyngdom; yt betokenes ye vij gyfes of ye
holy gost. Ye bybyll beres wyttnes yt god named Criso-
f. 128 lyte ye x. ston to / Moyses for to signifye ye x. commaund-
menttes of ye law.

XI.   Onycles & Sardon & Calcidoyn are waxen togeder
in ye land of Tyr & of Indye & in ye land of Araby; &
yai ben of diuers colours & yai be gretly wertwed. &
euerychon by yam-selfe a naturel ston. Onycles is a name;
& when he has rybbe3 white as veyne3 oyer as rose or
blew or roget, & he haue noght lytyll of blake, Onycle is
his name be ye scriptur. Onycles makes a man noble &
hardy & courtes, & he sal haue lyfe enogh on hym, & he
sal encresse hym in plente of gudes, & he sal kep hym in
helth yt beres hym, as ye buk says. Onycles makes a man
to drem on nyghtes & spek with his lufe ded slepynge, &
he sal haue gud mynd yerof in ye morynge if it be nedfull.
Bot he yt beres hym has mony fayr grace. Ye glos says yt
ye Onycles white & blake semes a man is nayle, & signi-
fies yam yt ouercomes ye vyolence of ye flesche, &, also
ouercomes ye holy men ye frel[t]e3[1] of ye flesche, & yai
be-leueth[2] noght ye hardnes of ye ston with ye deuyll, yt
is ye synfull man yt slepys in his synn. Yus says ye glose of
f. 128v Moyses, yt ye Onycles natturel yt has on hym / red &
white: whit be-tokenes ye wysdom yt comes fro god & ye
chastite yt is ye fellow to Ihesu criste. Ye bybyll says yt ye
onycles was in ye iiij tyr appon ye pyce Aaron, for it be-
tokenes ye iiij Euangelistes yt has naylle3 as a man & as
an Egle & as a lyon; & yus signifie3 ye Onycles of diuers
colours.

XII.   Berels is a ston yt has ye colour of an Egle when
ye sonn smyttes appon hym; & he comes[3] of ye land of
ynde. Ye ryall beral agayn ye son[4] it castes [fir].[5] Ye

---

[1] MS. frelle3.
[2] Third e above the line.
[3] First minim of m above the line.
[4] sto crossed through before son.
[5] MS. for.

buke telle*s* y*t* ye berell noresches lofe betwen me*n* &
wome*n*; & know well y*t·*ye wate*r* y*t* berell has lyen in is
myche worth for seke [e]e*n*[1]; & he y*t* drynke*s* of ye wate*r*
y*t* ye berel has lyen in, he thar noght rak of euyl blod ne
of rotyng ne of feu*er*; & he y*t* bere*s* it is mekyll ye mor
worschoped. Y*e* holy wryte telle*s* y*t* ye berel falle*s* noght
for to be cutt, bot he wyll be playn & pullesched. When
ye son smytte*s* appon a berel, & he be cutt, it be-tokenes
ye first p*re*chou*r* of holy kyrke y*t* p*re*ched ye baptym of
f. 129 Ih*e*su c*r*iste. Y*e* / bybyll beres wytnes y*t* god named ye
berell ye xij ston, y*t* signified ye xij appestolle*s* y*t* p*re*ched
ye baptym. Saynte [Iohn][2] telle*s* in ye Apokalips y*t* he saw
ye berel ye viij ston vnd*er* ye p*ar*durabill cite; y*t* signifyes
ye place y*er* ye vpryssyng sal ben. & y*us* says ye autorite:
if a ma*n* sett a berel to his naked flesch agayn ye sonn, ye
fyr y*t* goys out of ye berel sal bren his flesch; y*t* signifyes
ye me*n* y*t* sem[l]es[3] yai*m*self to gud me*n* & to holy y*t* be
brinynge of ye fyr of charyte.

Now ʒe haue hard ye vertues & ye significacou*n*s of ye
xij stones, y*t* god named of hys mouth to Moyses ye p*ro*-
fett; & ye xj y*t* saynte Iohn saw y*t* bar & sustened p*ar*adys
ʒe hafe herd ye vert*us* & ye significacou*n*s of ye viij; now
we wyll say of ye iiij y*t* ye buke & ye autorite says.

XIII.   Baleys is a ston y*t* saynte Iohn named Iagonce, &
he drawe*s* to ye colo*ur* of a Ruby; & he is fund in a town
y*t* is betwen two sees. Iagonce drawe*s* hy*m* to ye colo*ur* of
ye ruby, bot he nys noght of y*t* man*er* whe*n* he is noght
f. 129v fund / y*er* as me*n* fynde*s* ye ruby. For [h]e[4] chaunches &
he amende*s* his fayrnes in fayr wed*er*, & he is ye mor cler
when ye wed*er* is cler, & *m*or gentil of colo*ur*. He is ye
lord of Iagonce eft*er* ye ruby. Well may a ma*n* say y*t* ye
Iagunce is a ruby. Iagunce baleys, Iagunceʒ Safir, Iagunce
grinad, Iagonce Centeryn, yis[5] man*er* of stanes & of oy*er*
may a ma*n* clepe Iagonceʒ. The balyes is a well gud ston

---

[1] *MS*. men.
[2] *MS. omits.*
[3] *MS*. semes.
[4] *MS. ye*
[5] i *above the line.*

& a gentil & a fayr, for god has gyfyn ham many fayr vertus. Ye buk telles yt ye balyes dolyueris a man of ydel thoghtes & sorow, & he sal kel a man of lychery; & ye buk telles he yt beres a varay balyes & he schew hym to his enmy it thynkes his enmy loth yt he war noght accordyd with hym, & he yt beres hym emonge his enmys he may returne a-gayn hole & sond; & who-so tuches hym to a corner of his hall or of his chaumber or of his gardyn, wo[rm]e¹ may no₃te enter yt may do hym any harm. Saynte Iohn telles in hys glos apon ye Apokalips yt yis ston chaunges his colour agayn fayr weder, & yt he betokenes iiij wyse clerkes yt moues & spekes to ye Iue₃ after yt yai

f. 130 b[eys]², / [as]³ Saynt Paule yt spake to ye gud clerk & to ye Iewes efter yt yai wer, & he moued hym-selfe as ye gentil balyes yt moues hym-self agayn ye fayr wader. & yis lond yer yis ston is fund in ye land of Ethyope.⁴

XIV. Crisopas is a ston yt is born of ye land of ynd. Ye buk telles yt ye colour is gren & castes fyr on euery syde as gold. & he yt beres hym is full of gud graces, & whar-euer yt he comes men be ryght glad of his comynge. Ye glos of ye Apokalips says yt yis ston & hys colour betokenes yam yt leueth in peyn & in trauell & leues in charyte.

XV. Calcydoyn is a ston yt is of truble white, & he is oryentel. God almyghty has gyfyn to yis ston suche a vertu yt beres hym is well spekyng, of gud eloquense; & if he schew hym to his aduersary, in yt tym he sal ouer-comen hym; & if he be ouerled with wrong his ryght sale dolyuer hym. He yt Sardoyn & Onycles beres & Calci-doyn, he sal be well entached bot if he lesse it thurght synn. Calcydoyn beres grace. Yis ston & yis colour be-tokenes yai yt gaderys [y]a[r] bo[n]te.⁵ Ye glos of ye

f. 130v Apo- / kalips telles yt yis ston withdrawes gret speche; yt be-tokenes ye gud men yt withdrawes ye synfull men to gude warkes.

¹ *MS.* wopyne.
² *MS.* boghte.
³ *MS. omits.*
⁴ T *crossed through before* Ethyope.
⁵ *MS.* gaderys aboute.

E

XVI.   Sardoyn is a ston of red colo*ur* with a blake lyst. Yis ston by hym-self temp*eres* y*e* wreth of a ma*n*; & he sal mak a ma*n* rest well in y*e* nyght w*ith*-oute gret dremyng; & so he dos a-way fro a ma*n* euyle vyc*es* & euyl tho3thtes, & he sal make a ma*n* chast & gracyouse. Y*e* buke of y*e* Apokalips tell*es* y*t* Sardoyn be-tokenes yam y*t* suffers gret penaunce in y*er* bod*es* for y*e* lufe of our lord, & dysspysys y*er* flesch as synfull me*n*.

XVII.   Dyamaunde is a ston y*t* is first named in y*e* lapidari. Y*e* dyamaunde y*t* comes of ynd ben cleped male3 & be brou*n* of colo*ur* & of violet colo*ur*; & tho y*t* comes of Arabe ben called female3, & yai be mor blew. A Dyamaunde is no grett*er* yan a small note. Y*t* ston is y*e* hardyst of al stones for he kerues y*e* yrne & y*e* stell & al oy*er* stones. Y*er* may no ma*n* amend his fayrnes, noy*er* for to polysch hym ne for no oy*er* thynge bot in y*e* sam man*er* as yai ben wax & fund. Y*e* lapydary says y*t* god gafe a
f. 131   gret grace to/y*e* dyamaund has mony v*er*tus. A dyamaund gyf*es* to a ma*n* y*t* ber*es* hym strength & v*er*tu; & he sal kep a ma*n* fro dremynge & of fantasy & of venom; & also he kep*es* y*e* lymes & y*e* bones hole; yef a ma*n* fall of on hors oy*er* of oder best he sal kepe hym hole, so y*t* he haue gud belefe; & he dos a-way gastene3 y*t* comes be nyghtt*es*; & he dos a-way chydynge & wreth[1] & lychery; & he sal kep a ma*n* in y*e* poynte y*t* he fynd*es* hym of gud*es*, of wytt, of ryche3, noy*er* in hauo*ur*, ne kouet no3t to myche; & he dystroys lyghtly[2] chydyng. Al yes v*er*tus has y*e* Dyamaund, he y*t* ber*es* hy*m* chast. Dyamaund is a ma*n* defyne3 a-gayns his enmys, & he y*t* ber*es* hym y*e* mor sal lufe god gladly. Suld a woma*n* with child ber a Dyamaund, for he kep*es* well y*e* seed w*ith*in hir body, & y*e* child in y*e* body he kep*es* y*e* lym*me*3 hole. Y*e* buke tell*es* vs y*t* he most be born on y*e* lyft syde; and he y*t* wyl assay hym of his v*er*tus he most haue hym of trew byinge or of

---

[1] e *above the line.*
[2] lystely *crossed through before* lyghtly.

of fre gyft. Hym behoues for to be of holy lyfe y*t* so v*er*t*us*
a ston wyll ber.

De lapidibus p*r*esiosis et in q*ui*b*us* locis su*n*t.[1]

Men fynd*es* I-wryte y*t* Euax kyng of Arabe deuysed be
f. 131v letter*is*, & Neyron, / y*t* was a wys E*m*p*er*our efter Augustus
deuysed how mony man*er*s ben of p*re*cyous stones, &
how yai be named, & of what colo*ur* yai ben eu*er*ychon, &
in what contre yai ben fond, & what v*er*tus yai haue; & I
haue loked yis buk, & y*er*for I haue made yis lytill buke
y*t* is gud & lyght to ber, & yis I mad for my-selfe & for
a few of my frend*es*, for he y*t* p*ur*pusus a p*ri*ue thyng
[h]e[2] lesses ye worschope y*er*of, for it is noght p*re*ue y*t*
mony me*n* knaw*es*; y*er*for I haue ordand it for to gyfe to
iij of my frend*es*, for y*t* is w*ith*out nombrre, & to yam y*t*
lofues god.

XVIII.   Electoyr, y*t* myche is to prays, is engendred in
a Capon wombe of iij ʒer old, & so it wax*es* eft*er*ward.[3]
Yis ston passes neu*er* ye gretnes of a ben. Yis ston is lyk
to crystall oy*er* to cler wat*er*. Old me*n* gafe hym a name
Electoyr; & he y*t* wyll haue vyctory apon his enmy, &
y*t* he sal noght be ou*er*-comen of no ma*n*, ber yis ston in
a rynge of gold on his ryʒte[4] hand, & on y*t* oy*er* syde of ye
hond I-graue a knyght armyd, his swerd in his hand, &
f. 132 eft*er* y*t* lat syng ix messys apon ye rynge, / y*t* is to say iij
of ye Trinite, iij of ye Crosse, & iij of ye Martirs; & when
a ma*n* has yis ryng a-pon hym, lok y*t* he make no defayle
of synn. Thurght ye v*er*tu of yis ston ou*er*com Mylons
of his enmys, & many oy*er* knyght*es* has ou*er*com yar
batell*es* be v*er*tu of yis ston. & he staunches thrist if a
ma*n* set it in his mouthe; & ye Electoyr conquer*es* a ma*n*
in worschep*es* & p*er*formes ye holy; & he sal make a ma*n*
to be stabil & creabil[5] to al man*er* of thyng*es*; & a ma*n*
sal haue ye less wil to lychery; & it is gud to a woma*n* y*t*

---

[1] *At top of f.* 131 v *in different hand and ink.*
[2] *MS.* ye.
[3] *MS.* eft*er*warld.
[4] fyng*er* *crossed through before* ryʒte.
[5] g *crossed through before* creabil.

wil plesen hir husband; & yerfor he yt wyll knaw yis ber
i[t]¹ close in his mouthe.

De lapide herundinis et lapide.²

XIX.   Celidoyn is a ston yt is engendrid in ye wombe
of a swallow, for scho beres in hir wombe yt scho is worthy
to be slayn. Yerfor yis ston is not of ye nombre of ye stones
be-forsayd; but he is full and lytill and has no per in
strengh, bot he passys any gud ston in profitt; for yis ston
is of ij pecys and two colour, blak and red, and yt on and
ye toder is drawen out of ye swallow wombe. Yis ston is
gud for a lunatik³ man, and he⁴ sal hel lang sekenes, and
he sal mak hym yt beres hym fayr spekyng and plesaunte.
Yis ston most be wond in lyn cloth, / and he most be born
on ye left syd, and ye blake on ye sam maner; for yis
brynges many⁵ nedes to gud end, and makes wrethes of ye
kyng to passe a-way; and wen he is wesche in water he
helles sore eyn, and in lyn cloth he is gud for feuer.

XX.   Magnete is a ston yt men fyndes in yis contre,
bot it comes owt of ynd, and has ye colour of yirn, and he
sal be kynd draw vp ye yrn to hym yt is ner hym. & yis
ston is gud for to vndo charmez and nygramencye. & if
a man wil witt weder his wyf be a gud woman of hir body
or noght, set yis ston apon hir hed when scho slepes, &
anon if scho be a gud woman of⁶ hir body scho sal halsen
hir husband, and if scho be a neuyl woman scho sal slepe
still, for ye power yt ye ston has ye which syn. & if thefez
enter in on hows yt is full of clothe and of gud, and ye
theffez set brynyng Collez yerin and cast powder of ye
ston apon ye colles so yt ye smyche go vp and down in ye
hows, al men yt be in ye hows sal be turned vp and down
and it sal sem to hym yt all ye hows turned, and al ye men
wil fle away, and ye theffez may abyd all sur and tak
what yai wyll; & gretly is yis ston gud to make maryage

f. 132v

¹ MS. is.
² In different hand and ink.
³ MS. limatik.
⁴ s crossed through before he.
⁵ n above the line.
⁶ of above the line.

betwyx ma*n* and woma*n*, & for dropsy, & he wil hel thyng
y*t* is brynt.

f. 133 XXI.   Corayle is a ston y*t* is mad of *ye* fom of *ye* se and
ye dew; and *ye* wynd ber*es* it vpe in-to *ye* eyr, & *yer* it sal
congele & wex hard & be-comes a ston; & he has colo*ur*
of gernad red, & he is lik *ye* rote of a tre, & a ma*n* fynd*es*
non lang*er* yai*n* a pas lange; & he is gretly gud to hym y*t*
ber*es* hym, for he has m*er*uellous power, as tell*es* gret
Mast*er*s; yai say y*t* *ye* corall kep*es* a-way thonduerys &
tempest*es* whiche syd y*t* a ma*n* ber*es* him, oyer in hows or
in co*ur*t or in feld*es* or in ways or in gardyns; & wher som
of y*t* ston is cast in *ye* sed*es* he sal kep it fro al tempest of
wedd*er*, ne he wyl suffre no schadow of fend*es*. He gyff*es*
in cerins gud forton.

XXII.   Cornellyn is a ston y*t* is red of colo*ur*; & y*t* ston
me*n* suld not forgytt, for yof it hafe colo*ur* dirke he has
ryght a gud v*er*tue y*t* is noght for to be dysposed nor
forgytt; for whe*n* a ma*n* ber*es* it on his fyng*er* or a-bowt
his neke he sal se*ȝ* wreth & chidynge, & he sal staunche
blod on what lym it be, & on *ye* sam man*er* of a woma*n* y*t*
has blod of kynd.

XXIII.   Etrayte is a pr*e*cyuos ston y*t* is named *ye*[r]for[1]
fowll*es* to bryng furth byrd*es;* ye Egle ber*es* hy*m* of *ye* end
f. 133v of *ye* warld for to kep & defend / of his nest, y*t* no harm
com to hym of his bird*es*. Yis ston ber*es* a-nod*er* lytill ston
in his mouth, as it war w*ith* child; y*t* yai wast noght away,
or els y*t* yai trauell bot lytill for to be dolyu*er*ed, of y*t* ston
let[2] it be bond to hir left arme & it sal kepe *ye* woma*n* &
ye child on lyfe; & it[3] wil make a ma*n* & his wyfe lufe well
to-ged*er;* & for fallyng euyle; & if y*u* trast y*t* any ma*n* wil
anoy *ye*, if y*u* wylt assay hym, mak hym ett with *ye*, & sett
yis ston in his dysche apon his met y*t* he sal ett, & if he
hafe will for to anoy *ye*, whe*n* he tak*es* *ye* mete for to asay
he sal not swelle it down, & yan tak a-way *ye* ston & he

---

[1] *MS.* ye for.
[2] *MS.* lest.
[3] it *above the line.*

sal ett wiþ a gud wyll. Yis ston has colour gernad red, &
ye egle beres hym away in-to diuers contreȝ.

XXIV.   Selinete is a precyous ston yt is noȝt for to be
hyd. He is as gren as any erbe, & he is lyke to a Iaspe.
He kepes ye moment & ye tym of ye mone, & he cresses
& dyscresses wen ye mon cresses & dyscresses; & he is a
sory thyng a-gayns foull weder & tempest & yerfor he is
cleped ye holyston. & he is gud to recur lofe & for to syk,
& when a man beres hym in distreȝ of ye mone he makes
f. 134 mervellous wirkes & profers; & men says / yt it is fond in
ye lande of perse.

XXV.   Saramoyd is a precyous ston & has mony vertus.
When ye ayr is truble & gret wyndes, & when it thon-
dueres & lyghtynes, & when ye mystes departes, yan falles
yis ston of firmament; & yer may no man fynd yis ston bot
in a place yer ye thonder clepe falles, & yerfor is he cleped
saramond, for ye Iewes clepyd thonder seraym. He yt
beres yis ston chastely he may be smyttyn wiþ no thonder
ne wiþ no lyghtyng, nor ye hows yt ye ston is in may noght
be parsched for no weder; & he yt goys be water or be se
he sal neuer be drouned & he hafe yt ston wiþ hym; & yis
ston is gret help for to ouercomen batals; & he yt beres yis
ston sal slep sothly & drem treuly; & yis ston schynes as
it wer byrnynge; & it is lyk a ston yt is cleped pirope.

XXVI.   Elyscrope is a precyous ston yt has his nam efter
his doyng. He has a gren colour lyk an Emeraund. He
has mony vertus. If he be sett in a vessell wiþ water & ye
vessell be set in ye son-bem, he sal mak ye son sem al blody,
& he sall mak[1] a new inclypes in ye son, & it sal sem yt
f. 134v yer comes a strong rayn sodanlye / & anon efter be fayr
weder. & he yt beres hym sal knaw & tel mony thynges
yt be to com; & if a man gyfe hym to a man, if he be of gud
belefe he sal make hym fayr & lyght, & he sal make hym
haue long lyfe, & sal wiþdraw hym gretly fro women, &
he sal do away venom; & he yt beres hym may noȝte be

[1] MS. makeſ.

ouercomen nor be begyld. & yis vertu has yis ston of god; & ʒitt has he a gretter vertu & myʒty, for if he be set to ye erbe yt is of his awn name, if yt erbe be well sakerd & coniured, yer sal no man sen hym yt beres yt erbe. Yis ston comes of Ethyope, of Cyper & of Aufryk, & yis ston has frekeles as it were of blod, & is lyk emeraud.

XXVII. Espetyt is a ston yt sonderes in ye se, & he [is]¹ more precyous yan a ston yt is cleped Aram; & he is cler & red. & if a man cast hym in a pote boyland full of water thurght het of ye fyr, a-non he sal lefe boyllyng & becomen al blod be vertu of ye ston. Yt ston kepes fruttes fro snylles & fro wormes & fro harmes; & wen yis ston is sett in ye son he sal cast bemys as ye son & fyr, & he sal blemys yam yt lokes apon hym for his gret bryghtnes; & he sal kep hym yt beres hym sur when he is agast. & yis f. 135 ston beheues to be born apon ye hert, on ye lyft syd / yar ye hert lyes.

XXVIII. Ematite is a precyous ston yt has ye colour of gernad oder of yrn, & yis ston a-mendes blod, & he is gud for to kep² mans kynd, for he has vertu for to hele sekenes of ye eyn & makes hym cler, & if a man take of ye ston & menge it with ye gleyr of an ege, or els if a man wesche it with ye Ius of a pom-gernad, yan it helpes hym yt castes blod at hir mouthe, & also it wyl hele woundes yt be anoyntyd yer-with; and also it with-drawes ye flour of kynd fro wemen, & ye powder of yis withdrawes ded flesch fro a wound, & also it helles ye flyx; & if yis ston be wesch with old wyn yan wyl he hele woundes of stan[g]yng³ of an eddir; & when it is melled with hony yan is he gud. Yis ston has ye colour of yrn or of rose, & he comes of Aufryke or of ethyope or of Arabe.

XXXIX. Galatite is a precyous ston & has colour sondr, & if a man temper it with hony & drynke it fastyng, he sal make hym hafe mylk; & if a man take a thred of

¹ MS. omits.
² kep above the line.
³ MS. stanyng.

woll & sett it thrught ye hole of ye ston & b[er] it[1] abowt
his neke, he sal haue gret plente of mylk yt beres it; & if
a woman trauell of child, if yt ston be bond abowt hir hipe
f. 135v scho sal be son / dolyueryd. & yis ston was so gretly
alowyd of old men yt wend yt only yt ston gafe to hym
yt bar hym all ye gudenes yt oyer stones myȝte gyf. & if
a man hold it in his mouth, he sal dystemper & troble al
his pou[ers][2]; & when he is wel rubbyd he lythes ye Ius &
ye sauour of mylke.

XXX.   Panter is a precyous ston yt has many colours,
for he is blak, & red, & gren, & pale, & colour of rose;
& he yt has all yes colours to-geder & al dyuersed fro
other, & if yu set hym furth in ye son yu sal ouercomen all
yi enmys. & yis ston is cleped pantera for yt he is lyke to
a best yt is in ynd yt is cleped pantera, & he is of diuers
colours, & when he cryes ye lyons fleys a-way for ferd.

XXXI.   Apthalme is a precyous ston, bot I know noȝte
hys colour, bot his vertu is yt he helles almaner of soris of
yen; & he is patron & lord of theffes, for he kepes ye yen
of hym yt beres hym cler & scharp, & ye yen of yam yt
bes abowte er dirk & blynd, so yt theffes yt beres yis ston
may robe howses & no man sal lett hym.

XXXII.   Thegolite is a precyous ston yt is lyke to ye
rynd of an olyf tre. He is foul for to luk to, bot he is pre-
f. 136 cyous of vertu, for if a man temper hym / with water it
helles a man of ye ston in ye reynes & in bledder.

XXXIII.   Griseletre is a precyous ston yt has ye colour
of gold; & he is lyke to ye colour of laton; & he is a glad
thyng to be seyn in ye morow-tyd, & son efter he[3] sal
schew hym in a noyer colour to hym yt lokes appon hym;
& men says yt he has natur of fyr, for he is as son lyght
as he is sett to ye fyre.

---

[1] MS. buyte.
[2] MS. pounces.
[3] & crossed through before he.

XXXIV. Capuduascum is a ston yͭ makes a man alway lyght, & lettes noȝte a man is gudnes away nor be lesse yan yai war when he had ye ston; & he is gud for a woman yͭ trauelles of child in trew wedloke; & he makes men to lofe yͭ be dyscordabyll, & he gyffes a man gret grace of god & of ye pepyll. & he yͭ beres yis ston may noght be ouercomen in batayl. Also he helles a man of ye dropsy & of ye ston & of al sekenes; & if a man haue any sekenes in his body, wesch yis ston in water or in wyn & drynke it, & he sal be hole; & if he haue ony sor outward, wesche it with ye sam water & it sal be hole.

THE ASHMOLE LAPIDARY (MS. D)

THIS fragment on the virtues of stones is not of any especial interest except for its preoccupation with purely magical qualities. Some of its statements are ultimately derived from Marbode. We have not found any French or Latin text from which it is translated, and it may well be an original compilation.

ASHMOLE 1447. (MS. D)
LATE FIFTEENTH CENTURY

I   HERE BEGYNYS THE VERTUS OF STOUNYS.

Ovtalmus ys a stoune, yf he be wrappyd yn a lory[ll]¹ leue and bere it on thy w[r]yste,² hytt schall make the ynvysebell, and he callyth the patroun of theffy3.

Constantume hath þe same vertu.

II   SILONICUS

Thys ys³ a stoune that grovyth yn the mowthe of a snaylle, and whan the moun wyxyth he wyxyth, and whan the mone wanyt he wannyt. Philosopherys sayn that a tellyt the presagys that ben to cume.

III   THOPHASION

Thys stoune ys yleke to golde, and yff he be pvt yn eny water bovllyent thou mayste pvt thynne hande and svffre the hete of the water thrugh the vertu of thys stoune.

IV   MEDAS ORDINATIS⁴

Thys ys a stoune, effe he be hold vnder thy toung and þu thynke on any nede that schall be do oþer may be do, a-non ryght a remevyth to þi herte þt hyt may not be do away for no thyng.

---

¹ MS. loryff.
² MS. wyste.
³ stoune if he be wrapp crossed through before ys.
⁴ Letter cancelled before second i.

V ALECTORIUS.

Alectorius. Thys ys a stoune of whyte[1] crestall, and
p. 38 he ys drave ovte of a kockys wombe / or elste of a henyes
after-warde that hys y-hellyd ouer x yere, and some sayne
after j yere; and he ys beter that ys drawe oute of a kock
decreppyth,[2] and he ys þe mechelnys of a bene. A makyt
a man lecherous and kend. And holde hym vnder þi tonge,
a-non he woll quinche þy therste.

CELIDONIUS

VI. On ys blacke and a-nother ys rvsty. Wrappyn hym
ynn a lynnyn clothe other elles lether, and lyen hym vnder
þy lyfte arme, he schall make kyend and plesynge. The
blacke ys god·for þe feuerys and abryngyng a Iourne to a
god ende. And þey byth drawe out of þe wome of a swolwe
yn the monythe of Avgust, and ij stonys byth y-founde
kyndely one a swalwe.

---

[1] h *above the line.*
[2] departy *crossed through before* decrepytt.

RICHARDOUNE'S VERSES (MS. E.)

THESE verses are an interesting example of the use of the lore of precious stones, other than the Apocalyptic stones, in a moralizing work. The inclusion of alabaster makes it possible that the list given is ultimately derived from the Anglo-Norman Alphabetical Lapidary,[1] and all the stones mentioned but Carbuncle and Auripigment are to be found there, though not always with the properties alluded to in the poem.

B.M. ADDIT. 34360 (MS. E.)

LATE FIFTEENTH CENTURY

An Hymne vpon Christs being *ye* true
stone vpon *ye* cross by Richardoune.[2]

f. 58r   Gentilnesse[3] and curtesie wold be rewarded*e*
  Of al creatures resonab[l]e[4] in semblable wise,
  Without feyneng or grucchyng of hert enharded*e*.
  Of verray trewe lou*er*s this is the guyse,
 5 Rooted*e* vpon vertu to worship for to arise
  In word*e* & thought and dede knyt al in oone,
  Nat variable ne movyng, but as a stidefast stone.
 Nunpower nor pouerte makith none excuse
  Of theym that love fectually, by cause of dispence,
 10 Al trewe lou*er*s put it in refuse,
  Holdith them content and payed with loves p*re*sence,
  Of theym that meane wele out on absence,
  Nat variable ne movyng but knyt al in oone
  In thought, worde and dede as a stidefast stone.

---

[1] Studer & Evans, op. cit., p. 204.
[2] *This title is given in the 'Catalogue,' fol. 3.*
[3] *Line begins with capital E; g (red) in left margin.*
[4] *MS.* resonabe.

15 Many stones ther ben of vertues commendable,
    As Alabanstre, Allectory and Auripigment,
    Asteron, Adamas, stones tretable,
    Amatistes, Asterites, suche stones I ment
    As wil nat in wethers nor blastes ben blent,
20   Nat variable ne movyng, but knytte al in oone
    In thought, worde and dede as a stidefast stone.
  Suche stones of vertue most commende I
    As swagis Ire and staunchis enmyte,
    And love refourmes, and hath the victory,
25   In creatures resonable commendide to be;
    Of a stone most precious now[1] late see,
    In thought, worde and dede knytte all in oone,
    Lapis xristus, a passyng stidefast stone.
  Mo stones there bene whiche I reherse shal,
30   As Berille, Celidone, the Charbuncle goode,
    Cipres, Cersopas, most shyneng of all,
    The coral clere, flux staunchyng bloode,
    The goode Saphir, most mekest in moode,
    Nat variable ne movyng, but knyt al in oone,
35   In thought, worde and dede a stidefast stone.
  The grene smaragde that is medicinable
    Ayenst tempeste, sikenes and fantasy,
    The Serenice, in love nat variable,
    The Sardius that makith men hardy
40   As champioun stronge, of hert most myghti,
    Nat variable ne movyng, but knyt al in oone
    In worde, thoughte and dede as a stidefast stone.
  Al other stones whiche bene precious,
    That men may se, ful of pure delite—
45   But I of force must be compendious,
    Therfor of theym no further wil I write,
    But of a stone of vertue most parfite,
    In thought, worde and dede knyt[2] al in one,
    Lapis Angularis, a passyng stidefast stone.

[1] now *above the line.*
[2] knyt *above the line in different hand and ink.*

50 Go, litel cedule, ande do thy besy cure
   Al variaunce to avoyde and doublenesse.
   To euery persone do parfite plesure,
   Groundede in love with parfite stidefastnesse.
   Suche love groundede in trowth and stabilnesse
55 In thought, worde and dede knyt al in oone,
   Super hanc petram, a verray stidefast stone. Amen.

        Columbina apparuisti Eleyson
        Verba Auctoris quod Richardown.

THE PETERBOROUGH LAPIDARY (MS. F)

THIS lapidary is chiefly remarkable for its length and for the variety of sources from which it was compiled. The main sources are the *De proprietatibus rerum* of Bartholomaeus Anglicus (whence all the references to Diascorides, Avicenna, Platearius and most of the references to Isidore are derived), the Anglo-Norman Alphabetical Lapidary, the two Anglo-Norman Prose Lapidaries, and the French Lapidary of King Philip or an English version of it not identical with our MS. B. It would appear that the author used John of Trevisa's English translation of Bartholomaeus Anglicus, but he freely paraphrases it at intervals. Besides these he makes occasional use of Marbode, the First Anglo-Norman Verse Adaptation of the first French version of Marbode, and of a Lapidary of the type preserved in Bodleian MS. Digby 13. In fact there is nothing original to be found in the lapidary, though in a few instances the sources have eluded us.[1] Yet it is not without interest, as illustrating both the many sources that united to form the late mediaeval scientific tradition and the attempt to include them all in an encyclopaedic scheme. We have no indication of the author's identity, nor is it known if the manuscript has always been at Peterborough. It is obvious that it must have been written somewhere where the author had access to a library unusually rich in its collection of books on precious stones. The Lapidary has not been published before.

PETERBOROUGH 33 (MS. F)

f. 1   This is þe boke þat euax kyng of Arabe sent to tyberi off rom, of all maner of precius stones as well of her names, vertues, as of here colours & her contreys þat þey ben founde ynn, & of the prevyng & of the assaying howȝ ye schul know hem. Also he seythe that no man schall be in

---

[1] Some may be in relation with the Lapidary wrongly ascribed to Mandeville, and some with that of Thomas Cantimpratensis.

dowte þat god haþe set & put gret vertu in worde, stone &
erbe, by the wyche, if it so be þat men be not of mysbeleue
& Also owte of dedly synne, & many [wonder]full¹ mervailes myȝt be wrowȝt þorow her vertues. And also he
seiþe þat god takeþ stones for a precius tresowur. &
therfor I propose to certifey her names folwyng in ordere
herafter by the A b C, boþe of the bok of euax of All þe
stones þat seint Iohne euangelist & apostell þe which
were schewde to him in heuen wene he lay in cristes lape;
And also of stones of Auycene, ysodor, Diascorides,
Plynius, dias, bartholomus, Richard rufus, & many other
þat treten of precious stones.   And so to begyne I schall
re[h]e[r]se² her colours, vertues, contreys & places þat
þey com owt of.

I.   Absittus is a stone þat is sum-wat of blaces colour,
a partie drawyng to the colour of red, & he is good evyn
weiȝtes & mesors, & he takeþ het of the fire & so lasteþ
xij dayis. Ysidore seyþe þat he is a precius stone, blake &
hevy & strakyd with ·red strakys & red weynes. tº de
gemmis, ysidre.

II.   Achate is a stone fownd in þe orient in a flom which
is cleped achate; & some seyþ þat he comeþ owte of cecyl,
& ther is founde; & he is of many maners; þat one is blak
& ouergirde with whiȝt veynes, & so he haþe al a whiȝt
crose, & he haþe whiȝt figures as of a crosse. Dias. And
such þer bene þat haue branchis, figured as trees & as leuys,
hedys, þat kynde haþe put to. And some þer ben grene as of
iaspe, dipped with red droppis; and þis maner of achate is
clepid of myche folk Diodropie, þat mych is of vertu &
miche yn device of lapidarus. And such Achates þer bene
that han gold veynis. Ðe scriptur tellit vs þat þer bene som
of colour of gold & of ensens & of mirre & of coral
droppid. Ðis achat temporeth softly & comforteþ old men.
And þer is an oder colour as coral, he hath gret [p]oynctes³
as gold; and anoþer that haþe þe smell of myrre, and

¹ MS. & owde & full.
² MS. rerese.
³ MS. yoynctes.

anoþer þat haþe colour as wexe. All þe maner of achates
ben god aȝens venymm & aȝens biȝting of serpentes & he
kepeþ A man fro euell þinges; & he encresite strengþe &
makeþ god spekyng togeder & creable & of goode colour;
he geueþ gode consayl & he makeþ good beleue, he holpeþ
the [p]lesauns¹ to god & to þe wordell. And he seiþe þat
þer is an achat þat is blak & haþe forme of many kyndes,
as semeing of kinges or of princes, for suche is his apparacion of your lord þat swet figure; in þis maner is his know-
yng. / Also som seyn þat þer is oon & is browȝt owȝt of a
contrey lyk to coral, & anoþer lik to wexe of gret valewe.

 Also bartholomewe seiþe: accipe lapidem achatem
dicitur est niger habens albas venas & iste facit vincere
periclam & vires confert cordibus & facit homineibus
gratum potentem & placentem iocunde & secundum &
iuuat contra aduersa.

 Also we fynd in redyng of old bokes þat þer is such an
achates þat woso put it in an her[b]e² þat is clepid þe gold,
& put it in his fist close, no man may se hem. As þe bokes
seyne, þis maner sueþ þe sone; þis maner of achate is green
droppid with red. Moyses put þis achates vpon þe brest of
arone his broder, & was blak & had whiȝt branches; &
þis stone was set in þe þrid corner of þe brist of arone. Also
þer is of anoþer maner of achate which is founde in creta,
as diascorides seiþ, & it haþe a blewe weyne. And þer is
anoþer kinde, þe which cometh oute of Inde, with red
droppis, as ysidore seith. Men trowen þat þe fyft maner
þer-of helpiþ wich-crafte, for þer-with þei changen tempest
& stauncheþ ryvers and stremes, as it is seid.

 Also dias seiþe þat þe same kend is gode to schappes &
ymages of kinges & to schew lykenes of sc[ha]pis³; & þe
maner kynde of creata changeþ perels, & makeþ graciose,
plesyng, & fayr spekyng & shewyng, & yeueþ myȝth &
strengþe. Ðe maner of ston of ynd com-fort þe [s]yȝt⁴ &

¹ MS. blesauns. See note.
² MS. herke.
³ MS. sclepis.
⁴ MS. lyȝt.

F

help*it* aȝens w[e]ny*m*,[1] & it smellith swet & it be nyȝt, as dias seiþe.

III.   Andromada is a ston*e* of iiij man*er* liknes, & is lik to silu*er*, & of hard*nes*, lik to þe diamau*n*t; & he is fou*n*de in þe red se, & he makeþ a ma*n* ys wite to stedefastnes.

IV.   Achites is nom*o*bred amo*n*ges þe stones þ*at* be good; þe egle sekeþe hi*m* i*n* þe vtterist p*ar*te of þe wordil, & he berith to his nest to defend. Ðis ston hath a-noþ*er* ston w*ith*-y*n* him & is moche worthe to weme*n* w*ith* child, þ*at* sche lese not her child; & þey schull ber it in her left side. And a ma*n* þ*at* bereth it, he holdeth hi*m* in a me*n* statt, & defendiþ oldnes, & he e*n*ncrecith riches; & he þ*at* beriþ hi*m* schall be wolbelouid & avau*n*sed; & it makeþ a child to encrese & kepiþ his wytt, & helþe & doþe awaye þe fowle euell. And yf a ma*n* haue to anoþer suspecio*n* of yuel, do put þ*is* ston vndir þe dische þ*at* he schall ett of, & he schall mow ett no mett til þe ston be don*e* awaye. And þ*is* ston is round, & is fovnde i*n* de gret see of occian; & it is good & helpi*n*g to me*n* i*n* batail, & kep a ma*n* sobre; & som seyn*e* it is found i*n* þe egle nest. See mor of þ*is* ston i*n* Etite.

V.   Adamas *vel* asius is a ston þ*at* is liȝt i*n* beri*n*g, & his colo*ur* is witȝt i*n* him [w*ith*][2] b[l]ak[3] tacchis; & hoso will preue hi*m*, ley hi*m* vpon his tonge & frot hit a litel, & Ano*n* a schall wax whitt*er* þen he was befor. And who-soo berith þ*is* ston scall nat haue þe goute nor be potagr*e*, ne no*n* oþ*er* euel schal fal i*n* his legis; & yf eny yuel comeþ, brek this sto*n* i*n*to povder & dri*n*k it w*ith* wy*n*e, & þen scall be hol.

f. 2   Require vlterius i*n* diamo*n*de.

VI.   Adamant is a ston of his na*m*e, þ*at* no ma*n* may be ou*er*-come whe*n* a ma*n* bereþ it vpon hi*m*. And all-so ley it vpon*e* an Andefeld of yren*e* or of stell, & smyte

---

[1] *MS.* wny*m*.
[2] *MS. omits.*
[3] *MS.* bak.

þer vpone with a gret hamer of yrene, for [mor][1] is apeired
þe hamer & þe anfeld þen is þe ston, & so a man may
preve & þe adamant be worþ or no. And þow it be so þat
a man may by no engenns of yrun brek it, in hot new blod
of a gote boke & it will in schort tyme breke & departe
into many parties. And also þes vertues it haþe, þat hoso
berith it vpone him dar not not dred of þe blody flyx ne of
þe fowle agewe, ne no þefes schal tak him, ne he schall not
fale in no such greuance ne harme. And he þat bereth it
schal not be ouercome in bataile. Also a man must close
him in golde, & he most ber him on his lefte honde &
while þu berist & be owte of dedly synne þer schal no
wikkid spret ne[2] enfy of mankynd do þe harme þer as þe
adamant ȝeueþ lyȝt, ne he schall dey sclepyng, ne no pride
ouercome him, ne evel swendes schall hant him; & þu
schal be curtes & loue goddes seruyse; & it schall defend
þe of þin enemye. Lok þu do no dedly synne while þu hast
þis adamant vpone þe. Ðis preved euax kyng of araby &
oþer many mo.

Require vlterius in magnetes.

VII.   Agatten is a stone, & it is lik þe skyn of a lion.
Some clepiþ it agapis. Yf a man be wounded with eny egge
tole with þe poynte, tak þat stone agatene & wassh him in
clene water, & þen ley it to þe wounde, & it schall draue by
þe vertu of þis ston all þe wenem owte of þe wounde. And if
eny scorpion or eny serpent stynge eny best, mak þis ston
to powder & ley it opone þe wounde or drinke it with wiȝt
wyne, & þey sall be hol. Wyles þu berest þe stone þu schal
loue goddys servise; þis preuede þe emperour Tiberius.

VIII.   Alistores vel alettoria is a ston whiȝt shynynge
lik to cristal water þu schald fynd him onder An old cok or
vnder an old capene; wene þey ben passed vij yer old þey
will gendir þis stone in her wombe, & þis stone is clepid
alistores. Ðese ben his vertues: he þat berith þis ston

---

[1] Not in MS.
[2] be crossed through before ne.

vpone him, he schal be hardy on his enemyes; he þat bereþ
ouer his helme, he schale neuer be discomfet in werre.

Also dias seiþ, who-so berith þis stone he schal be a
conquerour. Also who-so bereþ þis stone vpone, he schall
be lecherowse & amarowse of wommen, & a fayr speker.
And yf he haue eny opostome in his body, mak powder of
þis stone & drinke it, & he schall be hole; þis preued
croantis in battaile.

Some men seyn þat þis stone groweth fro iij ȝer age til
he be vij ȝer old, & it is founde in þe capons wombe; & it
is lyke trobel cristall. And yf a man haue gret þurst, put
þis ston in his mouþe & it schal help him anon. Also a man
or a womman may not conceyue, ber þis stone vpone him
& þey schal conceyue anoon. And it is godd for a woman
þat will haue of her lord or of her master. Also þis ston
makeþ a woman to be delyuerd [of]¹ child & encresþ well
mylk, so it be vsed beforn m[ete].²

f. 2v Also many kynges han had þe victorie in battail & it
helpiȝt myche in cases. And he schall be gracius þat bereþ.
Also dias seyþe þat þis stone exciteþ þe seruice of venus; &
he makeþ a man gracius, & stedfast, & victoriose, & wise,
& redy, & connynge in plee, & it acordeth frendes &
quencheþ þrist in þe mowthe.

IX.   Alabastre is a stone þat is cendre & whiȝt when it
is grounde. Whoso drinkeþ him with eysel, he is good for
all maner sores in þe fote or in þe knee.

X.   Alabanda is a ston of þe kyngdom of Asie; & þis
alabanda is myche lyke þe colour of sardayne; & he makeþ
scharpnes of iuges. Ysodre seyþ þat þis ston alabanda is
a precius ston, cler & comndable rede as sardines; þe vertu
þerof exciteþ & echeþ blode.

XI.   Alemandyne comeþ owte of a lonnde þat is clepid
dayse, þat [is]³ clepid asabrace. It resembleþ mych to
sardyne, þat yvel it is know þe ton fro þe odere.

¹ MS. omits of.
² Only m left at edge of page.
³ MS. omits is.

XII. Alpitistes is a red stonе schynyng, & it is of such
vertu þat it leteþ þe cawdryn of cedyng or boylyng, &
coleþ þe water in schorte time. It doþe away þe briddes of
þe londe þat is swet, & it fordoþe medlynges, & makeþ a
man hole; and put it in þe sonne beme & it зeueþ bryзtnes
as it werе feirе; and yf þu wolt berе it þu most berе it onе
þy riзth side.

XIII. Albestus or asbestus is a stonе þat comeþ owte of
þe contrey of archady. Ðis ston haþ coler lik to þe colour
of yrenе, & it is a wonderе kynd, for if he oones liзth
he with-holdeþ mych feyгe, & þer may welneзt no þeng
quenche þe lieзt of him. Ðat stonе is made with so crafty
þinges of which naciouns þ[at]¹ tak with sacrelege won-
drede; for in a temple of venus is made a candelstik onе þe
which was a lantren so brenyngе þat it miзt not be quenched
with tempest ne with raynе, as ysodre seiþe, ll° xvj° t° de
gemmis.

XIV. Aristinctus is a ston riзt hardy. Yf a man smyteþe
onе it will flawmy sperkyls as it wer feyrе owte of þis stone;
& ley it vponе herdis of flex, & . . . . . .² herdes with þe
powder þer as þu art brent, it schal helе þe brennyng;
also þu myзest smyзte fir þer-of vponе herdis.

XV. Amatitus is a ston like to purpull red as. . . .² wyne
or red rose in color. Ðe boke telleþ vs þat þis ston is comfortable to him þat bereþ it when wild bestees comen to him;
& it is mych comfortable in all sorow[s].³ And it holdeþ a
man in gode beleive & strongе boþe to body & to soule to
him þat bereþ it worþely & clenly. And whoso bereþ him
schall singe clerly & with gode voys. And as þe boke of
Moyses tellith þe, he þat bereþ him schall⁴ be welcomе
beforе þe kynges and lordes, & delyuerly he schall worche
þe craft þat he entermeteþ of, And it makeþ a man mek.
Whoso bereþ þis stone schall haue in him þe more mynde⁵

---

¹MS. þey.
²Illegible.
³MS. sorowþ.
⁴MS. schall schall.
⁵MS. l myndе.

of god, & be gracious. Also whoso bereþ þis [a]metist[1] no euel spret schal haue pover to don him harme; neiþer he schal haue no yuel dremyng anyȝt; neþer in feyre ne in

f. 3 water / neiþer feuer, ne he schal dred; & his catel schall encrese, & his enemy schall neuer ouercome him in a riȝtfull qwarell; neiþer he schall be prisoned ne dy withoute repentauns of his misdedes, ne long be in presoun, but if it be in relegius; ne no horse schall founde vnder him, he he schall not assent to eny tresoun, neþer horse þat he re[d]yþ[2] one schall neuer haue þe wormes ne trenche. Also isodre seiþe þat amitistus is pu[r]þel[3] red in color, & is medeled with þe color of violet, as it were a blasinge rose, & liȝtly casting ow[t][4] as it were schinyng bemes þat ȝiuen liȝt. Also ysed seyþ þat þer is a-noder kynde which is myche lyke to blow & he is not al f[i]ry[5] but he haþe vertu of ·hete, and þer ben v kendes þer-of as þias seyþ. Also diasçorides seiþ þat þe purpel red is most noble & better þen þe oþer, for þe vertu of helpit aȝen dronknes, & makeþ a man to worche, & putteþ away ydel þoutȝtes & maketh gode vnderstondyng; & it is nessh, so þat mene may graue þeryne & writhe. Of þis color schul kynges cloþe hem when þei holden her courtes.

XVI. Anittida is stone lik to oþer stones þat begynnen by a; & his vertu is, if þu hast him þu maist commaund þe devell to þe, & he schal bere ouer þe se & þu wolt, & he schal do þe no harme.

XVII. Adredamian lapis formi quasi tessera quadre
Dicitur argenti representare colorem
Cuius duricies quasi duricies adamantis
Ipse maris rubri mixtis reperitur arenis
Quam magus affirmat tantem virtutis haberi
Vt possit presens animos sedere volentes.

[1] MS. metist.
[2] MS. reyþ.
[3] MS. pupel.
[4] MS. ow.
[5] MS. fry.

XVIII.   Aracontalides is a stone þat men clepeþ lime-cons brynge it in to ynd. It is purpill blak. If a man wasshe his mowþe & hold it vnnder his townge, as longe as þe mone is waxyng, a man may dy[uyn]¹ fro þe morne to mydday, & þe cours to-for day, & wehen sche is prime þen last her post al daye riȝt as when sche is of xv dayes full of age; his strengþe sholdith no lengere.

XIX.   Aricheces is a stone red shinyng as brennyng fire; & if þu wilt preve him, þrowȝt him into þe feyre & it schall wax pale. He þat bereþ þe stone & he be sike he schall neuer be hole.

XX.   Akamanda² schineþ like water, & he is founde in þe water or reuer of nilus; and he is gode to a man þat bereþ him; þer schal no dedly wreþe ouercome him whilis he haþ it vpone him, so þat he lese not his vertue.

XXI.   Asterides & adiamante be wel ny lyke, for þey ben closed like togeder. Đis ston asterides is like a stare þer is no s[o]ne³ so trobel þat schal cast clernes one him & þe firmament schal clere. All þe vertues he haþe as þes oþer þat begynneþ with a befor þis. Asterides is wyȝth & conteyneþ þe lyȝt þerynn I-closed, as it wer a ster goinge withyne, & maketh the sonne bemes lyȝt.

XXII.   Astrion is a ston & it is lyk cristall, for he takeþ no colour, as schinyng lik þe sterres ben vp, for of þe sterres he takeþ his colour. Also þer is anoþer stone of þe same colour þat mene clepen arechetes, & he schyneþ as brenyng feyr, as it is be-for seyd. Đis stone is founden in ynde, & in þe medel of þe stone þere is schynyng like a ster with clerenes of þe ful mone, & he haþ þe nam þat is clepid astris, / for yf it is set in þe sterelyȝt it takeþ lyȝt of him, as Isodre seyþ, t° de cristall.

XXIII.   Argirites is a ston lyk to syluer with golden spekkys.

¹ MS. dyne.
² kadaman crossed through above.
³ MS. slne.

XXIV.   Andromia is lyk þerto in colour, & it is a ston with þe colour of siluer; and Isodre seyþ it is iiij cornerd in schap as ben þe corners of a diamounde; & it is as stronge as þe ademant; & wyches seyen þat it haþe þat name for men wenen þat it refryneþ hastines & wraþe of hertes, as Isodr seyþ, s° de gemmis.

Berellus

XXV.   Berel is a stone & is browȝt owte of ynd, & it is myche worþe. Đis stone is lyk water & also myche lyk cristall; & it haþe a rounde schap, some of gretnes of a napill & some lese. And whene þe sone schineþ, whiche comeþ owte of þe londe of ynde, þe rial berel casteþ feyr aȝens þe sone. The boke telliþ vs þat berell norschit loue betvxe man and woman; and wyȝt it well þe water where in it haþe leye his mych worþe to sor yene. And whoso drynk þe water þat it haþe leye in, it kepiþ him fro ȝexyng, & doþe away þe chafing of þe liuer; and whoso bereþ it schal be myche worchyped. The boke of dyuynyte seyþ to vs þat þe berell schal nat be scharp but pleyne & pul-shid, when þe sone schynyth. The bible seyþ to vs þat owre lord god bad moyses to set berel þe xij stone in þe brest of arone. Sent Iohne seyþe in apocalyps þat þe berell is þe heyest in þe fundament. Also whoso beriþ nyȝ to his flesche þe berel aȝens þe sone, þe feyr þat comeþ owte of catcheþ¹ þe flesche; also þei þat taken þe berell & holden aȝens þe hote sone & holden lynen cloþ or flax or cotone, & þat schall wax one feyre þorowe of þe sone & þe vertu of þe stone. Ised seyþ þat þer bene x maners kynd of berel, & he haþe pale greynes, & þey schynne toward þe colour of gold; & þis ston cummeþ oute of ynde. Dias seyþe þe vertues of berell þat is most palle, þat berell is best aȝens stryfe, & makeþ þat a man may not be ouercum. Also he makeþ a man to be sufferable. Also he yeueþ gode witte, & he is gode aȝens þe seknes of þe liuer, and also aȝens cherkyng & bolkyng; & he helpt most þen yne, & it brennit his hond þat bereþ it if it is holden before þe sone

---

¹ cha *crossed through before* catcheþ.

and makeþ a man of¹ grete astate & he loueþ will matremonye, and he holdeþ al þe sorow of þe splene.

Berellus is a stone þat is wiȝt, somwhat grene; as it
semeþ to þeyn yene-siȝt, a fowle of þe see is peyntyd
withyn, & aboue a fase of a best which[is]² corniclam. If
þu berest þis stone in a rynge, put a litel sauen vndire þe
left kne, & þu schalt neuer be wroþ with þe woman þat þu
hast weddid; also yf þu hast yuel in þin yne, grynd þis
stone to powder, temper it with water, whas þeyn yen &
þu schal be hole. Also it is seyd þat cristall is a maner kend
of berell, & haþe pale greynes þer-of schinyng toward þe
coleur of gold. Ðat stone cumeth owt of ynde.

XXVI. Bericia is a ston, & he is like water. He is gode
for swellyng in mennes belus; bet þat stone & grynd
him to smal pouder, & drenk him, & he schal be hol of his
swellyng of þe beleys.

f. 4 XXVII. Belloculyis is a stone, & he is like to berell.
With-in him þer is a pirnell of clernes, & a-bowte him þer
is a blak cirkel schynyng lyke ȝelowȝ gold. He þat bereþ
þis stone schall neuer be dede in baytayle for no egge tole.

XXVIII. Badda is a stone þat is well yuell to fynnd
aboue all þe stones þat ben, for it schal neuer be founde but
yf a man kerfe þe schip bordes, for it stekeþ so strongly
þerin þat men may do it no harme, & no man may gete it
with-owte keruyng of þe tre; & it haþe þe coler of rede, &
semeþ all rede.

XXIX. Betumques is a stone of þe contrey of acherdes,
& he is colour lyk to yerne; & he is of merwelows maners;
& he is of þis kynde: if he be oones take & put to þe feyr,
he schall bren all day & ever mor lastyng.

XXX. Baleis is a ston þat seynt Iohne cleped Iagounce;
& it þrawit him to þe colour of rubie; & it is founde in a
yel þat men clepen coracle, bytwene þe sees; & in þat yel
so clepid is þis stone Iagounce founde, & it drawiþ to þe

¹ g crossed through before of.
² MS. omits.

colour of rubie, but he is not of þat maner, for when he is
founde in places where men fynd him, þe rubies changen
hem & amend his fayrenes aȝens fayr tyme, & þe mor þey
ben clere when þe tyme is cler. Ðe Iagaunce baleis is of
mor gentil colour after þe rubie. Iagounce baleis; Iagounce
saphir; Iagounce granet; Iagounce ce[t]ryn[1]; Iagounce þe
gentil baleis. Owre lord ȝaue þer to many feyr vertues.
The boke tellyþ vs þat whoso bereþ þe very bayleis, &
he schew it to his enemyis, he may turne aȝen hol & save;
and whoso towcheþ þe iiij corners of his chambere or of his
hall or of his gardyne, wormes ne tempest schal do no
harme to þat howse. Also þat stone chayngeþ aȝens fayr
tyme, & mendyþ her colour. Ðe ston is found in an yle . . .[2]
in the lond of Crope.

XXXI.   Crisolide recembleþ mich to þe water of þe see,
& castyþ a flawme a[s][3] it wer of gold by euery syde. Ðe
boke seyþ þat it were gode to bere amoung kyndly stones;
and who-so be owte of dedly synne & of schrewdnes, he
may enter into many cowrtes & contreys with eny aȝen-
seyng; and all men schall bere grace to him. And as þe
bokes tellen vs þat who-so haþe crisolide persed & put
þorow a brestell here of an asse he schall mow go a-monge
develles, & hafe hem by nyȝt with-owt eny dowt; and as
bokes seyþ þat who-so beryþ þis stone he schall [kepe][4] his
body trewly. It schall be bore on þe lefte syde. Crisolide
comeþ owte of ethiopie. Also crisolide bereþ colour of þe
see water & of gold. Sent Iohne seyþe in þe apocolyps þat
he sey crisolide þe vj ston in þe fundament of þe wery kyngdome. The bible seyþ þat crysolide was in the brest of
aarone. Also Ised seyþe þat þer is anoþer maner of crisolide
þat is clepid crisoletus, & he is colerd as gold; & he is well
fayer in syȝt in þe moruntyde, & þen as þe daye passeþ his
coler waxeþ dyme. Ðis stone takeþ most soone & if to be
set by þe feyr anone it waxeþ into a lyȝe.

---

[1] MS. cerryn.
[2] *Illegible.*
[3] *MS.* a.
[4] MS. *omits.*

XXXII.   Calcidonice is a ston of white pale coler, as it
wer a trobel whitnes; & it comeþ owt of þe est, & it is lik
f. 4v to cristal; & he þat bereþ / him schall [be]¹ wel spekyng
& ful of gret eloquens; & if he [haue]¹ eny ple or cause,
schwe þe stone to his aduersary, & it schall helpe him in
his cause, & if he pleded with wrounge it helpit him in his
riȝt.   He þat bereþ þe sardyne, þe onycle & calsidonye, he
schall be wel enttacched, but yf he lese his vertu þorowȝ
synne.   The calsedony bereþ grace to him þat bereþ him;
and if a man be iuged þorow fals iugement þis wol nat leue
fro him þat he schall not be lost from him; & he schall loue
þe seruice of god whiles he bereþ him clen.   Also Isod
seyþe þat þe ston is gendryd of reyne of yower lordes as it
is seyd; and he is founde in þe full of þe mone; & he is not
founde but of iij colours, as þe lapidare seyþ þat all kynde
þer-of with-þraweþ² grauynge, & drawyþ to him-self
strawe if he be het or chafyd.   Ised seyþe if þis ston be
persed & Ibore makeþ a man to haue maystre in causes,
and it helpit aȝen iapis & scornes of feendes, & kepeþ
& saueth vertues as diascorides seyþc.

XXXIII.   Crisopas is a stone & it is brouȝt oute of þe
lond of ynde.   Ðe bokes tellyne vs þat his colour is gren,
& þey ben lyk hogges yen, & þey caste oute as gold by al
sydes.   Who-so bereþ it, men schal be glad & ioyfull of his
commyng.   This crisopas comeþ owte of ynd þe more. And
som men seyen his colour is lyk þe Iues of apples, & he
schewit lyke to gold; and [he]³ þat bereþ him schall be ful
of grace, & be loued of all men & women. And some men
seyne þat þis ston comeþ oute of ethiope⁴; & he schyneþ
moche in þe nyȝt.

XXXIV.   Chilindris lapis volubil in modum columpne
quaidra coegit.

XXXV.   Coramis albus et durus.

¹ MS. omits.
² wᵗ above the line.
³ MS. omits.
⁴ Egype crossed through before ethiope.

XXXVI.   Cemedia lapis q*uis* i*nue*n*itur* i*n* cerebr*o* pisc*is* eiusde*m* nom*in*is.

XXXVII.   Cemieus lapis flamme*us* a color*e* dittus.

XXXVIII.   Calluca e*st* gemma viridis color*is*.

XXXIX.   Cristallus is a ston*e* þ*at* co*n*ceyueþ wel fyre of þe son*e* bem.   Also make poud*er* þ*er*-of, gif it to þe nurse to þry*n*ke, & it schal i*n*crese her mylke & multiplye it anon*e*.   Also c*r*istall haþ þ*at* vertue, þ*at* if eny ston*e* haþe lost his v*er*tu þorow3 synne, let hi*m* co*n*fes hi*m* of his sy*n*ne, & take & wasche þe c*r*istall i*n* feyr wat*er* & towche þe ston þerewyþ, & ano*n* he schall tak his v*er*tu a3e*n* by þe v*er*tu of c*r*istall.   Som me*n* sey*n* þ*at* he is harded by gret cold, & so he becomeþ c*r*istall.   Also he kepeþ a ma*n* chast, & makeþ a ma*n* myche worchipid; and me*n* seyn*e* þ*at* it come owte of ynde & of araby; and old anceters telli*n* þ*at* it is harde*n* by froste; and some me*n* co*n*trarie*n* þe old maisters; and so many co*n*traries þ*er* bene þ*at* it is not of so gret coldnes.   Also Ised seyþe c*r*istall is a bri3t ston*e* & colerd w*ith* watery coler.   Ma*n*ye trowe*n* þ*at* snowe or yesse is mad hard i*n* spas of ma*n*y yers, & þ*er*-for þe grekes 3afe a name þ*er*-to, þ*at* it is ge*n*dred in aseie & i*n* cipres & namely in þe norþe mow*n*tens þ*er* þe so*n*ne is most ferue*n*t i*n* somer, & þ*er*for þey maken yesse to dur*e* lou*n*g, & þ*at* þey clepe*n* c*r*istall.   Ðis stone, Iset anon*e* i*n* þe sone, it takeþ feyr*e* & ly3t þ*at* he setteþ drie táddestoles afeyr.   His vse is ordeyned to dry*n*k and worchep, no od*er* þi*n*ge but what cold þyng may suffr*e*.   Also dias seyþ of c*r*istal, & seyþe þ*at* it is hard & torned i*n*to a sto*n*, not only by v*er*tu of stre*n*gþe of cold but mor by erdly v*er*tu.   Ðe colo*ur* þ*er* of is lyk to yesse.   Also þre*n*k it & it helpit a3e*n*s colica passio.

f. 5

Hu*n*c & tritum quida*m* cu*m* melle propina*n*t
    p*ar*tib*us* i*n*fantes qu*ibus* assygna*n*tur alendi
Qu*o* potu credu*n*t repleti vbera latte.

XL.   Celidonie is a ston*e* þ*at* me*n* fynd i*n* þe wo*m*be of a swalow.   Sche is not feyr, but not for þe*n* sche is moche valow*ur* & mor þe*n* eny oþ*er* stones i*n* profyte.   Of þes

stones þer ben too maneres; þer bene þe one blake & þat
oþer red; þe red is gode aȝens a malady þat men clepen
lunatix, wherby he falieþ, & wherby he is foolych &
wytles & falleþ þer-with long tyme; let him ber þis ston &
it will make him well to spek & wel to be loued and . . .[1]
But þe blak stone, & a man bere it in such maner, it schal
help to do grete þynges. It helpeþ aȝens malices of gret
princes & kynges. Ðe water þat it is wasshen in is myche
worþe to hot yueles. Also it is miche worþ þis stone, if it
be hold at þe sacrament & be wounden in linen cloþe,
withholdeþ þe feuer & aȝen stondeþ wycked humours þat
comen abowte in many maners; and if it be wasshen in[2]
clen water it is gode for sor yene.

XLI.   Coral is a ston þat groweþ in þe red see as an erbe
þat is gren, & when it is owte in þe eyr it wexyþ hard &
red & recembleth to a branche, & it is no more þen half a
fote, & it is mych louely to him þat bereþ it.   And þe old
autors seyn, ȝerastros, Methodorus, & þe gode autour
phytonas, it þedfendeþ tempest in þe plas þer it is, and þe
stone is gode to set in a vynnȝerd, or in gardynes or feldis,
for it kepeþ away tempest & all yuel, & makeþ þe fruyte
to multeply.   And he delyueriþ a man fro fantaseys; ane
it yeveþ a gode begynnyng & a gode endyng, & stancheþ
blod and he is gode for þe fowle yuel.   Ðis corall is lyke
raue flesch ywash, redische.   Also whoso bereþ þis stone
vpone him or one his fynger, he schal get loue; and if he
haue e[n]y[3] siknes vpone him he schal sone be hol.   Also
powder of þis stone ydronke is riȝt good for þe crampe.
Also ysodre seyþe in cci° de gemmis rubeis þat it foloweþ
þer þat as precyus stonnes þat margarite is amonge vs, so
preciose or more is þe coral amonge þe yendes.   Wycches
tellen þat þis stone wiþstondiþ lyȝtynge; and Ised sayþ þe
same, þat it putteþ away tempest & whirlewyndes.   All
auctours seyn þat corall is[4] gode & helping agayn þe fowle

---

[1] *Apparently* syde.
[2] & if ben *crossed through before* in.
[3] *MS.* ey.
[4] *MS.* corall is corall is.

yuell, for þe fendes gile, for schornyng, for to staunche
blode, for woundes, for þe crampe, for gardyns, for to
multepley fruyte, for make god beginnyng, for to make
gode endynng of causes & redes.   Also þer is wyȝt
corall, & it haþe all þe vertues þat þe rede coral haþe &
moo. If a man have sore yen, or sor teeþ, or sor in þe rofe
of þe mowþe þat be full of bleders, take þe wyȝt corall &
g[r]inde¹ him small, & temper it with water, & wissh þin yene
þerwith & þey mowthe & they teeþ, & þeyn bleders schall
be holl. Also yf a man or a woman haue þe blody menysone,
þrynk þe powder of þis ston, & þey schal be hole & if þu
wilt bere þis ston þu most perse him & þen bere þat stone.
All þe vertues he haþ as all þe stones that begenyne with
f. 5ᵛ C C C.

XLII.   Cymydia is a stone, & he is found in þe hedd of
a fisch; & is longe stone & a wiȝt. If a man bereþ him in
his mowþe þer schall no tempest in water do him harme
neder by lond, ne he schall neuer be scomfited in were.

XLIII.   Cymbria is a ston þat comeþ of a fissh of þe see,
& þat fyssh men clepen ȝele²; þis ston is wyȝt & dry as
chalk. He þat bereþ þis stone schall be mery & laxatyf,
& he schal neuer be gret scleper, ne he schal neuer tak
gret colde in water ne in londe.

XLIV.   Collorus is a stone, & it is lyke a sapher but he
[is]³ wyȝte in schynyng as water of the see. He þat bereþ
þis ston percede abowte his nyke schal neuer dedly wraþe of
euencristene; & he schall haue a man fro wyckyd spirites;
þat he deseyreþ riȝtfully he schal haue.

XLV.   Capnices is a stone lyke cristall; þu schalt not
knowe þat one fro þat oder, safe þis capnice is wyȝtter þen
þe cristall. He þat bereþ þis ston schal not haue þe dropsy,
& it schall defen him fro wyckyd enchauntementes; & if a
man be seke & drynk of þis ston he schal neuer be hole;
þis preued euax þe kynge.

¹ MS. ginde.
² Read cete?
³ MS. omits.

XLVI. Corinthe is a ston blac & rounde, & it is
myche worþe aȝens venymynge of bestes, as of adders &
oþer. If a man stamp it with oyle roset, & bereþ it amounge
wylde[1] best when he goþe in desert, & haue with corenthe,
he dar not reche of hurtyng of edders. Þe þrid maner is
more preysed, for it is one party scharp & one þat oþer
partie as it were yern grounde. A woman þat bereþ it one
here, it causeþ perel to þe chil in here wombe.

XLVII. Crapadoune, ne serpentes townge, ne many of
oþer stones to þe wych god haþe ȝeuen vertu be not
ynoumbred amonge þe xxxvj stones befor nemed, for carpa-
done is founde in þe hede of carpadonie þat is of vij ȝere
old & mor; & sche þat bereþ þis ston, wene sche meteþ
with a man comyng aȝens here, sche ryseþ vpone her fete
behynd with gret stre[n]gþe[2] by þe vertu of þis stone. And
þis stone is half broune & half wyȝt al abowte. And he
þat will haue þis stone, he most[3] take þe crepaud & put
him in a new pote of erþe, & make þer-in many holys, &
set it in an Ant-hell, & keuer þe pott aboue; And þen
schall þe antes ete þe crepaude all save þe bones, and þu
schalt fynde þe stone styk one þe hed of þe crepaude. And
he is god for venym, & he most be set in fyne gold; and
some seyne, þat it is blak and is gode for medecyne & for
venym, and þer as he is may no yuel be done. And he
makeþ a man & woman myȝty; also he makeþ a man to
incres fro day to day, & abounde in worthinnes. And
some seyne þat þer is one of þe colour of wax, & he is
gode to conquer batayls.

XLVIII. Caltophono is a stone þat is blake, & it makeþ
a man to haue a swete & cleyr voys. If a man bere þis
ston vpone him, he most be mek þat schall bere him.

XLIX. Caladista is a ston þat haþe þe colour lyk sendres.
Þe woman þat þrenkeþ it with oyle, it schall multepley
her mylke; but sche most vse it befor met or after

[1] Wᵗ hym crossed through above wylde.
[2] MS. stregþe.
[3] MS. he most he most.

badyng; and if it be perced & an her of wole of a schep
þat is with lambe & be put þorow, & hanked at þe
norseis neke, it scha mych awayl her; and if a woman
trauell with child, let her bynd it to her þeyȝe. And if a
woman make povder þer of & temper it with salt & water,

f. 6 & noynte here within & withowte, it schal awayll / myche.
And þe water avayleþ myche þe sch[e]pe[1] fro þe reme.
Also þe old autors seyn it schall as myche avayle as all.

L.   Corneole is a derke stone, & not-for-þan it haþe gret
vertu. It fordoþe wraþ, & it haþe colour like blake flessh,
and it well stanche blod of all membres, & namly wemmen
þat han ouermyche her flowres.

LI.   Calonite it is a stone þat is called fre, & he is lyk
to purpill color, & he is founde in ynde. If a man put him
in his mowþe erly in þe moruntide til þe owr of sixe in þe
waxinge of þe mone, he may deuyne al þat is after to come,
& encreseþ & decreseþ as þoþe þe mone; and whene þe
mone is pryme, þen duret his myȝt al day. Ðis stone wil
not bren with eny maner feyr. And some seyne it draweþ
Iaspyne colour. And he is mich worþ to ladies, for he
norsheþ loue & with-holdeþ loue. And he is god for the
tisik.
    And some seyne it comeþ owte of persce.

LII.   Cecolite is a stone þat is fowle to be-hold one, but
he is of a precius nature. Ðe ston leyd in water & ydrounk
a gode drawȝt þer-ofe, is god for þe reynes, and he is gode
to clense þe entrayles withyne forþe.

LIII.   Ceramus is a stone þat comeþ of araby, and who
þat bereþ it, þis stone, vpone him, it wole bere him fro
weders & horrible tempest & yuel eyris, as lyȝtnyng of fyr
& þonder. And some seyn þat it comeþ owte of grek; &
he wol be bor[2] mekely; and it haþe his name of a flume in
grek þat þis stone is founde in; and þis ston is god for flodes.
And he þat bereþ him schal not be drenched in eny flod;

[1] MS. schorpe.
[2] se crossed through before bor.

ne þer schall no howse, ne towne, ne marener in þe se be
anoyed with flod þer þis ston is. And he is gode fore
bateles & victories. And he ȝeueþ swet slepes & swete
dremes to a man. And some seyne þat he [is]¹ lyke to
cristall & coral for he is of suche dowble colowre. Also
ysidr & Lapidary seyn, when it þondreþ horrybly, þe feyr
of þe eyr leyȝtneþ, whene c[l]owdes² smyten togeder þis
ston falleþ fro heuen.

LIV. Cataricus is a stone, & is fownden in þe see, &
þer it is norsched. Þe ston is gode for leche-crafte, as for
ycche in þe body, for þe scabe, for serpige, & impetige.
Make powder þer-of, & ley it in veneger al a nyȝt; & þen
take þe powder of lyterg, of gold, & oyle of roses, &
make her-of an oynente & noynte þe sores þerwith.

LV. Coparius is a stone þat is bred in þe eyre, & some
callen it fouldre; & he falleþ with a tempest to þe erþe when
gret tempest of þondres & lyȝtnyng fallen, & it falleþ in
to þe erþe ix fote, & þe erþe reboundeþ aȝene agayne be
vertu of þe ston. And he þat secþ³ after him schall not fynd
him til ix dayes be passed. Þe man þat most ber þis ston
most kepe him clen fro lechery, & þen schall no tempest
do him harme in lond ne in vater ne no mysaueutur do him
harme ne come to him.

LVI. Cleridonius is a ston, & þer ben two of hem; þat
one is blak, þat oþer is red; & boþe þey ben rounde in
ligging. He þat bereþ þis in his left harme he schal not be
sclaw; & he schal be a feyr speker, & he schal be loued of
all men; and he þat bereþ þis blak stone, what þyng he
begenneþ ryȝtfully he scha mak a gode ende. And yf a
f. 6v mannes / yene dropene sore, make powdere of þis ston, &
wassh þyne yene þerwith, & þey schal be hole. Also for a
codidiane feuer & a tercian feuer, bynde þis stone in a red
sendell clowte, & ber it vpone þe, & þu schalt be hole.
Also yf a woman be in trauelyng of a child, by þe vertu of

¹ MS. omits.
² MS. cowdes.
³ c above the line.

G

þis ston sche schall be delyuerd wiþ gret peyne of her body, & þe chyld þis stone may towche ne dieþ.

LVII.   Carbuncculus is a precios stone, & he schineþ as feyre whose schynyng is not ouercom by nyȝt. It schineþ in derk places, & it semeþ as it were a feyr; & þer bene xij kyndes þer-of, & worþyest ben þo þat schynen & send owte leemes as feyre, as Ised. Also it is seyd þat þe carbunocyl is cleped so in grek, & it is gendryd in libia amonge þe tregodites. Of þis carbuncul þer is xij maneris of kendes of carbuncles. But þoo ben best þat han þe coleour of fire & þo ben closed in a wyȝt veyne. The best carbucul haþe þis propirtie: if it is þrowene[1] In þe feyre it is qwent as it were amonges dede colis, & it brennyt yf water be þorow þer-of. Anoder kynde of carbuccle is cleped starida sirus, & he haþe þat name of a plase of ynde in whiche he is founde In þis maner of kynd, as it were withyn hit bryȝt feyre ben ysey, as it were droppis of gold. And þes precious stones ben of gret price wiþoute comparison þen ben þe oder. And þer is anoþer maner kynd þat haþe signes, & he haþe þe name of smellynge of lanternys & þis preciowus stone is clepid remissus carbuncels, not þat it is chef carbuncclus; and here of dowbel maner of kynd, þat oone is wiþ bemes of purpull colour of red sylk; and þis kynd if it be hotte in þe sone wiþ fretyng of fynggers, it wol þraue to himself straues[2] & leevys of bokys. Also it is seyd þat it wiþstondet grauyng, & it is some tyme ygraue & Iprentyd in wex as it were wiþ byȝtyng of a best, as Ised seyþ. Amonge þe maner of kynd, of carbunccus, belagius is acounted, þat is red & briȝt, as dia seyþ. Also it is seyd þat þis maner of carbunccle is þe vayne of saphire. Belagius haþe a maner myȝt as it wer aboute sperkynge of fyre þat beclyppeþ him wiþowte, and þis is openly Iseyn yf men tak besily hede þer-to.

LVIII.   Crisopassus is a ston of ethiopie, & it is hide in lyȝt & seene in derkenes, for it is firy by nyȝt & goldy

---

[1] d crossed through before þrowene.
[2] r above the line

by day, as Isodre seyþe; þerfore he is hid be day, as it
were wesshynge, & waxeþ pal as gold. & anoþer maner
kynd þat is clepid crispassus is like in colour to a ston
þat is called prassius, & it [is]¹ grene as lyk, as it is be-
sprenge with certyne dropis of gold, as it is seyde in þe
lapidary of bartholomewe.

LIX. Diamand is a ston þat is named & dyuysed in
þe lapidary, for euax, kyng of araby, seyþ to vs þat diamand
þat comeþ owte of ynd ben clepid þe mal, & þey ben
brewen of colour & of violet, & þo þat comen owte of araby
ben clepid þe femal, & þey ben more whiȝt, resonable to
þe colour of cristall. A diamand is no mor þen a lytel note,
but he is mor hard of all stones. No man may amend him
of bewte ne polissh him, ne for no noþþyng. Of such
f. 7 maner þey ben founde and / bore in gold. Ðe lapidare seyþ
vs þat god ȝaue many fayre vertues & grace to þe diamond,
þat if a man bere it in strenþ & vertu, it kepiþ him fro
greuance, metinges & temtacions, & fro venym. Also it
kepiþ þe bones in þe membres hole, so-fere-forþ þat þu
schalt not fale of horse ne of oþer best but þat þe bone schal
be-leue hole, who þat bereþ it in clen leuyng. Also it defendiþ þe þred that comeþ be nyȝt; & it doþe away heuy
wrath & lechery; and it kepeþ a man in þe same poynt þat
he fyndeþ him, of prys, of wytte, of walew, of riches, &
encresyþ him in valew, in riches & good, ne he schal not be
made lese; & he schall be of lytel dispense if he clenly ber
it. A diamaund is myche worthe to be-hold one for wytles
men; and it defendeþ him fro his enemyis; & þat bereþ, he
schal þe mor loue god; also it kepeþ þe sed of man wyþinne
þe wombe of his wyfe, & it helpeþ þe child & kepeþ þe
childis membres hole. Ðe bokes seyne vs þat if a woman
be with child it most be borne one þe lefte seyd. And
whoso wil preue is vertu he most haue it of trew beying,
ore of ȝifte, & hoole & holy schal he be þat þis ston bereþ
in clennes; & it is most Iborne on þe lifte syde of a man
ore of a woman; & þen he haþe vertu. Also þis stone is not

¹ MS. omits.

made wiþ yerne ne stell ne noþer þinge may perse him, but wiþ þe hote blode of a gote buke.

LX.   Diadose is a stone which is pale, & he is found in water, & he is gode to avoid deuelis, & he þreueþ away mych derknes; and if it be set to a ded man he leseþ his kynd.   And þis stone is lyk to berell.   Diadosus is a ston riall & bryȝt as berell; & it is able to haue answeres of fendes, for exceteþ fendes & fantaȝies; and if it hap þat it towche a ded man, it leseþ his vertu, for that ston hateþ a ·ded man, & he is scoymes of þinge þat is ouercom wiþ depe, as it seyd in bokes.

LXI.   Dionisa is a stone þat is blake as he schineþ as a riede stencelettes; & þis in clen water tri[bl]e¹ mak wyne brene, & so wiþ þe sauour of þis stone all dronkenes gooþe away; & all þe vater schall sauore of þe wyne by vertu of þis ston.

LXII.   Diodoma is a sto[n]² formed square & it haþe coler of siluer.   Men fynde in þe grauel of þe see.

LXIII.   Disparea is a ston whiche is found in libia, & his kynde such þat all hunttyng comeþ which þat is lykyng to him.   And þat bereþ þis stone may take þer-of ynowȝe, such vertu haþe þis ston.

LXIV.   Deadotes is a ston þat is lyke berrell.   Yf þu wolt preve him in þy mowþe, þy mowþe schal bren but þu put³ him owte þe rader.   He þat bereth þis ston, þer schall no fantasie ouercom him.   Also yf þis ston towche a ded body þris, this body schall aryse & mowe by vertu of þis ston, but he schall not speke neyþer doe.   And if þu wilt þu mayst comaund what deuel of hel þu wilt & þe devel schal do no man harme.   Ðis ston may not often be nempned, for a man schal neuer dye whiles þis ston is vpon him.

¹ MS. tride.
² MS. sto
³ but crossed through before put.

LXV.   Diaffinian is a stone & it is like berell, redyssh,
f. 7ᵛ palyssh; he þat bereþ þis ston schall neuer have / harme of
ny3t of no temtacion of deuel, ne he schall neuer haue þe
blody menysone ne þe palsey whiles he bereþ þis ston
vpone him.

LXVI.   Dianya is a ston, & is blak & haþe redyssh
schynyng.   Yf þu wil make wyne or all or water, it makeþ
gode sauor to drynke; and grynde þis ston & put it in þe
wyne or ale or water, & anoon it schall make þe licor of
good sauour to drynke & doþe no harme.

LXVII.   Draconitidis is a stone, & it is in a dragones hed.
Some men clepen him escarbuncle.   He schyneþ clerly.
Non oþer vertu knowe I not þat it haþ; but in-as-mych for
it is clere, lordes putten it in here tresor to kepe.

LXVIII.   Esmeraude is a ston þat ouerpasseþ al þe
grennesse of grenhede; and þe bokes seyne vs þat þe
esmeraude & þe prames ben growyng togeders; and þe
esmeraude comeþ owte of þe lond of tyre by a water of
paradis.   Nero haþe a myrrour of þis ston wherein he loked,
& he wyst by þe vertu of þis stone al þat he wole seke or
deseyre.   It encresseþ ryches & makeþ word of man
dredfull.   Also is myche worþe a3ens þe gowte & a3ens
tempest & a3enes lechery, & it is gode souerenly for þe
sy3te to be-holdyn.   Wit it wel, he þat bereþ it vpone him
þe more he schal led his body in clennes, & þe les to loue
vnclennes boþe of body & soule, & he schall haue þe mor
loue to þinke one his soule, & þe more to loue clene
beryng, & þe mor to loue gode workys.   Also þis ston
bereþ him fro tempest.   God himself 3aue such vertu þerto,
and þe beyble seyþe þat þe esmeraude was the t[h]rid¹ ston
named of god vpone þe brest of aaron.   Seint Iohne seyþe
in þe apocalyps þat he sawe þe emeraude þe iiij stone
vndere þe verry kyngdom.   Also þer is a maner of beestes
cleped gryffonnes þat kepen þe emaraudes vpone þe flod
of paradyse in þe lond of syre; & þe bestes han iiij fete &

¹ MS. trid.

ij wyngis; þe body befor & wynges ben in þe maner of an
egle, & behynde [in]¹ maner of a lion; and þer bene a
maner of folk þat ben cleped aropolis, & þey han but oo
ye in þe medys of þe forhed; & þese comen to seke þe
emerawde all armede one þe water & taken him, & þe
bestes beforseyd comen rennynge & flyeng, & wold take
þe aropoles by here power & mych angwyssh hem, & egre
ben to tak hem, but þey ben armed, þey may do hem no
harme to tak hem.

LXIX.   Elitropia is a ston, & is of scuch kynde, yf a
man put in a vessell ful of water aȝens þe sone it schal make
þe sone rede & in a lytel tyme, & he schall make þe vessel
to cast owte þe water as it² reyneþ, and profiteþ myche to
him þat bereþ it. Hit ȝeveþ a man gode fame, & also it
stancheþ blode, also it is gode aȝens venymes & fylþes;
and who þat takeþ þe erbe clepid elytrepie & þe charme þat
longeþ þerto, & if he put it with þe ston, he schall mow go
where he will. Ðys ston comeþ owte of ethiope & egypte
& of auffryk, as it were blody. Ðys ston is gode befor
many oþer stones; for god ȝafe him þat vertu & strenge,
þat þe man þat setteþ him in a pleyn vessel & in clen water
aȝens þe sone, as it is befor seyd; þe cause is that he is apropred to þe clypsse; also who þat bereþ him schal be of gret
f. 8 purchese, & he bereþ a man in gret helpe, / & makeþ a man
to be of gret renoun. And some men seyne þat he is
sumwhat like to þe emaraude; & he is cebled with red
seyinctes; & he is a-Iuged to clyppsse, and he schall make
þe eyr troble & reyne; and he makeþ gret d[i]unaciouns³
& gode fame.

Somme men seyne þat þis stone is som-what lyke to
smaragdus, but he is not so grene, but grene veynes
spreyng owte of him, redyssh like dropis of blode. And
some mene seyne þat he is founde in a asse hede; for þis
ston elitropia makeþ þe asse blynd. And whoso bereþ þis
stone schall neuer be blynde, & his syȝt schall neuer fayle

¹ MS. omits in.
² it rey crossed through before it.
³ MS. dunaciouns.

him. Allso towche a wounde with þis ston & þe wounde schall neuer rote; also wasse þis ston in wyne, & he schal neuer haue þe iawndyse. Ðis ston makeþ fayr weder & cler, & he haþe many mo vertues. Also Ised seyþe þat þis ston discerneþ þe foly of enchaunthementes, & of wyches þat haue lykyng in pryde of her owne wondres þat þey begyle men with wondres þat þey worchin, as it is befor seyd. Also þat þis stone is gode & commendabyle for it stancheþ blode & putteþ away wenym, and he þat bereþ þis ston may not be begyled. Also þis elitropia is gren, & spreynede with red droppes & waynes as colour of blode, & haþe þe name & effecte & doynge of eclypsse of þe sonne, as it is befor seyde.

> Nam si iungatur eius de nomine herbe
> Carmine legitime verbeque sacrata potenti
> Subtrait humanis occlis quem cunque gerentem.

LXX.   Etite, de egle, is a ston & haþe many vertues. If a man will þe harme, put þis ston vndyre his dissh or in his disshe which he schal ete of, & he schall ete no mete whil þat ston is þer. Also he is gode for wymmen þat trauelyng with child. Also he makeþ a man riche & kynde. Also som men seyn þat þis ston etite is lyk to lynen cloþe wytest; & with-in him þer is anoder ston þat is blake. Ðe egle setteþ[1] him in the este & swoloweþ him, & when he will byeld his neste he leveþ him in a corner of his nest. Than dar no oder fowle cum to his neste, for þey wene þat egle be in his neste.. If a man be aferde of poyson of mete or drynke, lete þis ston towche þe mete or drynke viij tymes & it schall neuer do him harme. Also yf þis ston be bounden to a womens lefte arme in trauelynge sche schall be delyuerd withoute payne. Also dias seyþ þe vertu of þis ston: it makeþ a man sobre, & it encresseþ riches & loue, and he[l]peþ[2] to victory & fauour, & letteþ & with-stondeþ þe fallyng of him þat han þe fallyng yuell; and if a man haue suspecien of venym, tak[3] þis ston & ley it vnder

---

[1] l. getteþ or fetteþ?
[2] MS. hepeþ.
[3] be in þe mete crossed through before tak

his mete, & if þe venym be in þe mete he schal not swalow
þe mete whilis þis ston is þer-in, & if þe ston be tak away
he schal not tary to swolow þat mete, as Ised seyþe.

LXXI.   Epistidio is a ston þat is precious, & it is seid
þat it is rede; & he is gode for cold & he is gode for
fruytes in þe erþe & for bredis, & he is god also for hayle
& frostes, þat þu put him agaynst þe sonne. Also he makeþ
branches as feyre. Also he makeþ al dowtable þinges I put
into sikernes.

LXXII.   Exacontalito is a ston of sexti colours. Þis
ston makeþ myche þe strenge of a lytel mane. And þis ston
f. 8v is founde amonge þe trogocdotes / in þe contrey of libie.

LXXIII.   Egestes is a ston þat is founde in þe contre of
archade. Þis stone haþe þe color of yerne; & anoþer suche
þer is þat is þe female; and whene sche conceyueþ, sche
conceyueþ anoder stone. Þe vertu is more worþe to
wymmen trauelynge in chyld-beryng, for sche schal þe
soner be delyuerd.

LXXIV.   Enydros is a stone & droppeþ away, &
mylteþ note, & it is neuer þe lesse, & is alway swetyng;
& he is not wele grete, and he is founde in arabie in þe
rede see, & he haþe senblaunt of cristall. Yf a man hold
þis stone in þe sone-beme, it scheweþ to a man all þe colors
of þe reynbowe. Enydros, þat ston, wepeþ alwaye as it
were by sprenginge of a ful well with droppyng teres, &
welleþ alway. And þerto it is seyd þat it is hard to tell þe
cause þerof. For if þe droppis were of þe substaunce of þe
ston wellyng, whi is not þe ston lese & melteþ away; and
if a þing deencreseþ & put not aʒens þat þing þat goeþ
owte; but as it semeþ me, it may be þat þe vertu of þe ston
makeþ þe eyre þik þat is nyʒt þerto, & tornet into water,
& so it semet þat comeþ owte of þe ston, neuer-þe-lese it
comeþ owte of þe substance of þe eyre þat is abowte
þe ston.

LXXV.   Exebenius is a stone, & he is whitest, & þe
growne is lyk golde. If a woman be syke in her bely, take

þis stone & grinde it, & let here drynk þe powder with
wyȝte wyne & sche schall be hole.

LXXVI.   Epetites is a stone redyssh sumwhat in schynyng, & if þu willt preue him holde þis ston in boylyng
water, & þe water waxe colde by vertu of þis stone; also
preue him, holde þis stone aȝens þe sonne, & owte of þe
ston schall springe oute rayes aȝens þe soon. Also he is
gode for women þat trauelyng with chyld, and for wykkyd
wormes & wicked tempestes; and if a man may not do his
will with a woman, take þis ston & bynde it vpone the
reynes & he schall do what he will. Also it doþe away
wordely wraþ. Al dis seyþe Ised & dias.

LXXVII.   Excoleritos is a litel ston, for it disteyned &
dyuersed with fowrty colors, & it is full bryȝt, and þat
bryȝtnes makeþ me[n]¹ þat loken þer-on for to quake; and
þis ston is fonde in libie amonge þe trogodites.

LXXVIII.   Firigins is a ston, & it haþe vertues of schynyng oþer colour. Ðis ston is gode if it be dronkyne with
sauen for þe gowte; also it is gode for to bere abowte for
þe palsey.

LXXIX.   Fimionis is a ston, & he þat bereþ him þer
schal neuer no venym do him harme, ne he schal not be
longe in drede, ne no vnkend auentur schal come to him;
also yf he begyn eny gode þynge he schal mak a gode ende;
also he schal not haue no wraþe, ne dred, ne non anoye of
lord ne lady. Also he þat bereþ þis ston schal neuer be
brent; also he schall neuer be wonded ne hurte. Ðese
vertues & many mo þis ston haþe.

LXXX.   Fedus is a ston for medecine. If it be grounden
to small pouder, tak of þat pouder & womans mylke &
medel him well togeder, so þat be of a man child, & wassh
þe sore yen wel þer-with, & þey schall be hole; and yf eny
f. 9 body haue / yuell in his . . .² take þe mylke³ of a schepe

¹ MS. me.
² Illegible. First three letters apparently pet, followed by four or five letters.
³ l above the line.

þat was a lambe þe same ȝere & þe pouder of þis ston, so
þat he be a masculyn schepe & be wyȝt of schyne; let him
drynke þat is potagre of þis medecyne & he schal be hole;
but he muste drynke a lytell at onys for hys brayn; If he
drynke mekel at ones, his brayne will fayle him.

LXXXI.   Fensites is a stone, & is rede. Ðe man or
woman þat bereþ þis ston vpone hir ryȝte arme, þer schall
neuer no wraþ of no maner man do him harme, so þat he
be in clen leuyng & þe ston haue his kynde.

LXXXII.   Florendanius is a ston of many vertues &
ful[v]i[1] coloris. Yf eny body hange þis ston abowte his
neke it helpeþ an euell þat is cleped arthetica. Also ȝ[e]f[2]
þis stone be holden hard in a mannes hand, a schall bren
his honnde, & þerfor þu must smartly towche him.

LXXXIII.   Gagatis, þat is gete. He groweþ in a contrey þat men clepen licio, & it recembleþ myche to þe
ademant; & faylet but lytell but þe best in þe world is in
þe world is in breteyn maior, þat now is clepid ynglond.
Ðat ston is blake, schynyng, lyȝt & playn, & he is of
many vertues; and when he is chafed by rubbyng or by
fretyng it draueþ to him þe strees þat ben abowte him; and
it brenneþ in water; & it is gode to ber to him þat haþe
swellyng in sckyn or in flessh as a man þat is founded. Ðe
powder of him ywassh in a litel water clenseþ a man is teeþ
& makeþ him faste. When a man brenneþ it & he haue þe
gowte, anone as he feleþ þe odor & þe smell þerof þe
gowte goeþ away. Also bren him, & þe smell þerof dreueþ
away edders; & myche it worþe to him þat han her wombe
ouerturned. And it fordoeþ wiche craft & charmes; also it
dispreveþ maydenhede; also yf a woman trauell of child,
of a drynk of þe water þat it haþe leye yne iij dayes & iij
nyȝtes smertly sche schall be delyuerd with þe grace of
gode. Also yf a man or woman may not pise for þe ston,
take þe powder of geete & drynke it lewke-warme with red
wyne or with swete cowes mylke, & he schall pise anoon &

---

[1] MS. fulti.
[2] MS. ȝf.

þe ston schal al to brek. Also he is good for þe fowle yuell; let him sauour to þe geete when it is brent. Also it is good to a man or a woman yf þey bled byneþe, forþe tak a pane with quyk colis, & let þe seke sitte bare aboven clear iij dayes arowe, it schall stanche. Also who bereþ þis ston abowte his nek, þer schall no serpent do him harme. Also with þis ston and a erbe þu myȝtest tie þe wildest beest in þe forest þat he schold nat meve. Also þe fumusite þerof exciteþ menstrua if it is withdraw by eny happe. Also it is seyd þat it swageþ ache in þe wombe, or yf þe stomake be torned by eny way. Also it helpeþ her þat is travelyng of child. Ised seyþ of þis stone it wole brene in water, & it is qwenched with oyle, & þat is a wondre þyng.

LXXXIV. Gerastie is a stone of blacis color, & it is of gret price. Yf it be wasshe, put into a mannes mowþe vpone his tonge, þat yf a-noþer man þynke eny þyng of him he schall know his þouȝt anoone. And yf a man wyl know his vertu, anoynt his body with hony or mylke, & set himself þer as ben many fleyes, & put þis ston in his f. 9v mowþe, & þer / scall no fley euer neyȝ him. And some men callen þis stone genardus.

LXXXV. Gagantruels is a stone, & is lik to þe skyn of a kyd. Đe princes beren þe ston with hem into batayl, ase þe chasen away her enmyes. Ercules ascaped all his enemyis & many perelles by vertu of þis stone.

LXXXVI. Galactida is a ston, & is myche lyke to asshen; & yf he be dronke in mylke he restoreþ mylke; but it most be vsed befor mete; & sche þat bereþ it is good for child-berynge. And it kep schepe fro scabbys, & makeþ full of mylk. Đis stone galactides haþe many dyuers names. Some clepen him gracitem & egipcis smaragene, & his ryȝt name is galactida. Also men clepen him gan-ancten & fenichom & letorgone & we clepen him oblianus. He þat bereþ þis stone, his will schall be fulfelled. If þu wilt know þis ston, it smelleþ lyke . . .[1] hony; & grynde him to powder & he schalle waxe whiȝt. And if a woman

[1] *Illegible.*

drynk þe pouder sche schall hawe plente of mylke; and yf[1]
þe stone be persyd and hanggyd abowt her neke that is
with childe, sche schall be deliuerid anon withowt any
perell. And if þe child be scabbyd, washe him with þe
mylke of a schepe or þe sone ryse, and he schall be hole.
And if her teþe be sor, wesh hem with þe mylke. And yef
thou bere þe ston þu schalte be glade, and þu schalte neuer
dyy in batell nor neuer be a-ferryd. Also yef a woman may
not be deliuerid, tye þe stone to here lefte thee with a þerde
of wole of schepe. This galaxide is swete in taste and
sauoure; yf hee be smyttyn, þer will come owt a[2] maner of
swete mylke, as ysaidre sayd. This stone iclowsid distrow-
billyth þe wyt; and yef hit be bore abowte þe neke hit
makyth brestes full of mylke. And yef hee be medillyd
with watter & salte and spronge abowte þe feldes, then þe
schepe schall be full of mylke. Also hee schall clense
sckabbys as diases. And yef hit be bownd to þe theys hit
makyþ yessy byrth.

LXXXVII. Garsius is acowntyd amonge þe stonys, and
hit is not lefe, for hit haþ no prophete but that hee is
grene. Also þer bene odere that haþe small venys blodi.[3]
The þirde maner haue iij maners and be figuryd whit. Isid
saiþe þis stone schall neuer be hotte with fyre and dias
saiþe the same.

LXXXVIII. Galcido uel gelacid is a ston that is like
þe Addemand, for he haþe noo vertu to noo medisyne, for
he is colde as anny yse and þerfor he is put to noo medisyne ne in l[e]se[4] a manere as do oder stones for he will not
be schafyd be noo fyre.

LXXXIX. Hieme is a stone þe wiche a best berethe,
the wiche is clepide hieme, in þe bale of his ye; this stone,
as holde autors seyne schall make a man diuinable, for yef
f. 10 / a man haue it vnder his tonge, so that his mowth be clen
wassh, for then he haþe his strengeþ. Also yf he be bore,

---

[1] MS. and yf and yf.
[2] mylk crossed through before a.
[3] MS. blodinth (?)
[4] MS. lse.

þis ston, vndyr his tonge, he schall sey þe soþe to what man þat askeþ him.

XC. Macedone is a stone þat yf women ber him if sche trauayl of child sche schall neuer be delyuerd til þat stone be tak awaye.

XCI. Herimacius is a stone, & his color is in maner lyke þe mayle of an hawke; þe vertues of him can I not fynde ȝet.

XCII. Hispannen est gemma quae reperitur in littoribus hispaniensis occeainis ignee & perlucede.

XCIII. Iaspes. Ðer bene þer of xvij¹ maners colours, & þey ben founde in well depe parties of þe wourdyll; but he þat is grene aȝens þe daye, he is godly, & when he is blake dropes he [is]² lese worþe. And when it is dropped with rede & it is grene, & he schapyd after the old schape, he is lorde of all the iaspe; þis is þe moste precius Iaspe. Ðes iaspes ben founde in many parteys of the world; þose bene here vertues: Iaspes is good aȝens all maner of wormes; and oone be stonge with wenym or any oder maner poysone, & he be brouȝt in eny maner stede as iaspe is, he schal choyn[g]e³ anoon owte of color; and it schall stanche blode be resone of him þat haþe gode beleue, or of menysone, or feuer, or dropsye; and whosoo beholdeþ iaspe aȝens daye, he schall expounde dremes and also mych worþe to woman þat trauelyþ of child; if sche haue it vpone her sche schall þe soner be delyuerd. Iaspes kepethe a mane fro his aduersarys; and whoso bereþ him he most kepe clene lyfe. Ðe bok telleþ vs þat þe goode iaspe is grene and moyses set þis ston in þe brest of arone. Sent Iohn seyþe in apocolyps þat he say in heuenly kyndome of ierusalem þat þe ferst fundament wase Iaspe. Ðe grenest Iaspe is a caladone. He þat bereþ þis stone schal neuer⁴ dey in water, ne his enemy schal ouercomen him. A man

¹ x above the line.
² MS. omits.
³ MS. choynde.
⁴ MS. nereuer.

schall let graue in þis stone yarmede, & a ȝerd in his honde,
with a stoole abowȝt his neke & a ȝerde þat schold be
of[1] olyuetre; & his vertu is gret in siluer þen in gold;
also þer is one þat is a blak colour. And some seyn þat þe
Iaspe is of xvij maner colours; & þat is blak is mor myȝt
& worþe, & gre[t]er[2] of valew & of vertu for he comforteþ many men of fantome. Also Ised seyþ þat one of þe
iaspes is fonde in þe hed of a edder which is clepid aspis;
and þis ston iaspis is but lytell. Som men seyn þat it is a
stone of wonder vertu; & þis stone is named after aspis.
Dias seyþe þat þe best iaspis is founde in þe moyntens of
sicia, & gripes kepen þis stone as þey don smaragdus.

XCIV.   Iagunce is a ston, & is of many maners. Ðe
gret iacunce is rede & it is of gentyl maner & of gret
vertu.   It kepeþ a man trew, and it makeþ a man to beholden trew. Anoder Iagunce, & is of ȝelow colour, & it
is called citri. Ðes ij maners of iagunce ben of þes vertus,
þat when a man putteþ him in his moweþ he makeþ a man
riȝt cold; and he þat bereþ it vpon him may go into anoþer
contre withowte dred, & he schal be worchipid in his oste
howse; in al maner þyng þat he askeþ it resonable it schal
not be hid fro him; & þis stone schal be put in golde. Some
men seyne þat þer ben iiij maner iagunces; þat one is full of
g[r]eynes,[3] þat oþer ȝelow, þe þryd is pleyn; and þey comforteþ weyn suspecio[n]se[4] & heuynes; & he is allmost as
hard as adyamont; & he wol be bor in rynges or at a
manes nyke, & þen he may go save wher he wolle. And
f. 10v some seyn þat / he comeþ owte of yende þe mor. Also he
is gode for medesyns. Al þes iagunce be red brownyssh,
and þer iiij maners of hem, þat oone is gryned, þat oder is
ful of vaynes, þe þryd is pleyn. The tho maners of stones
þu schalt preue hem in þe feyr, wil be cler & lyȝt; þe pleyn
iacyuncte will suffre no feyr, but he is good to distroy a
felone & to stanche blode, and yf þu pers him & binde

---

[1] MS. be of be of.
[2] MS. grener.
[3] MS. geynes.
[4] MS. suspeciose.

him abowte þey naked flysh þer schal no tempest do þe harme. Þe ryȝt colour is as þe firmament þat makeþ þe daye, and þus þu schalt him knowe.

XCV. Irunde is a stone & is founde in de wombe of a bryde þat men callen þe swalowȝe in englyssh; þe ȝonge briddys, while þey be in þe nest, þe wombe schall be kytte, & in þe mowþe ȝe schul fynde iij maners of stones, oon blak, anoþer redyssh, anoþer of diuers colours. Item celidonus est lapis palydus & fuscus & aliquantulum obscurus quasi perforetur; causas aduersatur, & virtutes conseruat, vt dicit albertus. Þat ston þat is blak is gode for sor yene, of what cause so þat it be, & it comforteþ þe syȝt. Þat oder þat is of dyuers colours is aȝens caduce men for to han or abowte her neck; it helpeþ þat he schal neuer haue it more. Also þis stone it makeþ scharp syȝt; and also drye it & make pouder of it, & it helpeþ þe squynacye. Also þe erbe with þe stone is profitable.

XCVI. Iacincte is a stone myche clyr, & it is of iij maners; þat oone is of violet colour, þe oder of red, þe iij color as . . .[1] Al þes ben gode for medcyns, and þorowȝ her strengeþ and hir vertu þey done away al idel þowȝtes & hewynes; and who þat bereþ it vpon him, he may go savely wher he wole, and he schal be myche worchiped in all places. And he comeþ owte of þe mor Inde, & he wold be set in gold. Þis iacincet, as men seyne, he [is][2] blowȝ & grene of colour, þicke & derk as purpull colour; & he is lyke to þe reynbowe, & he is of such colour. Ised seyþ þis stone þat is founde in ethiope is best, & is not to cler ne to dyme, but mene & temperat betwyx shynyng. And Ised seyþ þat ston schyneþ not alweye liche, for in cler wedyr he is cler befor þe yene, & in derke wedder it is derke & dymme; also Ised seyþe in þe morun cold, if it is þerin. And it is most hard to graue yne, neuerþe-lese it may be graue ynne & ywryten & ymarked with þe stone adamans. As ysed seyd þat þe stone iacincte is

[1] Illegible.
[2] MS. omits.

now blew, now redyssh, now purpill color, now briȝt
blew; & þer ben iij maners of kyndes for ben citrin &
some blew; but amonge shuch the blew is beste. Also þis
ston is wondyrful, for confermeþ most to þe eyre, for in
dym weddyr he is dym, & in cler wedder he is clere; and
so þis ston haþe a syngler vertu, for it ȝefeþ gladnes & is
contrary to malyncole qualite, & he haþe vertu of comfort,
as it is seyd in þe kynd þerof, Iacinctus haþe vertu of com-
fort; & he doþe awaye al elyngenese & sorow, & also
veyne suspeciosnes, & withstondeþ dyuerse pestolens þat
comen ofte of a corupte eyre; & it ȝeweþ strenge & vertu
to membres & lyfe to þe synewis & ȝeveþ good sauor &
swet & hollsom; & it lyke to þe saphur. Also dias seyþe,
& al men þat treten of precious stones seyn, that þe iacinte
is lyke þe saphur in color & substans, þe mor vertues he is;
and such iacincte withstondeþ venymes, & is contrary to
poysone, as dias seyþ; þer is a herbe of þe same name is
lyk þerto in many þinges, þow it be not lyke in walew, as
Ised seyþe.

f. 11 XCVII.   Iapectes is a stone, & þer bene many of dyuers
colours & of many maners; for he that bereþ þis ston
vpone him he may wel goo in-to batayl & ouercom his
aduersaryis, & it kepeþ a man riȝt hardy & ful of mych
godnes.

XCVIII.   Iacinctornicta is a ston, & he is myche lyke
to cristal; & if it towche a man is heer it waxiþ blak.
Oþer vertues know I noon.

XCIX.   Iren is a stone, & it haþe[1] þese vertues. Take
þis & ley it vpone a manis brest or woman brest sleping &
þey schall tel al þat þey han doune. Also ber þis ston in þey
purse, for it schal do awaye all fantasies in þe brayne. Yf
þu wilt fynd þis stone, go to þe lampwynch neste whene he
leyd yren,[2] & tak a glasse cuppe & ley it above þe nest &
styk ij roddes on crose wyse above, & þe[n][3] will þe

---

[1] is erased before haþe.
[2] MS. ley dyren.
[3] MS. þe.

lapwynche fle to þe rede see & fete a ston, & towche þer-
with þe glase cuppe, & þe coppe will breke & þe ston will
fale doune into þe nest & so he bryngeþ forþe his bryddes.
And þe ston haþe many mo vertues then I can tell.

C. Indres is a preciose stone þat þe raven feccheþ at þe
red see or in ynde. Take þe stone & put it in a rynge, &
þen take a lefe of laureal & wynd þe ryng þeryn, & towche
þerwith feters or lokys & þey schall vndo. Also [tak]¹ þe
ston & put it in þey mowþe & þu schalt have vndyrston-
dyng of all langgages. Also þis ston putteþ awaye all
wraþes & yre. Also he þat haþe þis ston abowte him he
schall neuer fayle goode wyle þat he leueþ in þis worle. &
þis ston is of many colors & rownde. And þus þu mayst
have þis stone, go to þe raven is neste when he haþe leyþe
& tak adowne þe eyerne & feþer him hard, & þen ber þyn
to þe nest aзen; & þe raven will fle to þe red see or in to
ynde & fyche þis stone & [put]² it amonge her eyrne
st[y]ryng³ it with his byle al abowte, & þe eyren schall
waxe rawe, & so he brengeþ forþe his bryddys by wertu
of þe ston.

CI. Ipacon est lapis qui nascitur in libia ad quem cur-
ru[n]t⁴ omnes bestis tanquam ad refugium & . . . & . . .
ne noceant animalia.

CII. Irachie is a ston; þe man þat bereþ him schal nat
be bytten with fleyes, neyþer stonge with bene as Dias
seyþe; & men supposeþ it helpeþ aзens venym.

CIII. Molas is a ston, & his vertu is not but when
mone is at full; he most scharply be draw vp & when þe
sone schyneþ vpone him, & then he takeþ is full vertu.

CIV. Ligurie is a stone of ynde fonden vpon þe flode
þat is cleped Quendis; & þer is a best wiche is cleped lynse,
& he kepeþ & withholdeþ þis stone wel depe in his þrote

¹ MS. omits.
² MS. omits.
³ MS. stryng
⁴ MS. currut.

H

for the gret vertu þerof schuld nat cum to vs. Þe bokes
tellen vs þat þer ben many maners liguries, but þe best is
he þat haþe þe color of goldy. And also þer ben such þat
ben lyke þe color of mire, & some of þe color of encens; &
som þer ben þat ben like þe color to ȝelow grenehed, &
som of þe color of mylk; as a maister deuysed þat þer ij
maners of topacie. Moyses seyþe vs þat þer ben some of
þe color of Iagounce. Owr lorde ȝaue to þis ston many feyr
vertues it heleþ þe iaundyse; & it restryneþ a man fro . . .[1]
vices. Also he is god aȝens þe gowte, & it clenseþ a man
f. 11v of sorowes, & it helpeþ þe / stomak. Ligure pleseþ a man
þat is wraþfull, & gladeþ him; also he stancheþ þe blody
menyson & þe bledyng membres. And þe bokes tellen vs
þat þis ston is good to ladys, for þis ston schal make hem
plesyng to her lordes. Also þis ston coleþ a man of gret
hetes if it is put in his mowþe. Also who-so towcheþ a
manes sor eyne, it schal dryue owte þe yuel & þe blode.
And wite it well þat þis stone haþe be cleped by many oþer
names, but owr autours clepeþ it ligurie. Moyses clepeþ
þe best ox, & þe vertu of þis lymes telleþ vs Iob; þese
lechores men aȝens þe lymes shold we haue þe vertu in vs
þat sig[n]ifieþ[2] chastite; also þe best befor seyd þat dyggeþ
þe erþe to hid þe ston. The bible seyþe vs þat þis ston was
pute in þe þryd corner in þe brest of arone. Also it helpeþ
a mane of þe excesse & of þe meneson, & he amendeþ þe
ache of þe stomak, & makeþ þe entrals of a man hole.
Also Ised seyþ þat þer is a best þat is cleped lynx, & þe ston
lygurius comeþ of þe beste, & it is gendryd in þe grauel of
þe see of þe vryng of þe same best. Also he draweþ straw
to himself.

CV.   Lange serp[e]nt[3] is of many colors, & he is of
schap a tonge; but þis ston is broun, blak, & þe . . .[1] red
aȝens þe mone, is þerin most vertu, & þefendeþ a mane fro
venym, and yf a mane be poysened it kepeþ him; & þerfor
þey put it in seluer befor kyngis & princes & befor oder

---

[1] Illegible.
[2] *MS.* sigifieþ.
[3] *MS.* serpnt.

gret lordes at her metes & dryŋkes. Ðu myȝtes set þyn
boþe in gold & iŋ siluer; and meŋ fynd him in many places
in þe see grauel of þe gret bretone.

CVI.   Laparie is a ston, & he fonde of contreis of libie,
& his kynd is mych of wyld bestes, for he is gode for
huŋters wheŋ þey have no houŋde. For wheŋ he þat bereþ
þis ston vpone him schal not[1] haþe iŋ huŋtyng. Ised seyþe
þe laparie comeþ owte of þe contre of cirtes. Ðe propirte
of þis ston, þat wild bestes comeŋ to þe stones presense &
beholden þerone; and for bestes þat may not be taked with
hondes, þey taken & tollen him. with þe syȝt & schynyŋg
only of þe laparia.

CVII.   Magnes is a stone þat is fonde among to maneris
of folkes, þat one cleped trogadite, & oþer is cleped ynde;
& iŋ þat contre meŋ fynd him, & he haþe þe color of yerŋ.
Delder þe enchanter vsed it myche, for he wist wel þat it
helped mych to enchantemenes; and after him vsed it
mych þe mervelows enchauntere Cierce, was a womaŋ.
Amoŋge all oþer experyiŋneces it is founde & knowen &
it is soþe of a mane & of his wife, as it is seyd after iŋ þe
verses. Also yf a thefe enter into an howse for to stell, &
yf he tak a quyk bronde of fyr & . . .[2] Also þis ston makeþ
loue betwen maŋ & woman, & gyfeþ a maŋ grace to spek
swetly; and yf a maŋ yf it to drynk iŋ oyle to him þat haueþ
þe dropsy it schal porge him. And þe powder is good for
brenyŋg. Also whoso bereþ þis stoŋ schal neuer be wroþe
with his wyfe, ne þe wyfe with þe hosbone. Also he þat
hath a felon, dryŋke þe powder þerof, & he schall be hole.
Also yf a womaŋ dryŋke þe powder þerof sche schal be
baren; and yf a man dryŋke iiij times he schal lese his
genetralis. And yf þu þrawe þe powder þerof in þe feyr, al
þe meŋ þat loken in þe feyr schal wene þat þe howse schal
fal downe. Ðis stone is fonden in þe see of ynde; þis is ryȝt
gode to be set iŋ a rynge aȝure. Also Isodre seyþ, þis
magnete is a ston of ynde, colored somdel as yern; & it is

[1] *MS.* not not.
[2] Illegible.

f. 12 fonde in Iudea amonge þe trogodites, & draweþ / to himself yern; & it is founde in ynde, so þat it makeþ as it
were a scheyne of yerne with ryngis, as Ised seyþe; þerfor
in þe comen speche þis yerne is clepid quyk yerne. Ðe
myȝth & þe vertu þerof is so gret, as austen seyþe, þat ane
a ston be sete vnder a vessel of gold or off brase or.yerne
set þervpone, by mouyng of þe stone þat is byneþe, yerne
schall moue þat is aboue. Also it is seyd that þer is in
anoþer contre in a tempill an ymage[1] of yerne, & it semeþ
þat ymage hangeþ be þe eyre. And in ethiopa is anoþer
maner of kynd of magnes þat forsakeþ yerne & dryueþ
away fro it self. Also þe magnes draweþ þe eyrne in to a
corner; & þe mòr blew þe mor better he is. Also diascorides
& lapidarie seyen þat þis ston reconcileþ & acordeþ lowe
betwene men & her wyfes. Also it ȝeueþ grace & feyernes
in speche & in worde. Also a drynke Imad of hony & of
wyne it helpeþ þe dropsi & þe splen & þe fallyng yuel, &
also for brenyng. Plata seyþe þat wyches vse namly of þis
stone. Also þis stone magnes is drye in þe [þ]ry[d][2] þegre.
And þer ben moyntens in þe see of schilce magnes, & þerfor þey drawen to him & brekyne schippis þat ben Inayled
with yerne. Also þe powder of audamant, put it into a
woynde, it draweþ owte yerne of þe wounde. Also auycen
seyþe þat þe[3] pouder of þe adamant, þe quantyte of ij
drammes, with þe Iues of fenel, is gode for þe dropsy &
aȝens þe splene & for fallyng of heere.

CVIII.   Saphyr is a ston ryȝt comly one a ryng vpone a
kyngis fynger; & god haue ȝeve to him myche grace.
Men taken him in[4] general[5] lymbe in a flod of þe eest
besydes a roche of þe see, & þat þey ben so fonde. Some
ben mor gentill þen oþer; þo þat ben most gentill of color
& most lyke Inde, þey semble to þe clen color of heuen;
& in þe dep waters ben founde saphirs þat ben derke, &

---

[1] yis alone also it crossed through—ymage added above.
[2] MS. dryþ.
[3] Iuys of fenel is g crossed through before þe.
[4] aȝen crossed through before in.
[5] Read grauel of (?)

þey ben ful of vertues & better, þe[n]¹ clene oþer maner
saphirs þat ben lasse worþe, & þey ben vertues & full of
grace. Ðese iij maners of saphirs distrowen fowlnes &
envy, & comforteþ þe body & membres, & letteþ þe man
fro enprisonyng; & he þat with þe saphir towcheþ þe iiij
places of þe prison or of þe cheynes, if he haue gode beleue
he schal be delyuerd by vertu of þe ston þat god haþe gyfe
to þe saphire & granted. The bok tellen vs þat þe saphir
is wel good to acord men togidder, & to brek wychecraft; & it is mych worþe to hele byles & swellyng; if it be
geven to him þat haþe byles or swellyng with-in þe body,
anon he schall be hole by vertu þat gode haþe gyuen þerto;
and it schall kele þe body of hot syknes, & do away þe
sorowȝ of þe hede, & it helpeþ þe seknes of goomes, &
chaseþ owte þe ange of yene. And þe boke seyþe þat gode
counseyleþe him to ber it clenly, for it makeþ a man to haue
wyte & myȝt; þey schuld leve a clen lyfe þat beren þis
vertues stone. Ðe boke telleþ vs þat þe saphir is of þe color
of hevene. Also sente Iohn seyþe in þe apocalyps þe saphir
was þe secund fundament in þe heuenly ierusalem. Also þe
saphir schold be wassh in mylke & Idronke, & for all
yuellis in a mannes body, & for ache of þe hede & for þe
palesye. Ðe best saphirs ben þoo þat ben in þe este or in
ynde, & namly if it haþe as it were powder of gold ymedeld
þeryn. Ðis saphir stone is þyke & not passyng bryȝt, as
Ised seyþe. Ðis ston is most Iprysed in þe lapidary; & for
he is so noble & so excellent, þerfor he is clepid gemma
gemmarum, as it wer chef of precios stones, for kepeþ þe
f. 12v body & saveþ / þe lymes hole & sounde; & he haþe a
bryȝt ster, by þe bryȝtnes of þat sterre & þerby his vertu is
knowen Also þer is anoder maner of saphir which is cleped
sirtices, & he is founde fast by þat plasis þat is cleped
cirtes, amonge þe grauell of þe see libicum. Also dias seyþ
þat he is founde in þe veynes of vermylon, þis laȝurine is
founde; also þe sam vaynes of saphir in² þe myddell & as it
wer in þe wombe is a certen kynde of carbuccle yfounde;

¹ MS. þe.
² MS. in in.

þerfor many men suppose þat þe saphir is carbuccles moder; for many men seyn þat þe carbuccle is gendyr in þe saphir veynes; & many men seyn þat þe carbuccle is sodenle beschawed[1] with a certen blew lyke of þe kynde of saphir, as dias seyþe. Also he haþe vertu to confort & to glade þe hert þerfor. It is seyd þat he helpeþ aȝens þe cardeacle & aȝens al malyncoly passiouns; þerfor it stancheþ rennyng & swetyng that comeþ to swyþe. Also dias seyþe þe same; ande he haþe vertu to stanche blode; & so þe saphir of þe eest stancheþ bledyng at þe nose if it is leyd to þe temples. Also he haþe a syngler vertu þat þe saphir abateþ bolnynges & swellynges of postomes þat is clepid antrax, for he putteþ þe myȝt of ventosite & þe malice of þe postom, for he ouercomeþ & putteþ owte þe wodnes þerof, & suffereþ not þe smeke þerof to come to þe hert; for his malice infecteþ þe spirites. Also his vertu is contrary to venym, & he qwencheþ it euery dele. And so yf þu wilt preve it, [put][2] an attorcope in a box, & hal a very saphir of ynde at þe mowþe a while, & by vertu þerof he is ouercome & dyeþ as it wer sodenly, as dias seyþ, & þe sam I haue asayd oftyn in many diuers places. Also his vertu kepeþ & saveþ þe syȝt & clenseþ þe yene of fylþe withowte eny greuance. Ðerfor it is wryten in bokes þat it takeþ away þe ache of þe forhede. Also þis ston was of gret autorite in old tyme, þat men seyd þat þey wold holowȝ it to hir god, & so it was syngulerly holowed to her god appolyne. For when naciouns axedet consel of appolyn in tyme of sacrifice, þey hope to be certefy & to haue answer þe raþer if saphir[3] ston wer present as Dias seyþe. And þer is þe soþe þat þey þat vsen nygramancie seyn þat þe mowene haue answer of god & mor Iherd by þe saphir þen be oþer precios stones. And also wycches louen syngulerly wel þis stone, for þey byleuen þat þey done certeyn wonders by þe vertu of þis ston. Also þis ston doþe away sorow and dred, & putteþ fere, & makeþ a man bold & hardy & mayster & wictor; and it makeþ þe hert stedfast in godnes,

[1] ? Read beschadewed.
[2] MS. omits.
[3] saf crossed through before saphire.

& it makeþ a man meke & myld & godly. Et qui portat eum castissimus esse iubetur.

CIX. Smaraddus is a ston most precios of al grene stones, as Ised seyþe. Men in þe old tyme ȝaue þerto þe þryd dignyte after margarites. And smaragdus haþe þe name aboue al precios stones of gren colors. For it is seyd þat all gren erbis & all gren stones þat ben precios ben not so g[r]en¹ in color as is þis ston smaragdus, for it passeþ in grennes erbes and grase & twygges or sprotte for he enfecteþ þe eyr abowte him with his passyng gren color, as Ised seyþ; & his color abateþ not in þe sone in no maner

f. 13 wyse. No þyng comforteþ / þe eyene þat greue mor þen þis ston; for if þe body þerof is clensed, þen ymage ben þerin as it wer a mirror. For þe Emperor Cesareus vsed to see Fyȝting of swerd-men in þis ston, as Ised seyþ. And þerof ben xij maner of kyndes, þat þe most noble ben yfounde in acia, þat is in gente scitica, & bredam holdeþ þe second pelase.² And smaragdus ben fonde vndir stonnes & in chynnes þerof when þe norþen wynde bloweþ, for þe erþe is vnhilled & þe stones smaragdus schinen amonge þe stones, for in southe wynd grauel & sonde be most Imoved. Ðe egipcions han þe iij smaragdus, & þey ben fonde in metel or ine ore of brase, but þey gleymyng for þey haue spekes lyke vnto brase or to lede or to salte. Ðowȝ þe smaragdus ben grene by kende, ȝit þer ben oþer smaragdus þat gone owte of kynde, for þey ben vnworch-iped by veynes of brase & þe ben called calce smaragdus. All þes seyþ Ised. And þis ston is Itak & beneme fro gryfes; and plente of smaragdus may not be fonde, for gret grifes letten þe comyng of men be þe wey þat ledeþ þerto, as Ised seyþ. Also þis ston multeplyeþ his grene color; of him comeþ a beme þat þeyþ þe eyre abowte him & makeþ him grene. Ðe body þerof is cler & of myrror kynde, & scheweþ figures, ymages & schappis of þynges þat ben mor nyȝ þerto; and it haþe a ȝifte of kynde, a benefite of vertu, to saue & to hell dyuerse syknes & yuell.

¹ MS. gen.
² First e above the line

Also dias seyþ he increseþ riches, & makeþ men to haue
goode wordes & feyre, & euydence of & cause of plee. If
þis ston is hanged abowte þe neke, it helpeþ emitritene &
þe fallyng yuel, & saueþ & comforteþ febell syʒt; & he
chasteþ lecheres meuynges, & makeþ gode mend; & it
helpeþ aʒens al fantaʒies & iapes of fendes, & ceseþ
tempest & stancheþ blod. And it is seyd þat it helpeþ hem
þat vsen to dyuyne & gessen what schall fall, a[s][1] it is
seyd in bokes. Also whoso bereþ þis stone smaragdus in
clene lyfe, his syʒt schal neuer fayl him, & his colour schal
euer be fayer, & he schal be loued of all men & women,
ne he schal neuer be trayed, ne neuer lese his gode, but
euer encrese in riches & loue, & it kepeþ fro al myshappis
& disestes.

CX.   Sardis is a precious stone, & he is of a red colour,
as it wer red erþe; & he[2] haþe þe name for he was first
founde in sardis, as Ised seyþ. For, as þe glose vpone þe
apocalips seyþe, þowʒ þis stone be preciose & fayre, ʒit
many men counte him lest worþe amonge preciose stones;
for as þey sey, owte take schynyng þer is no profite þerwiþ
but þat only þe stone onix may not greue in his presenss;
for as it is seyd, þat þis ston onichul haþe some yuel pro-
pirtes, & he may not schew hem yn dede in þe presens of
þis stone sardus. And dias seyþe þat ouer þis vertu sardus
haþe many oder vertues. Of sardius þer ben x maner of
kyndes, but þe best comeþ owte of sardius; & he is gode
for . . .[3] for encreseþ ioye & putteþ away dred; & he makeþ
a mane bold & hardy, & he schappeþ þe wyle. And þe
ston onyx may not grefe in his presens. Also he seyþe þat
sardous þat is all red kepeþ his berer fro enchanthementes
& fro wyche-crafte. Also þe lapidarie seyþ þat sardius &
grenas & alamandines & iagunces ben wexyng togiders;
but þe iagunce haþe þe vertu of al þese stones, & it is þe
most fine þyng of þe verld, for his colour is gentil & red;
& it makeþ a man glad & to dwele in ʒonge & trewþe; &

[1] MS. at.
[2] MS. he he he.
[3] Illegible.

he makeþ a man to forȝete his contrariosite & his beyng;
and dowȝt þe nowȝt as of no styng worme ne wild best.
Also men may passen perlose water mych þe raþer. And
whoso haþe it vpone his fynggere, mych þe leuer he schall
f. 13v recyue geestes to herbarowȝ; / and when he schaweþ þe
iagunce ston, of þat he preye to men resonably it schal not
be hid fro him. Also þe boke telleþ vs þat god named fyrst
þis stone, & was of color of þe erþe, of red erþe wherof god
made fyrst man, adam, in þe feld of Damaske, wherof we
be of þe self behetyng, & þerfor named god þis ston first,
& in þat it is of þe self color. Sent Iohn seyþe in þe apocolyps þat he saue þis ston in þe vj fondament of þe very
kyngdome.

CXI.   Sardonix. Þis stone haþe þe name of ij stones of
sardius & onix, as Ised seyþ; & he is of iij colors; for þe
blak is of þe lowest, & þe whitȝ of þe medel, þe rede as
vermylon is hiest. Only þis ston takeþ not only of þe wax
when he is þer-in. And it is fonde in araby & in ynde. &
þerof ben v maners of kynde, but which hym haþe moste
many colours, & most distingned, & is most pyche, he is
best. It is seyd þat he putteþ awaye lechery, & makeþ a
man mek & chast. Þe lapidarie seyþe þat þis ston sardonix
is a ston redissh reednes & blakkyssh. Þis ston by himself
adaunteþ wreþe of a man & makeþ him rest wel by nyȝt
withowte myche dremyng or noyng tacches, & it doþe
awaye noyng vices fro men & kepeþ him chast & schame-
fast & graciose.

CXII.   Serpentyne is a stone of dyuerse colours, & it
comeþ owte of perce, & it is red, blak & grene; for þe
panter is of diuers colours, þerfor þis stone haþe þe name
of panter, for al maner beestes maken myche of þe best
because of his bewete & of his coloures and his swet smel.
And he þat bereþ þis ston vpone him he is gladly kept fro
all yuelles; and also he is gode for venym.

CXIII.   Topaces is a stone þat haþe a ȝelowe color, and
þer ben moo þen oone maner, þat one of þe eest; and owte
of araby comeþ þe best. Topaces makeþ cold a malady þat

is cleped þe feyr; and þe feyr þat is quenched wiþ topace
schal neuer wax after. Ðe boke seyþe þe topace draweþ
him to semblence of þe·mone which is fowle & reyne, þen
þis ston is more fowle; and when þe ȝonge mone is most
fayr, þen it is mor fayr of color & gentil. He þat bereþ þis
ston schall loue to lede his body chastly, & þen mor to loke
heuenly wayes. Ðe bible seyþ þis ston was þe ij stone vpone[1]
þe brest of aarone, þe which haþe þe color of gold. Sent
Iohn seyþe in þe apocolyps þat he say þis stone in þe ix
fundement of þe [e]uerlastyng[2] cite. By þe morn kynges
sholden bleþly beholdene topace, for he gefeþ hem gode
remembrance to loke to þe rial lyf[3] þat he schal haue,
which is c[r]owned[4] in heuen, þat schal neuer fayl. Also
þo þat beholden many stones in sobernes tornen mor her
syȝt to þe topacie. Holy writ seyþe þat þe topace such as
he vaxeþ is best; but it is not so pleyn ne no hete may be
pulisched of him, þerfor he leseþ not his strengþe.[5] Also
þis topacie comeþ owte of a flode of þe eest orient, and of
þes þer ben ij maners, but þat oone is mor cler þen þe oder.
And þe[6] mone is cler, þe ston is cler, and when þe mone is
troble þe ston is troble; & he schal be set in gold. Also
Ised seyþe þat þis ston is a schyny[n]g[7] kynge & wiþ al
colowurs schyneþ; & it was forst Ifonde in a yel of arabie,
in þe whiche yle-londe þe trogadite wer disesed wiþ honger
& tempest; & þey dyggen vp rotes of herbis, & þer þey
found þis ston þer-with, & þey clepid it testamnebulis; þer-
after schipmen souȝten & founde it, & cleped it topazim
in þe langga[g]e[8] of þe trogadites; þerfor þis ston þat was so
y-sowȝt & founde is cleped topazius,[9] and it haþe name of þe
londe of topazim in her langage, & it[10] is seyng siche; & it is þe

---

[1] MS. vp vpone.
[2] MS. uerlastyng.
[3] lyk crossed through before lyf.
[4] MS. chowned.
[5] syȝ[t] crossed through before strengþe.
[6] eche crossed through before þe.
[7] MS. schynyg.
[8] MS. langgae.
[9] a above the line.
[10] MS. & it & it.

f. 14 most grete of precios stones.[1] Plinius wrote þat a/ston of þis
kynde was yfonde so grete & so myche þat philade[l]phe[2]
made an ymage þer-of, iiij cubites of lengþe. Also in þe
glose vpone þe apocalyps it is seyþ in þis maner: þe more
scarse þis topazius is, þe mor preciose he is; and he haþe
ij colors as it were of gold & clere eyre. And he schyneþ
most when he is smeten with þe soone-beme, and passeþ in
clernes al oþer stones þat ben precios; & he comforteþ men
& beestes to behold & þer to loke þer-vpone. And if
þu wypest þis ston he wole be more derk, & if þu love him
in his owen kend he wol be mor cler; and in the tresor of
kyngges no þyng is mor cler nor mor preciose þen þis
preciose ston is; for clernes of himself he takeþ to him þe
clernes of all oþer preciose stones þat ben abowte him. And
it is seyd þat he foloweþ þe course of þe mone, & þerfor
he helpeþ aзens þe passioun of lynatik folke; and so it seyd
in þe lapidairy, þat as þe mone is more ful or lasse so effecte
is mor of þis ston or lesse. Also he stancheþ blode, & he
helpeþ hem þat han þe emoroides & swageþ him. And he
wold not suffre feruent water for to boile, as it is seyd in
bokes. Dias seyþe þat it asswageþ boþe wraþ & sorowз, &
it helpeþ aзens yuel þowзtes & frenesey, & aзens soden
deþe. And he haþe þe schap of a mirror; and þe ymage þat
is þeryne is seene in a holowз myrror. Also, if þu preve þis
ston, put him in a hote water þat is boylyng, & if he lese
his colour þen he is nowзt.

CXIV. Margarita is chef of al stons þat ben wyзt &
preciose, as Ised seyþ. And it haþe þe name margarita for
it is founde in shellis which ben cokelis or in mosclys & in
schellfyssh of þe see; þis bredyng is schellfyssh, & it is
genderd of þe dewe of heuen, which dewe þe schell fissh
receyueþ in certen tymes of þe зer, of þe which dew margarites comen. Some ben cleped vnyons, & þey han a
conable name, for þer is oonly one Ifonde & neuer ij
togeder; and þe whiзt margarites ben better þen þe зelow,
& þo þat ben conceyued of þe morow dew ben made dym

---

[1] MS. strones.
[2] MS. philadephe.

wiþ þe eyr of euentyde: hucusque Isodorus. Also some ben
fonde which ben perced kenly, & þe ben better þen þat
oþer; and some ben persed by crafte, as Plato seyþ. And
þey ben best wyȝt, cler & rownde; & þey han vertu of
comfort by al kend þerof; and somme seyne þat þey com-
forten lymes & membris, for it clenseþ him of superfluite
of humours & fasten þe lymes, & helpen aȝen þe cordiacle
passioun & aȝens swonyng of hert, & aȝens febilnes of
Flux by cause of medecyne, & Also aȝens rennyng of blod,
& aȝens þe flyx of þe wombe, as plato seyþ. Also in plato
it is seyd þat margarites ben gendred of þe morow dewe, &
some mor & some lesse, but it is trowed þat no margarite
groweþ past halfe a fote. Also it is seyd þat when lyȝt-
nynge or þundri[n]ge¹ falleþ, when þe margarite schold bred
of þe dew þat it resseyueþ, þe schel closeþ be most soden
strengeþ & þe gendringes faileþ & is cast owte. Þe best &
most [n]oblyst² margarites comen owt of ynde & of old
brytayn.

CXV. Medus is a precios ston, & is fonde in þe lond of
medeis, and it is sumtyme grene & sumtime blak, as Diascorides seyþe. And som sey þat he is founde in þe sowþe
londe. Þis ston ȝeueþ boþe deþe & lyfe. Þe vertu of þis
stone is aȝenst blynndnes of yȝene, & aȝens potagre, if it
be temperd wiþ þe mylk of a woman þat norschiþ a man
child. Also it is gode for ache of þe reynes & ek for þe
frenesey; & if þe blak stone be leyd in water, & lete
dri[n]ke³ þe water, it distroyeþ spwyng & ouercomyng of
þe stomak; and if þe forhed eider þe yene be wasshin þer /
wiþ, it distroyeþ wonderly þe webbe þat greueþ þe syȝt;
& if he drynk þis licor he schal be dede. Þis ston is blak,
but his vertues ben whiȝte when þey helpen & blak whene
þey noyene. Som men seyn þat þe mylk beforseyd schold
be gode for yene þat ben blynd. And who distempereþ it
wiþ þe mylk of a schepe þat haþe not had but oone lambe,
& it be a male, it schal helpe þe potagre & þe syknes of

f. 14v

¹ MS. þundrige.
² MS. oblyst.
³ MS. drike.

oþer lymes; & it will be tempered in siluer, & when it is
temperid þen [ȝ]if[1] it to þe seke bodi with wyne; and when
he is distempered with water he haþe ale his kynde; and
afterward it schal be ȝeuen to Wassh with yene, & þey schol
be hole.

CXVI.   Onychinus is a stone of ynde & of arabie. He
haþe in himself color ymedeled lyke þe mayle of onix. Ðe
onix of y[nd]e[2] haþe colour of fyre with whiȝt veynes &
strakes, and þe ston onix of arabie haþe blak vaynes. And
þer [ben][3] v maner of kyndes; oone is sardonix, & he haþe
þat name of cumpanye of tweyne, of þe which stones of þe
onix & rednes of þe sardius, as it is seyd ynnermor in þe
sardonice. Also it is seyd þat þis ston onix haþe many
noyful effectes, as dias seyþe, for if it is borne abowte þe
neke eyþer fynger, he exciteþ sorowȝ & elyngnese & dred,
& it multeplyeþ plee, & ȝeueþ þe hert to contencioun &
strife, & exciteþ in childre noyful superfluyte of spetel; and
it may not noye neiþer greue in þe precens of þe stone
sardius. Ðis stone onix is cler & of þe kynd of mirroures,
þerfor ymages & schappis ben yseyne þeryne as it wer in a
mirror, but þat is dyuersely & derkely, as dias seyþe.

CXVII.   Obxianus is a stone þat if a man ber him þer
schall neuer sweuenes to him harme, ne no man schall spek
him harme, so þat þe ston shyne vpone him. Also ber it
vpone þe and þow schalt neuer have yuel deþe.

CXVIII.   Oblyx is a stone & is lik to horn of a mannis
nayle, & mydes as it were colour of whiȝt. Whoso bereþ
þis stone schal be de fyrst þat schal be scomfite in batayle.

CXIX.   Enysus is a stone, who þat bereþ it schall neuer
have rest in his slepe. No noþer vertu know I in him. To
preue him, frote him on þy tonge, & þy mowþe schal be
blak.

CXX.   Melotes is a stone, & it haþe þat name for swetnes
þat comeþ owte þerof, as wer hony, as Ised seyþ; & it

[1] MS. if.
[2] MS. yie.
[3] MS. omits.

haþe ij colours, it is lyk gren on þat oone syde, & lyke hony one þat oþer syde.

CXXI.   Merites is a preciose stone, & it haþe þat name for it is lyk to myrre color; & if it is wronge or pressed it smelleþ swete as narde.

CXXII.   Rubie is a red stone shynyng, & he strengþiþ al stones þat ben rede, as þe boke telleþ. Ðe gentel rubie þat is fyne & clene is lord of al stones, & he is also as water of wateris. It haþe vertu above all oþer precios stones, & he is of shuch lordschip þat when he þat comeþ bereþ it amonge oþer men, all þey schul do him honor & grace, & al men mak ioye of his comynge. Ðe boke telleþ vs þat þe beestes þat drinke of þe water wher þe rubie haþe be wete yne schul be hole of her siknes; & he þat haþe discomfort in goddis beleve, & behold þis stone, it schall comforte him & make him to forȝete his contrariosite bi vertu þat gode haþe ȝeuen þerto. It fedeþ a man & comforteþ his hert & his body, & it wynneþ a man lordship. Ðer ben iij gret rubies, & ben fonde in þe londe of libie in a flod of paradise. Moyses put þis stone in þe brest of aarone in þe ij corner of þe xij stones. Also þis stone clenseþ yene & comforteþ þe body. And þe fyne rubie is founde in þe londe of libie in a flome þat comeþ owte of paradise; & he wole be seet in fyne gold. Also he makeþ a man welbelouid with lord & lady. Ðe water þat it is wasshen yne, it distroyeþ þe moren of bestes & of men. Ðe man þat bereþ þis ston schal be neuer ouercom in ple ne in batayl, & þis seyþ euax kyng & emperowr.

f. 15 CXXIII.   Letates is a ston, & it is lyk in color to an attercop or an yrene or a spider. He þat bereþ þis stone schal neuer be harmed with eny wenym, nor þe place þat he lyeþ yne. And yf a woman be ful of blod, bynd þis stone to her forhed with a lynen cloþe, & it schal staynche here. And yf a old man haue þis stone vpone him, þe mor he bloweþ þe feyre, þe mor schal it quenche.

CXXIV.   Litugures is a stone þat þefendeþ mennes howses fro mysauentures boþe for man & woman; & yf a woman be in trauel of child, it schal helpe her if sche drinke it in powder.

CXXV. Lincis is a stone of þe dace, þat if a man be sike in his bely, grynd þis stone & drinke it with wyȝt wyne & he schal be hole. And yf a man haue withyne him 'la cursum' men clepeþ, schal helpe him.

CXXVI. Litigerus is a stone like to lede & siluer, but he haþe litel vertu.

CXXVII. Lontucerius is a stone, & he is profitable for a man þat wil tak venyson priuely, & for huntyng & for fowlyng.

CXXVIII. Lasulus is a stone þat is a stone ryȝt gode for medecyns; & also yf a man haue þe feuer quartene, take & grynd þis stone & drynke it with water of rose, & he schal be hole þorowȝ þe vertu of þis stone.

CXXIX. Molochites is a grene stone, & it is lyk to smaradus, but it is more boystous gren þen þe smaragdus,[1] & so it haþe þe name after þe color of malues, as Ised seyd, & he is bred in araby. & he is ful nessh in substance, & neuer-þe-lesse it is ful profitable, as Diascorides seyþ, for it kepeþ & saueþ childryn fro noyfull yuelys & happes; & whoso bereþ it in his lyf syde, þer schal no wykkyd þynge greue him.

CXXX. Marble is clepid marmor, & he haþe þe name of grekes for grenesse, as Ised seyþ. Also marbole ben noble stons, & þey ben prysed for speckes of diuerse colors, for marble is endles; & þer bene þerof many maner of kendes, but þey ben not all hewen owte of rokk. And þer bene maner of marbles as it is founde in many dyuers landes & places vnder þe erþe, as marble of lacedomonia, & þat is grene & precius, & þat marble is cleped ophites, for it is specked like an edder. Marble purpurices comeþ owte of egypt, & it is rody with punctes amonge, & it haþe þat name purpurices, for he is red as purpil. And þer bene

[1] ra *above the line.*

many maners of kynde of marble, as alabastrum & parium,
& of him we shul speke ynner mor. Also a-noder maner
of kynde is cleped coralicitum, & it is founde in asia, & it
passeþ not ij cubites in mesure, & it is wyȝt as yuory, &
some han wyȝt speckes in dyuerse proposions. Also anoþer
kynde is cleped telaicum, & it is spreynt with golden
speckes, & it is founde in de contrey of egipt, & it is
kendly schapen to make þerone colliria & oynemenes þat
helpen yene. Oder kendes of marble breden in qwarreis
& in roches, as marble þat is clepid marble dounche, &
þerof is made pilors & pawmentes & towres; also þer is
anoþer maner kynde which is cleped charistium, & it is
grene & beest; & it haþe þe name of aspeton, for men þat
grauen loue it wel for þe gren color, for it comforteþ wel
þe syȝt. Also þer is anoder kynde þat is cleped virundicum,
& it groweþ in india, & it makeþ þyng þat is froted with
lyke to gold, & þerfor it haþe þat name; also Ised seyþe,
liº xvj; and þer he setteþ an ensample of many dyuerse
marble, is mor sade, mor hard, mor stronge & feyre, mor
profitable þen oþer stones.   In þe veynes þerof þer is
founden diuerse materes as ben precios stones; for þe
hardnes þerof is most hard to grauen, & for cold &
sondynes þerof it is best to kepe in spicire & oynementes
ouer all oder þynges.   We may wonder þat marble stones
be not hewen ne clouen with yerne ne with stele ne with
hamer ne with sawe, as þey ben with a plate of lede ysete
betwyx nessh shynglis eiþer spones, for with led & with
yere marble stones ben hewe & ycloven & Iplaned as for
small stones.

f. 15v CXXXI.   Noset crapendien is a precios stone, somdell
wyhiȝt, and þerof ben diuerse colores; and it is seyd þat þis
ston is taken owte of þe todes hede, & it is then clensed
in stronge wyne & water, as Dias seyþe.   And sometyme
þe schape of þe tode semeþ þerin, with schappen fete &
brod.   Ðis stone helpit aȝens byȝtynges of serpentes & of
crepyng wormes, & aȝens venym, for in presense of venym

he varyeþ, & brenneþ his fi[n]gres[1] þat towcheþ him, &
schold boþe be yclosed y fer as dias seyþe.

CXXXII. Niger is a stone, & men clepen it galanticen.
Ðe vertu of þis stone is þat yf a man hold it in his mowþe, or
ley it one his tonge, & put him in wax or in hony, what
man þat will him harme schall haue no power but come to
him & telle him. And he þat bereþ him schal be loved of
all men, & his vertues increse. And yf a man will asay him,
bynde þis stone vpone her reynes, & þer schall neuer
woman leye.aȝens her wyll; and if a man may not do his
kende, bynde it to his naked flessh, & he schall do so
myche þat þe rede blod schal come after. Ȝit yf þu wylt
preue þis stone better, take þis stone & put mylk in hony
togeder, & anoynt þee, & þer schall no fley towche þe
after.

CXXXIII. Uytrum is glas in englyssh. Ysed seyþe
þat þis glasse is a stone somdel whiȝt, & he may be hewe
& cloue, & he is ful clere. It dissolueþ, tempereþ, &
draweþ, & clenseþ & wasteþ superfluitte of humors. Also
Ised seyde, l° xvj° cc° ij°, þat uytrum haþe þat name of þe
contre of uytrea in egypt; & þerof medecyns ben made, &
þerwith bodyes & clodes ben waschen. Ðe kynd þerof is
not fer fro þe kende of salt, & it is mad ryȝt as salt in
drynes in old clyues. Ðe [f]oome[2] þerof is cleped affroni-
cum, & it is genderd of þe droppyng of dowues in þe contre
of asie, after it is dryed with þe hete of þe sone; & when it
is best dryed þen it is schynyng[3] as Ised seyþe. And Platea
seith that nitrum is a veyne[4] of þe erþe & it is hote & drey,
lyȝt rede oþer wyȝt or citrin, & it is better sower, &
somdell salt in sauor. Uytrum abateþ fatnes if it is taken
in þe mowþe, & consumeþ & wasteþ glyme humors. Ðe
powder þerof confecte in clarefyd hony worshipeþ þe fase,
& clenseþ scabbes & qwiter of þe stomak & of þe guttes, if it
come of a postome; & it clenseþ luys & scabbes of þe hede,

---

[1] MS. figures.
[2] MS. soome.
[3] MS. doubtful.
[4] And Platea ... veyne almost illegible.

I

& it sleeþ wormes of þe eeren, & it c[l]enseþ[1] most *perfite*
þe qwyter & scabbes; & put vyneger þerto, & it helpeþ
gnawenge[s][2] & swellyng. Also it helpeþ aȝens þe dropsi, &
clenseþ dymnes of yene, if it is medeld *with* hony; & it
sleeþ venim[3] & distroyeþ it, & *with*stondeþ myȝtly þe palsy
of þe tong, as platearius seyþ. Also dias seyþ þat uytrum is
hote & drye in þe ende of þe þryd degre. And it laxeþ &
clenseþ, as Ised seyþe. Also glas, as auycen seyþ, is amonge
stones as a fowle is amonge men, for it receyueþ al maner
of colors & peyntynges. & it is cleped vitrum for 'vy,' his
vertu, is bryȝt & cler & lyȝt schinyng, & þorowȝ all þat is conceyued in...[4] in metayl & in vaynes of erþe whiche is hidde.
Al maner licor is seene owteward, as it is wyne, & is
yschewed as it wer to yen closed þat loke þeroone, as Ised
seyþe. Also glas was fyrst yfonde besydes tholamayda, in
þe clyfe besydes þe reuer þat spryngeþ owte of þe fote of þe
monteyn of carmelo, whiles þe chepmen reyned; þerfor
vpone þe grauell vpone þat reyne shypmen mad feyre of
clottes ymedeled *with* bryȝt grauell, & þerof rane stremes
of new leycor þat was þe begynnyng of glas, as Ised seyþe.
Now glas is mad of asshen of trees & of erbes *with* full
stronge blastes of feyre, *with* þe wiche it is nowe medeld
with now glas, now bras, now boþe torned into glas. When
glas is Imolten in þe fornes & perfyȝtly clensed, þen he
f. 16 takeþ puernes, bryȝtnes & clernes. Glas is died / *with* al
maner of colors, so þat it foloweþ iacinctus, smaragdus, &
oþer precios stones in color & bryȝtnes. Also it is pleyant,
so þat it receyueþ ful sone dyuerse & contrarie schappis by
blast of þe glasier; & it is sometyme ybete & somtyme
ygraue as siluer. Also Ised seyþe þat no metall is mor able
to make of mirrores þen is glas, neyþer to receyue peynture;
but it is most worthid wyȝh glas ȝat is nyx to cristall in
color; For it is oft ychose befor siluer & gold to drinke in,
as Ised seyþ. Also þis he seyþ, þat þe stone Osianus is
rekened amonge þe kend of glas, & þis ston is somtyme

---

[1] *MS.* chenseþ.
[2] *MS.* gnawengeþ.
[3] hony *crossed through before* venim.
[4] Illegible.

grene & somtyme glas, & it is cler & bryȝt, & it is cleped
Speclaris & is with fatti liȝt. Of þis stone many men maken
precios stones, & to contrefet, as Ised seyþ. And al glas
haþ þis propirte, þat it is most plyant whiles it is in meltyng
hote & nessh, & it is most brotel when it is cold & hard,
& yf it be brok it may not be amended withowt meltyng
aȝen. But þer was oone had mad plyant glas þat myȝt be
amended and wrowȝt with hamer. Also Ised seyþ þat oone
browȝt a wiole made of such glas befor tiberius þe emperor,
& þrew it down aȝen þe grownde, & was not ibroke but
Ibend & yfold, & he riȝthed it & amended it with a hamer;
þen þe emperor let smyt of his hed anone, lest, if þat craft
wer Iknow, gold schold be worse þen glas, & oþer metal
schold be litel worþe. For sikerly if glas were not brotel, it
schold be aconted mor worþe þen a wessel of gold, as Ised
seyþ. Ðen glas is clene & pure, & specialy bryȝt & clere,
& ymages & schadowes ben seyne þerin; & it is plyant
when it is molten & hote, & brotel when it is cold & hard;
& it receyueþ al color; & it foloweþ precios stones more in
color þen in walew, & it clenseþ fylþe & superfluite.
Auycen seyþe þe powder þerof clenseþ teþe & doþe away
welkes of yene; & it helpeþ gretly aȝens þe stone of þe
blader & of þe reynes, yf it be dronk with wyne.

CXXXIV.   Orides is a stone of color, & he is gode
aȝens venym & aȝens byȝtyng of wode bestes; and he þat
bereþ it vpone him may sikerly goo þorow desertes &
hermytagies. Anoþer maner is had, & þat is grene & it
haþe wyȝt ioyntes, & heleþ a man fro contrariosnes; also in
goote of þe syde he is scharp vpone þat oþer syd; he is
pleyne. Ðe woman þat bereþ him may conceyue no child,
& if she be with chyld sche schal lese her chyld.

CXXXV.   Onicle is a stone þat comeþ owte of ynd &
of Arabie; & Onycle, Sardius & calcidine ben drawing
togeder. Onycle kepeþ a man hardy, coragies & wroþe.
And yf he bere him in his fynger or abowt his nyke, he
kepeþ him saaf & encreseþ his bewte. Ðe onycle is blak of
color & his vertu is in gold. He doeþ away fantaȝies, &

makeþ a man to hawe gret dremes, & he makeþ a man hardy in fyȝt; & he helpeþ a man in plee, & so to conquer his ryȝt; & he wole not be myche loke þerone. Midas þe boke telleþ vs it makeþ a man to speke to his dede frend by nyȝt in metyng; & if it fal to drem in þe morow, þen þe dede is in travel. He þat bereþ it schal haue many gode graces. Ðe bible seyþe þat þe Onycle was in þe fowerþ corner of þe brest of arone.

CXXXVI.   Optalio is a stone þat is cleped opalus. Also it is a stone distingned with colores of diuerse precios stones, as Ised seyþe, þat þerin is þe feyr of carbuncle, þe schynyng purpur of þe amatist, þe bryȝt color of þe smaragdus, & colors schynen þeryne with a maner dyuersite of þe contrey of ynde in wyhche he is brede; and it is trowed þe he haþe as many vertues as colors. Of þis opatallio it is seyde in þe lapidary þat he kepeþ & saueþ yene, & kepeþ him cler & scharp & withowte greuance; and þer is a syknes þat blyndeþ menis yen with a maner of clowde & smyteþ him with a maner blyndnes which is cleped anancia, so þat þey mow not se neyþer to take hede wat is befor her yene; / þerfor it is seyd þat he most sikere pattron of þeves, as seyþe þe lapidary.

f. 16ᵛ

CXXXVII.   Orites is a stone, & þer-of ben iij maners; þat one is blak, þat oþer is lyke hony or waxe, þe iij is gren with blak spekkes. He þat bereþ þis ston shall neuer have harme of beest. Yf þu will preue þis ston, þrow him into þe feyre; yf þu may fynd him, kepe him wel, for þat is þe ryȝt orist. Ðe þryd ston kepiþ knowlech; he is like hony in þat one syde, þat oþer part is pleyne & lyȝt, & in þe oþer part playne as it were a clouce. He þat bereþ schal neuer gete chyld, ne no woman conceyue while it is vpone him; & yf a woman be in travelyng of chyld, sche schal soone be delyuerd weþer sche will or will not.

CXXXVIII.   Pirite is a stone, þat whoso draweþ him he will not abyd with him. His kend is to be towched lyȝtly, & he most hold it softly in his honde; & yf a man streyn him hard he wol bren his hond; or fret him one his fynger, his fynger schall bren. Pirite is red lyȝt, lyk to þe qualyte of þe eyre; mych feyre is þer-in, & oft sprynges to men owte þerof. And he haþe his name of pire, þat is to sey feyre.

CXXXIX. Piante is a stone þat comeþ owte of macedony of þe kyngdom; & he is god for womans kende, for he makeþ lytel labore of woman, & he is gode for a woman þat¹ conceyueþ, & makeþ a woman to chyld, & he is myche helpyng to þe fadere & to þe moder, & it is god for wraþe.

CXL. Prassio is a stone, & it comeþ owte of macedony of þat kyngdome; and he is god for womans kend, for he makeþ lytel þe labur of women, for he is² good for conceyuyng, & it makeþ a woman sone to have chyld. Also he helpeþ mych to þe fader & moder; and it is good aȝens wraþ. Ðis ston prassio is grene as leke, & he comforteþ myche þe syȝt; & he is founde sometyme with red droppes, & sometyme dystyngned with wyȝt dropes. Of þis stone it is seyd in bokes þat no profite is þerwith but þat he is grene, & wyrschypeþ mych gold.

CXLI. Panteros is a stone, & comeþ of a best þat haþe many colors. If a man bere þis stone, it is god for yuel neyȝ-bores. Ðis ston panterone is of dyuers colors ysprenge & dystyngned dyuersly; also he is seyne blak, rede, gren, pale purpil & ȝelowȝ, & also bryȝt gren in colour. And þis stone makeþ a man bold & hardy, so þat he schal not be ouercome þat day þat he seeþ him ȝerly at þe sone reysyng, as it is seyd in dyuers bokes.

CXLII. Prosultes is a stone þat haþ þe same vertu þat þe flent haþe, for he wole tende feyre.

CXLIII. Parius is a stone of þe kend of þe noble & gentil marbul, for he [is]³ precios. Also Ised seyþ þat ston is founde in þe lond of paroun, & þerfor it is cleped paryus. Ðe quantete þerof passeþ lances & . . . & it is good to kepe

¹ kend *crossed through before* þat.
² he *crossed through before* is.
³ *MS. omits.*

in spycery & oynemenꝛes. Also Ised seyþ, & þe glose
vpon ester seyþ, þat parius is a kend of most whiʒt marbul,
& þerfor it be token of chas[ti]te.[1]

CXLIV.   Proinces is a stone of femal kend, as it is seyd,
for somtyme he conceyueþ & bereþ such anoþer stone.
Also he helpeþ women þat ben with child, as Dias seyþ.

CXLV.   Periot is a stone þat is lyʒt grene.

[1] *MS.* chasitte.

THE SLOANE LAPIDARY (MS. G.)

THE lapidary is a free translation of the Second Anglo-Norman Prose Lapidary,[1] a text written before 1243. The Anglo-Norman text has a verse prologue in one MS., and a prose prologue, based on that of Marbode's lapidary, in the others; neither of these appears in the Sloane Lapidary, which starts without any preliminaries with Diamond. It gives all the sections of the Anglo-Norman Lapidary but those on Cornelian, Chalcophonos, Lyncurium, and Turquoise, and adds two sections on Toad-stones and Serpents' Tongues from the same source as that used for the articles on these stones in the Peterborough Lapidary. The translator occasionally shortens the text of the Anglo-Norman Lapidary, and frequently misunderstands it, but makes hardly any independent modifications. His version is independent of the translation of the Anglo-Norman Lapidary made or used by the author of the Peterborough Lapidary. The text has not been published before.

SLOANE 2628 (MS. G.)

f. 14v   Of pretious Stones.

I   EUAX

Diamonde comes from Inde and some from Arabie; that wich cometh from Inde is clipped males, ye other female. The male is [broun][2] appon[3] light shininge, ye female is whit & bewtifull of coulor like Cristall. Thes diamonds is very pretious to thee and of great hardnesse, for thay will graue in Iron or steele, taking no harme. If a man weare it, it strenghen him & kepith him from dreming in his sleepe, from faintnes and from poyson, from wroth & chiding. It sendeth & helpeth men to great worth. It defendeth a man from his enemies, & kepeth

---

[1] Studer & Evans, p. 119.
[2] MS. omits.
[3] MS. mappon, with m crossed through.

119

a man in good estate wher he findeth him; it comforte a
man witt, & support him of ritches. And though a man
f. 15 do fall downe from a cart or a wale he shall / not break any
of his bones if the stone be on him; it doth away all
ded[som]¹ sompnes yt cometh by night. It destroyth
Lechery; and he shall not lightly be acombred so yt he
feare god. And it will keepe the seede of a mans body
within a womans body, so yt the children's limmes shall
not be wrong ne crooked. And it must be sett in the
mettle of steele & bore of a mans left halfe.

II   SAPHIR

It cometh from ye strem Iorden & is found in grauell
of bythen. It is good for kings, queenes & great lords;
it shineth as a faire coulor of Inde bright & other
coulors. The best Saphir commeth from the red sea, it is
f. 15v dim² & shineth; it is provd to be of grat vertue, / but
some of more vertue then other. Our lord loued it so well
ye saphir that he cald it holy, pretious, & geme of gemes.
When a man holdeth the saphir he shall haue in thought
and in hart ye bliss and ye lykni[n]g³ of hert. It comforteth
man hart & limms, it keeps man from poyson, & it helpeth
him out of prison yt is imprisoned; for he shall touch his
bonds therwith & ye irons of ye prison that he is in shall
breake. It is good for to accord peple together, to heale a
mans byles & swelling. If a man haue an Impostume in
his body, if he stoope it & drinck it in milk it shall vanish
away throug ye vertue yt god hath giuen it. It helpeth a
f. 16r man yt hath to much heate in him, / and avoydeth the hot
evell yt cometh by sweting, and helpeth the hedach & sore
eyes. It geueth good cownsell to ye man yt bereth it on
him, & the man yt vseth him much he shall be chast. It
destroith witch-craft. It ought to be set in gold and bore
on the right side of a man.

¹ MS. ded wan (?).
² MS. drim (?).
³ MS. lyknig.

III   EMERAUDE

It is greene & cometh from the Streame of Paradis
And of Sirie.   Those of Siria are ye best.   This stone
multiplieth a mans goods; if he bere it on him & keepe it
cleene, it maketh him to be of word & fortune wyse.   It is
good for the knawing gowt of a man, it mendeth the sight
of a man, & doth a-way great tempests of wethers.   It
f. 16v voydeth lechery, For God gaue it such vertue; / And to a
man that kepeth it, his body and members should be euer
cleane and without euell.   It must be set in gold of ye best
and bore on ye right side[1] of a man.

IV   ADAMAND

It cometh from ye land of Inde, it is lyk to rust of
Iron.   It droweth to him vertues many one.   And ther is
no stone so good for charmes as this.   For if a man will
preev his wyfe or his leman if thay be trewe and loue him,
Lay this stone vnder her hed & if she be trew she will
turne her toward him, if not she shall stir as a beast, And
make as though she falleth, and cry as if she had feard an
f. 17r vngodly sight.   And also may ye mariners / and Marchants
know ye wynd by the thickning of wether.   It accordeth
man and woman of loue together.   It is good for ye dropsy.
It geveth grace to man & woman, and good cownsell; and
it helpeth a man in great power & strengh.   And whoso
putteth it in wyne & afterward putteth in his mouth
helpeth him soone of hart breninge for euer.

V   IASPES

Yt is a stone of ix manners, & of many coulors.   And
thay ar fownd in many lands of the worlde.   But yt is best
yt is greene as is ye Emeraud Agenes ye day, but it is of
more greatness.   And when it is entayled of ye old entayle
f. 17v it hath red dropps. / And it is good for it helpeth a man of
ye dropsie & from ye feuers.   It helpeth a woman in bering
of children & deleverance, & kepeth of a man from

<hr>

[1] d *corrected from* g.

co[n]tertaking[1] & fiting, And doth a-way ye fantou*n*nes & feyntness of a man. It stayeth blood & ye bloody menison. It is v*er*tues better in silver than in gold ether in any other metals. And this stone will sweat against venomes for truth.

VI   CRISOLITE

It is like ye water of ye sea, & he hath in i[t][2] of his owne kind sparkells lyke to gold. He that bereth it on him shall do no trespas of sinne nor no evell of wickednes, nor to be acombred in no land or place, but be beloued of

f. 18r all people. / If it hath a hole thorough it, put a thred of silk through it & weare it, he shall driue away all evells & feinds ther w*i*th erly & late, for ye stone cometh fro*m* Ethiope. It shall be set in gold & bore on the left side of a man.

VII   TOPASE

It cometh fro*m* the fleme of the East Contry; ther be of 2 sorts, and they ar lyk gold in ye sea, but that ye one is clearer then ye other. It is good for a sicknes men call the fyes that cometh sodenly to a man. It followeth the moone of his owne kind. When the moon*e* fulleth & trobled is, tha[n][3] is the stone trobled, & whan the wede[r][4] is faire and cleare tha[n][3] shall ye stone be cleare & shineth. It

f. 18v keepes a man fro*m* sinne / & chast from all euell company. It must be set in gold.

VIII   ONICLE

It cometh fro*m* the land of Inde & of Arabie. And Onicles, Sardonyes & Calsidones be drawing to-gethere. This stone maketh a man hardy and stronge if it be bore about ones finger or neck; & if he haue desire to speake with his frend yt is dead, lay it vnder his hed & he shall haue conference w*i*th him in his sleepe. He is to be set in gold and is of one coulo*r*.

[1] *MS.* cotertaking.
[2] *MS.* in.
[3] *MS.* that.
[4] *MS.* wede.

IX   IAGNUCES

It is red of kind[1] and of gentle manner and couler and of
f. 19r great vertue. It maketh / a man to be glad and honest
and to keepe him-self true. Another kind of Iagnuce is
caled Iagnuce Citryne. Thes 2 be of such vertues if a man
put them in his mouth thay kill his thirst. And bore on
you may go far in-to cuntris with-out dred of beasts and
things that he seeth, and that that he goeth for shall soone
be fownd & not hid. And he dare not dread ne haue no
doubt of his host whersoeuer he be by land or water. He
is to be set in fine gold for it is his kind.

X   BALEYES

It cometh from an Ile betwixt the seas yt is called
f. 19v Counche. It is lyk Ruby of Coulor. / It cooleth much ye
heate of lechery. And who-so toucheth ther with in any
the fore halffe of his chamber, his howse or his herbere,
ther shall no wicked worme nor no euell pest shall not fall,
so yt harme shall be go. It defendeth[1] contention & strifes;
if a man beare it on him among his enemies they shall haue
no power to hurt him. This stone is to be sett in gold.

XI   AMATISTES

It is in couler lyke to purple & it is shining. It is
fownd in Inde ye more. It comforteth much a man both
in his body and in his soule. And if any wild beast come in
ye place he shall not feare him if ye stone be on him. It
comforteth the shipmen and helpeth those yt be dronken &
f. 20 miss/gouernd. It is to be sett in gold & in silver.

XII.   RUBIE

It overcometh all ye mervealous stones of beuty. Yet
some is clearer yen others, for ye cleare Rubie is of so
gentle coulor lyke a burning cole. He is lord and king of
stones and of all gemms. It hath ye vertue of xii stones. It is

---

[1] Coulor *crossed through before* kind.
[2] *MS.* defendendeth.

of so great value and price yt he yt beareth it ageinst ye people yey have all manner of joy of his comming, wich hath beene preved full oft. So ye sick beaste yt drinck water[1] that this stone is wett in ar holpen of ther sicknes. It driueth away all taches & ill conditions. It is sayd yt this stone is in ye fleme of paradice. It must be sett in gold.

f. 20v XIII   ALECTORIE

It waxeth in a capon shin, and when he is 4 years old it waxeth till he be 6 or 7, and then it is of strengh but no bigger than a beane, and it [is][2] like troubled christall. It procureth a man the victory of his enemies; it stancheth a mans thirst by being put in his mouth. It maketh enemies frends; it helpeth a mans speach and meaning and maketh him welbeloued. It helpeth a woman to conceaue with child; it helpeth loue betwixt man and wyfe; they ought not to commit ye sin of lechery that bereth it; and he yt will proue ye vertue of it must put it in his mouth.

XIV   CELIDOYNE

It is in the wombe and mawe of a swallow. It is not full & / faire, But it is of much bewty in him-selfe. It is of 2 maneres & of 2 coulors, ye one blew, ye other redd of kind. It is good for men yt be lunatick, and for men or weomen yt be in langour and dissese. It maketh a man full wyse in speach and wel beloued. It must be bore in a linnen cloth appon ye left syd of him. It helpeth to end a mans worke he hath begun. It helpeth greatly for menacing and for threatning of ye people, from wrath of king, lords & ladies. This stone washt in water, ye water helpeth sore eyes and for ye feuer; it doth away ye fleame of a man, it streyneth and openeth ye humors of a man yt ar in ye body of him. It shall be wownd & laid in a linnen cloth yt is died greene.

---

[1] ye *crossed through before* water.
[2] *MS.* it like.

XV   ELITROPE

It over-paseth many stons for vertu, for god gaue it
f. 21v such a strengh. / If it be put in a vesell of water against
ye sonne it semeth that ye water is all red, and then it is
bright and of his owen coulor. He yt beareth it on him shall
be a great purchaser and happi to gett goods; it keepeth ye
body in helth and of great verchue and power; it stencheth
blood; it is good only for venome and for venome wormes.
And[1] what man taketh a greas yt is called Solsicle, if it be
blesed with good words of god, yf he do touch the stone
ther with he may go without any dred. It cometh from ye
land of Ethiope and Africk. It is of swete colour as is ye
emerawd. And it hath dropps of blood.

XVI   CORALE

f. 22r   It waxeth in the sea as a grass, and when it is out / of
ye sea it is red and lyke a branch. It is no longer nor
greater then halfe a foote. And as old maistres[2] and authors
do wryte, it defendeth and kepeth a man from lightning,
thunder,[3] and from tempest of wether. It is good in a
vinierd or garden, it defendeth it from tempest. It makes
ye fruit to encrease. It helpeth a man from faintness. It
geueth man a good beginning and a good ending what
contry yt he taketh.

XVII   BERRELLE

Berelle and hires ar a part lyke to christall. Berelle
is a rownd stone, and Hires is full of sydes. The berell
casteth a faire coulor against the sonne. This berell
norosheth loue betwixt man and woman. The water that
thes stones ar washen in ar good for sore eyen, and being
f. 22v drunke it doth away heuenes of hart & sighings, and /
helping all maner of euells of a manns liuer, & for ye
feuers. Thes 2 cometh from ye lond of Inde.

---

[1] Solsicle if it be blessed of god *crossed through before* And.
[2] *MS.* m^{es}.
[3] & *crossed through before* thunder.

XVIII   ACHILLES

This stone the egles fetcheth from far Lands and bring them to ther nests forto defend and keepe thes bodies[1] safe. This stone hath an other stone within him. It is good for a woman with child that she lese it not nor no member of it. The people yt beare it on the left arme it kepeth them in age and helth, and in a good meane and estate, and increseth gretly a mans goods to-gethere, and maketh them well beloued; it causeth a good witt. It helpeth ye knawinge gowte; and if a man haue a suspition of an enemy, lay this f. 23r stone under thy tooth that thow dost eate with / though he be godly and connable toward him, he shall not [m]ow[2] eat no meate as long as it is there, and when it is away he shall eate at his pleasure. This stone is rownd and fownd in in the great sea. It is a good jewell for weomen in birth of child.

XIX   CRISOPAS

Cometh from Inde, and hath a coulour lyke a frute of a Appull, and it shineth as gold. The man yt beareth it on him shall be full of grace and right well beloved of all yt know him, be thay[3] man or woman.

XX   SILENTES

It [is][4] a stone of a greene coulour; its called ye holy stone. It followethe the moone, and kepeth loue be-twixt f. 23v man and woman, and it helpeth / men yt be in langor and dissese; it helpeth men yt be outlawed, wrongfully indited. Men find this stone in a land of Persia.

XXI   GAGANTURELS

Ar peckled lyke gotes ferr. If a man beare it on him when he goeth to a battell he shall chase and defend him from his enemies of all ye host. For sir hercules yt worthy knight escaped from many a perell and mortall battaile through the vertue of this stone in many a land.

---

[1] Read ther brides (?)
[2] MS. now.
[3] Two letters crossed through before thay.
[4] MS. It a.

XXII   BERUMQUES

Cometh from ye contry of Arcade; it hath a Coulor
as Iron. It is of a wonderfull kind, for if it be ones hott
f. 24r at / the fire he shall euer more afterward brenne of his
owne kind.

XXIII   COLONITE

Some calleth it Fore, and it doth shine, and it is of
purple cowlor, and it is black. Men find it in the land of
ynde. And if a man put it in his mouth as long as ye
m[o]n[1] is wex, and he must tell things to come from
ye morrow till the tyme of ye midday. And when ye
moone is at the prime then lasteth his power all ye day;
and it will never fade.

XXIV   GENATIDES

f. 24v   It is of such a kind that if / a man put it in his mouth,
so yt it be well washed before, he shall then see whatt
othere men think of him, and a woman shall not deny
him what he asketh. And thus shall a man proue the stone
diuers wyse: As anoynte a man with hony and milk and set
him naked in the sonn[2] wher many flyes ar, and if he bear
the stone in his mouth they shall not touch him, and put
away the stone and they will set vppon him and frett him
to the death in soth.

XXV   ORIDES

Is a pretty black of coulour, but he droweth a coulour
to him as he weare gold. He is good ageinst venome
f. 25r and hurting of wicked beasts. / He yt beareth this stone
on him may safly go through any wilderness or desert and
every-whear ells. He is greene and hath within him whit
spotts. He kepeth a man from stryfe. Another maner of
Orides yer is yt is sharpe on the one syde & plaine on
ye other. The weomen that beare it on them may not
conceue with child; for and she be with child she shall do
loose her child for euer.

[1] MS. man.
[2] MS. sonñ.

XXVI   CHRISTALL

Is cleare and white and it keepeth a man of his thirst.
Make powder of Christale & giue a woman to drinck &
it shall greatly multiply her milke. Touch ye Christall
with ye stone that hath lost his vertue through ye sine
f. 25v of him¹ / that beareth him vppon him, so yt he amend
him of his sinne² he shall returne his strengh as in his
kind through ye vertue of ye Christall stone.

XXVII   ALECTORIE

Hath a coulor lyke Askes. Weomen yt drinck ye
powder of it with milk it will encrease her milke, but
she must vse³ it befor meate, and after meate let it be beaten
smale and put in a linnen cloath and hung about her neck
with a thred of woll. If yis stone be bownd to woman yt
traveleth with child it helpeth her soone of deliverance.
And if a man do make pouder of it and strew it among
shepe that be well washed and cleand, they shall beare ye
smaller woll and be never more scabbed. It hath a coulor
f. 26r and sauor as milk, and it cometh from / the flemme of ye
Orients part.

XXVIII   IASPES

Ar of many coulors. Whoso goeth to battaile and hath
this stone will overcome all his enemies; him behoueth to
know when ye sonne ariseth, and then it shall helpe him
much against his enemies. It maketh a man hardy in
fight; and as many coulors as he hath so many vertues
hath he.

XXIX   CANSIDOYNE

Is of troubld whitness. If a man haue it vppon him in
his plea and shew it to his adversaries, he shall haue the
better of them and it helpeth much his case to ouercome
them.

¹ of him *repeated overleaf.*
² *MS.* sinñe.
³ *MS.* vseth *with* th *crossed* through.

f. 26v **XXX** ACATE

It is fownd in ye east in the fleume caled Acate.

1. It is of many diuers things, for one is black and it is gird with white lynes. It tempereth a mans thirst, it comforteth men of age, and the men that holdeth him close
2. in his fist he shall be invisible. Ther is another Acate of colour as Corall & it hath dropps as gold. And
3. another Acate doth smell as mirr. Another of coulor
4. as wex. All thes manner of Acate ar good ageinst venome, and against stinging of edders. It warnes a man of harme, and giueth him good cownsell, and maketh him beloved of god and man.

f. 27r **XXXI** CARNELEYNE

Is lyke a lump of flesh, and it nemath a man his wrath soone, and it strenghen the limmes of a man[1] that bleedeth. It comforteth a man or woman much of ther sicknese and dissease and to recover soone. Therfore wee ought for to loue it; it procures loue and pleasing to all men.

XXXII CRAPAUDINES

It is fownd in ye front of a toade, and the man yt bereth it on him, yt is of ye age of 7 years old and more. And ye Tode yt beareth it when he meeteth a man, he dresseth him fast in his harnes to hid him. This stone is /
f. 27v rownd and bright, of ye quantity of a beane and white all about; he yt nemeth it from ye tode let him tak a new pot of erth that hath all small[2] holes made there in, And put the pott in a great Emit hill full deepe that ye emetts may enter in, but keuer it fast about ye mouth, and a some tyme after take it oute and you shall find ye stone in ye front. It is good for verchue being borne, and it encreaseth a mans goods. This stone shall sitt in silver.

[1] *Two letters cancelled before* man.
[2] small *above the line.*

K

XXXIII   Tongs

of Adders ar of many Coulours as browne, black, but
f. 28r ar red ageinst ye mone. / They ar of more vertue, for
it kepeth a man from venome yt bereth it.   And he yt
hath it in his keeping if men will pursue him it will full
fast sweate.   And therfor it should be set in silver, both
for kings [&]¹ lords at ther meate, so yt they may be kept
ye safer from poyson.   It is good ether in silver or in gold,
and many do find it in many places betwixt ye grauell of
ye great sea beyonde ye greater britaine.

XXXIV   Lince

It cometh from Lince.   It is a proued gemme.   And
anothe[r]² manner of Lince cometh from bretaine ye
f. 28v More. / It is black and a playne stone, and when it is chafed
at ye fire it will draw into him strees of corne of his kind.
And he burneth in water & is quenched with oyle.³   It is
good for fleame yt is betwixt ye flesh & ye fell, As a man
yt is afownded.   It streineth ye kind of a woman aboue all
things when she burneth in her owne kind.   If a wooman
be naked in a bath, put the same powder of this stone in
the bath; if she be a mayd she shall not mooue far, if she
be none she shall stand vp in a great hast and pass away all
naked for shame.   It will aswage ye gowt if he smelleth to
f. 29r it.   And as soone as Adders smell / therof they fley away.
It is good against euell⁴ spirits and euells.   The man yt
bereth it knoweth well a woman if she be a maid or no.
And weomen that travayle with child do drink of ye water
that this stone hath lyen in iij draughts: Foorth-with she
shall be deliuered.

XXXV   Sardonyes

is of 2 coulors, red & black mingled together.   It
temporreth a mans wrath; it maketh a man to have good
rest bore on him; it maketh a woman of a good complexion
and chast.

¹ *MS. omits.*   **FINIS**
² *MS. anothe.*
³ *Three letters cancelled before* oyle.
⁴ *Two letters cancelled before* euell.

NOTES

THE OLD ENGLISH LAPIDARY

p. 13. I. HYACINTHUS. Probably derived from Isidore xvi, vii, 8: 'Est autem smaragdo subsimilis, sed crassi coloris.'

II. SAPPHIRUS. Isidore xvi, ix, 2: 'Sapphirus caeruleus est cum purpura, habens pulveres aureos sparsos.'

III. CHALCEDONIUS. Bede, Explan. Apocalipsis Cap. xxi: 'Chalcedonius quasi ignis lucernae pallenti specie renitet, et habet fulgorem sub dio non in domo.'

IV. SMARAGDUS. Bede: 'smaragdus nimiae viriditatis est.'

V. SARDONYX. Bede describes one kind of sardonyx: 'alius, quasi per humanum unguem sanguis eniteat.'

VI. ONYX. We have not found a source for this. Bede omits it. Isidore says: 'nigra est cum candidis zonis.'

VII. SARDIUS. Bede: 'Sardius, qui ex integro sanguinei coloris est.'

p. 14. VIII. BERYLLUS. Abbreviated from Bede: 'beryllus est quasi consideres aquam solis fulgore percussam.'

IX. CHRYSOPRASUS. A confused version of Isidore and Bede, who give 'aureus . . . guttis.'

X. Omitted in MS.

XI. TOPAZIUM. Bede describes one kind of topaz: 'unum [coloris] auri purissimi.'

XII. CARBUNCULUS. Bede follows Isidore on the amethyst in describing this stone: 'quasi rosae nitore, quasdamque leniter flammulas fundens.' Isidore describes the carbuncle (xvi, xiv, 2) 'quod sit ignitus ut carbo.'

XIII. ADAMAS. Isidore xvi, xiii, 2: 'Hic nulli cedit materiae, nec ferro quidem nec igni.'

XIV. MAGNES. Isidore xvi, iv, 1: 'probatur cum ferro adiunctus eius fecerit raptum.'

XV. ASBESTOS.
Claudea: Arcadia.
Isidore xvi, iv, 4: 'Asbestos Arcadiae lapis ferrei coloris, ab igne nomen sortitus eo quod accensus semel numquam extinguitur.'

XVI. PYRITES. Isidore xvi, iv, 5: 'Pyrites Persicus . . . hic tenentis manum . . . adurit.'

XVII. SELENITIS. Isidore xvi, iv, 6: 'Selenites ... interiorem eius candorem cum luna crescere atque deficere aiunt, gignitur in Persia.'

XVIII. ? ALECTORIAS. Isidore xvi, xiii, 8: 'crystallina specie.'

XIX. SYRTITIS. Isidore xvi, xiv, 10: 'Syrtitis vocata quoniam in litore Syrtium inventa primum est. In parte Lucaniae color huius croceus, intus stellas continens languidas, et sub nubilo renitentes.' We have found no mention of its use in salve.

XX. CATOCHITIS. Not in Isidore. Pliny xxxvii, 56: 'Catochitis Corsicae lapis est, caeteris major: mirabilis si vere traduntur, impostam manum veluti gummi retinens.'

XXI. MOCRITUM. We have not identified this stone.

XXII. ACHATES. This does not follow Isidore, but is a rather confused version of Pliny xxxvii, iii, 1: 'post hunc anulum [the ring of Polycrates] regia fama est Pyrrhi illius, qui adversus Romanos bellum gessit. Namque habuisse traditur achaten, in qua novem Musae et Apollo citharam tenens spectarentur, non arte, sed sponte naturae ita discurrentibus maculis, ut Musis quoque singulis redderentur insignia.'

LONDON LAPIDARY OF KING PHILIP
MS. B

P=Lapidaire du Roi Philippe, Bib. Nat. MS. français 2008

7, l. 4. **perireres:** P. perrieres.

5. **þe boke:** les liures.

8. **deuysed was:** nous deuise.

kyndelich: naturielx.

þat god hymself yave vertu in hem: et ce que Dieu mesmes en dit, ce que Moyse en dit, ce que Salomon en dit, ce que Saint Jehan l'euangeliste en dit, et ce que l'emperieour eracles en dit.

12. **mysbeleue of men:** mescreance des gens et la non foy aueucques les pechies.

17. **but ayeinseith:** on le desdit.

20. **in a moos clen & fine:** en ung parement de pur or fin.

21. **in foure corners, in every corner thre stones:** et commanda que elles fussent par iiij tyres, et en chacune tyre troyz pierrez.

23. **of Iche kyndely:** oniches naturielx.

shaape: entaillier.

stones: ligniez. (Pannier, who collated P with other MSS. gives 'entaillier ens les noms des douze ligniés.')

26. **oon:** les oniches.

33. **sare:** sarde.

8, l. 2. **named:** nomma a moyse le prophete.

4. **my lord:** not in P.

6. **he sigh . . . cite:** e vit paradis en maniere de une chitey.

7. **and the xj stones . . . kyngdome:** Cy vit xij pierres ez xij fondemens de la chitey du celestiel reyne.

10. **elleuen:** xij.

14. **þe elleuenth Iagounce:** l'onziesme Jagonce, la douziesme Oniche.

16. **of þe elleuen stones:** et de cellez.

23. **atte aarons . . . grete kyngdome:** en fondement du vray regne.

I. SARDIUS.

8, l. 25. **sardes, grenas . . . to-gedre:** Sardes, grenaus, alemandines et jagonces sont concrees ensemble.

27. **and is . . . worlde:** et est la plus fine.

29. **in youthe & trouthe:** en jouuente et en loiautey.

30. **mysbeyng**: mesaduenture.
31. **touchinge ne styngynge**: atouchement.
    of worme: de venin ne de vermine.
32. **passe þe rather**: trespasser.
33. **mochel þe lever . . . harbourgh**: plus liement l'en rechoit son hoste pour ly herbergier.
34. **sheweth hit**: il le monstre a son hoste.
35. **the boke**: les vrais.
36. **The verray boke**: La bible.
37. **and was**: pour ce qu'elle fut.
p. 19, l. 3. **of þe same colour**: de humayne couleur.
4. **wherof all we . . . traueile**: dont tous deuons estres frerez de ce mesmez pechie, et demourez en sommes en paine et en trauail.
9. **signifieth**: senefie en l'appocalipse.

II. TOPAZIUM.

p. 19, l. 16. **colith**: refroidist homme.
    & þe fis . . . after: Le fij qui est creuey ja puiz ne crestra.
17. **The boke**: Les liures.
19. **foule**: laide et pluuieuse.
22. **to loke . . . weye**: regarder a la celestielle vie paruenir.
    The Bible . . . diuinitees: La Bible nous dit.
28. **þe life corouned . . . neuer faile**: la vie couronnée du chiel qui ja ne faudra.
34. **with sobrete**: par bonne entention.
p. 20, l. 9. **and þerfore shulde . . . hym-self**: et que mielx y deust chacun entendre.
10. **For dauid . . . men**: Not in P. The sense of the English is not clear.

III. SMARAGDUS.

p. 20, l. 15. **Emeraudes amenden . . . uppon**: Esmeraude amende les yeulx et garde la veue d'empirer a cheluy qui en bonne creance la porte. Moult est bonne esmeraude a esgarder.
16. **Nero hade . . . loked in**: The text of P is corrupt.
18. **seche or witte**: cognoistre.
19. **maketh worde of man dredeful**: fait a homme parolle raisonnable.
20. **tempeste & lecherye**: tempeste.
21. **þe more he shal loue . . . clennesse**: plus voulentiers se maintient douchement.
24. **for god to this stone**: par la voulente de dieu qui a ceste pierre.
25. **first**: tierche.

26.   þerfore hit signifieth: et segnefie.

27.   of hym þat is ... Trinite: de la foy que les bons patriarches et prophetes oulrent sy grand et sy treffinement et qu'ilz en ont acquis la grant gloire du chiel.

28.   Seynt Iohn seith ... euangelistes: Not in P.

31.   seith us seynt Iohn: Les lyures nous dient.

p. 21, l. 1.   on þe water: sur le fleuue de paradis.

     and taken hem: Not in P.

2.   & wolden take ... to take hem: et lez destornent a leur pouuoir et moult sont angoisseuses et ardans en tollir mez ilx sont armes por ce toulir ne leur peuuent. Saint Jehan nous dit en l'apocalipse que il vit l'esmeraude la quarte pierre en fondement du vray regne. Ce segnefie la foy dez quatre euangelistes.

p. 21, l. 4.   The fyne ... Jhesu Xrist: La fine esmeraude nette gentil et tres vert segnefie la tresardante foy qu'ilx eurent en la benoiste Trinitey. Toux ceulx qui sont en ceste verdeur de foy ne ont que ung oyel, c'est Jhesucrist pour ensuyre Sa doctrine.

11.   cristen men: les bons crestiens qui sont bien fermes contre les temptations du deable.

IV. CARBUNCULUS.

p. 21, l. 1.   steyneth: vaint.   (The translator misread as *taint*.)

     Þe boke: les liurez.

17.   water of waters: gemme des gemmes. Elle enlumine les euures par nuit et par jour et moult esprent et enlumine l'er cler et toutes choses cleres.

27.   above othre stones: et voult par dessus les deulx aultres pierres qui grigneurs d'elle sont.

28.   Þer ben gretter ... rubie: Rubi est trouuey en la terre de libie.

29.   The bokes of moyses: La bible.

30.   what god commaunded: Not in P.

31.   corner ... mouce: tire des xij pierres sur la poitrine Aaron.

32.   & to liȝte ... of this worlde: Nulle clartey ne se prent a sa jentil et joieuse couleur. Les liures nous dient qu'elle senefie Jhesucrist qui est vraie lumiere qui vint en ce monde pour enluminer le peuple qui estoit en tenebres et en umbre de mort. Toux cheulx qui la clartey du noble ruby esgardent doyuent esgarder par digne contemplacion a la vraie lumiere Jhesucrist.

V. SAPPHIRUS.

p. 22, l. 14.   gracious & gode: moult gracieuse de dieu.

     men take him ... so founden: Il en y a de trois manieres, qui sont trouuees en libie en la grauelle du fleuue d'orient.

18. **clene colour ... then the clene:** au pur chiel en la parfondesse du fleuue est trouuey. Les obscurs sont trouuez plus hault.

21. **vertuouse:** vertueulx de dieu.

Thise maner: ces trois manieres.

22. **enuie:** folle enuie.

membres: membres enuiemment.

25. **yef he haue any:** Not in P.

beleue: creance en dieu.

27. **The boke:** les liures.

28. **þat ben in discencoun:** Not in P.

29. **biles:** boches.

30. **Also yef men yeue:** Qui trible safir et en donne.

31. **bile:** boche.

34. **sorowe:** douleur.

sekenes of þe gomes: jaunice.

p. 23, l. 1. **greuaunce:** chacie.

þe boke: les liures.

3. **this stone:** sy vertueuse pierre.

4. **The veray bokes tellen us:** Not in P.

5. **saphire:** le noble saphir.

for þe strencth ... gode: mes la forche de la haulte veue cest du soleil fait sembler que soit bleu.

10. **vnderstandyng:** regard.

11. **blisful blysse:** glorieuse joie du chiel.

12. **Cite a blisful saphire:** saphir ... chitey de glore.

15. **corner:** tire.

17. **in gode memoire of hym-selfe:** en bonne esperance.

VI. JASPIS.

p. 23, l. 19. **diuers colours:** diuerses couleurs et ont diuerses vertus.

20. **ful depe:** forennes.

21. **godely:** le milleur.

22. **lesse worth:** mains en vault.

23. **shape of þe olde shappe:** entailliez.

25. **all manner wormes:** toute vermine.

and yef ... maladie & colours: et se vermine est atouchie ou apportee en lieu ou le vray jaspe soit, il uertira ou muera vue de ses couleurs.

31. **descriue metynge:** garde de fantosme et fait homme puissant et sain.

33. **aduersaire:** contraire.

35. **gode:** Not in P.

36. **þe trewe peple of men:** la foi de la loialle gent.

lesse vnderstanding: simple entendement et croient fermement.

p. 24, l. 1. **þei be lewde men:** Not in P.

3. **bounden:** simple gent.

signifien jaspe: sont compareyz au jaspe.

4. **Moyses seith . . . sarazins:** La Bible nous dit que jaspe fut la tierche pierre de la segonde tire qui fuc mise sur la poitrine Aaron et dit Moise qu'elle destruit fantosme, car la foy de la segonde loy c'est de la benoiste Trinitey destruit la fantosme au deable et aux juifs et aux sarrazins.

7. **of Ierusalem:** Not in P.

8. **gode man . . . þat is cleped:** proudomme qui jaspe porte. La premiere est appellee foy la seconde esperance la tierce charitey.

VII. LYNCURIUM.

p. 24, l. 15. **ouenes:** forestz. (The translator apparently mistook the French word for *forneis* or something similar.)

21. **mylke:** letre.

22. **Teopatus:** Theophatus.

24. **many vertues:** plusieurs manierez de vertus.

25. **voideth vices:** destourbe homme de faire son contraire.

26. **all sorowes . . . stommak:** toutes les douleurs qu'il a eu l'estomac.

29. **The boke:** les liures.

30. **lovyng:** amees.

33. **& þis stone:** Sachiez que ceste pierre.

p. 25, l. 2. **oxe:** une maniere de beuf.

3. **this stone:** elle (i.e. the beast).

8. **eryen:** aerent.

wynnen: Not in P.

be holy predicacion: par saincte predication ce son lez bons prescheurs.

9. **corner:** tire.

of Ihesu Xrist: de saincte Eglise.

at thre tymes: au tiers temps.

VIII. ACHATES.

p. 25, l. 14. **founden in a flode:** trouuee en la terre d'inde en ung fleuue mesmes.

15. **whyte & blacke colours . . . of colour:** blancez chaintes de noyres chaintures et de telles ou il n'a que une chainture.

17. **& som þat haue . . . trees:** et de telles ou yl a figures comme de rames et comme de fieulez comme d'arbres.

18. **hedes:** testes et comme de bestes sy comme nature les a mises.

20. **dyodropie:** dyotrople (i.e. Heliotrope).
21. **muche in deuyse of þe lapidarie:** moult en deuise le lapidaire.
22. **golden veynes:** veines aux riues.
24. **coraulys dróped:** coural goutee est la milleur. Aucunes en ya de couleur d'or et telle ya qui est de couleur de chire.
25. **saueth an olde man . . . strencthe:** Not in P.
28. **in redynge:** Not in P.
29. **an herbe þat is cleped þe goulde:** une herbe essuyee.
31. **shewith the sone:** suit le solleil (i.e. Heliotrope).
33. **his brother:** Not in P.
p. 26, l. 2. **the Trinite . . . fruyte:** des sains hommes qui par bonnes oeurez font fruict pardurable.
3. **two significacions:** ceste segnefiance.
4. **as þe bokes tellen:** Not in P.
    corner: tire.

IX. AMETHYSTUS.

p. 26, l. 9. **blode newe shedde:** sanc martirie.
    The boke: les liures.
11. **all sorowes:** yvresse.
13. **of Moyses:** Not in P.
15. **Who-so bereth . . . ful graciouse:** Et cheluy qui ceste pierre porte se il requiert dieu il luy sera gracieulx.
17. **The scripture of diuinite:** La bible.
18. **colour þt þe Iewys:** couleur de pourpre et segnefie la robe de pourpre dont les Juifz.
20. **& for þat cause:** Not in P.
21. **Salamon:** la diuine page.
23. **god:** Jesuxrist.
    atte his deethe: devant sa mort.
24. **and the lordeshippe:** et doibt ramentenoir la seigneurie.

X. CHRYSOLITHUS.

p. 26, l. 27. **of golde:** de or de toutez pars.
    The boke: Les liures.
28. **amonges kyndely stones:** Not in P.
    who-so be oute of synne..grace to him: Qui nettement la porte n'est pas ort de pechie ne de mauuaistie. Cy peult doncques en haulte court entrer seurement sans contredit et grace luy porteront la gent.
30. **þe boke:** le lapidaire.

33. **with myght:** seurement sans doubter.

7, l. 1. **blisful:** precieuse.

2. **cyop:** ethiopie.

3. **Holy writte:** la bible.

4. **wisely lyuen here in erthe:** sagement conuersent au monde.

5. **The glose of the appocalipce:** Et dit moyse le prophette que dieu nomma crisolite la xe pierre pour segnefier les x commandemens de la loy. Saint Jehan dit en l'appochalipse que il vit crisolite vij^e pierre en fondement du vray regne. Ce segnefie les vii dons du saint esprit. La glose de l'appocalipse.

6. **þe holy predicacions & miracles of Ihesu Xrist:** les sainctes predicacions que font les bons prescheurs des miracles nostre seigneur Jhesucrist.

9. **Seynt John . . . lawe of god:** See above.

XI. ONYX.

, l. 17. **Sardoynes:** sardines et calcedoynes

19. **& vertues:** et moult vertueuses.

20. **whyte sydes or veines:** couleurs blances comme vaines.

21. **parscour . . . plloncket:** perces ou rougettes et il y a ne poy ne quant de noir oniche a nom selon le scripture.

23. **& gederith plente of gode:** Not in P.

24. **þat bereth hit:** qui la porte nettement.

25. **the boke:** le scripture.

speke: songier et parler.

26. **in metynge:** en songeant.

& yef he falle . . . traueile: et luy souvient au matin de ce don le mort est besoigneux.

29. **onycle wexith blak . . . god yafe þerto:** l'oniche blanc et noir ressemble a ongle de homme. et segnefie cheulx qui sourmontent les mollestes de la chair. quer aussy comme l'ongle est plus dur de la molle chair aussy la vollontey que les sains homes ont a Jhesucrist qui est la ferme pierre est plus dure que leur chair. et par bonne affection sourmontent lez molestes de la chair. mes ilz ne parviennent pas a la durte de la pierre au deable comme le pecheur fait qui s'endurchist et endort en son pechie.

35. **kyndely . . . colours:** Not in P.

37. **charite . . . Ihesu Xrist:** chastee que vient de la compaignie Ihesucrist.

8, l. 1. **corner:** tire.

of the moce: des pierres.

2. **þat haue the figures:** qui oulrent ongle.

XII. BERYLLUS.

p. 28, l. 7.   **shyneth:** y fiert.

8.   **riall:** ront.

   The boke: les liures.

9.   **þe water:** et sachies que l'eue.

12.   **yixing:** senglont.

13.   **shall be muche worshipped:** est honnourez.

   The bokes of diuinite: les liures.

16.   **shyneth þervppon . . . heete:** y fiert et il n'est entailly il brulle qui le tient.

18.   **deueles:** le diable.

19.   **her enfourmynges ne her temptacions:** sa fourme ne sa fantosme.

20.   **Oure lorde . . . twelue apostles:** dieu nomma la XIIᵉ pierre beril. ce segnefie les xii appotres.

22.   **cristendome:** le baptesme de Jhesucrist.

24.   **þe holy age:** le viijᵉ aage.

25.   **þe auctorites:** le lapidaire.

28.   **fired with charite & bren of hemself:** qui enflambes sont de la chaleur de charitey et de ces sains hommes mesmes espranent.

30.   **The nature of Baleys:** See below.

32.   **named:** nomma de sa bouche.

33.   **& þe elleuen . . . named:** entre lesquellez en y a huit de celles mesmement que saint Jehan l'euangeliste vit en fondement de la celestiel cytey c'est paradis. Vous en auez ouy les vertus et les segnefiances apres vous diron des aultres quatre pierres que saint Jehan nomma. les vertus et les segnefiances ainxy que promis le vous auion au commenchement de ceste œuure. Du Ballais.

XIII. BALAS.

p. 28, l. 34.   **First:** Not in P.

p. 29, l 1.   **oracle . . . ful gode stone:** toracle. En ceste isle qui est ainxy appellee naist cette pierre. Jagonce retret a couleur de ruby mes n'est pas de celle maniere car elle n'est pas trouuee la ou l'en treuue le ruby. elle mue et amende sa beautey contre le beau temps. moult en est plus clere quant le temps est cler et de plus jentil couleur. Cest le sire des pierres apres le ruby. Bien peult l'en dire jagonce ruby jagonce ballaiz jagonce saphir jagonce grenat jagonce citrin. yces manieres de pierres et d'aultres peult l'en appeler jagonce. Moult par est bonne pierre gentil et belle ballais.

11.   **veray:** Not in P.

13.   **The bokes:** le scripture.

16. **safe:** sain et sauf.
18. **worme:** vermine.
    harme ne greuaunce: ny atouchera ja qui mal y faiche.
20. **feire tyme:** beau temps et contre le laid.
21. **clerkes & maistres:** les tressages mestres.
26. **cyop:** d'ethioppe.

XIV. CHRYSOPRASUS.

p. 29, l. 28. **Crisophas:** crisopas.
30. **swynes eyen:** jus de poreaulx.
31. **who-so berith hit . . . commynge:** cheluy qui la porte est gracieulx de plusieurs bonnes graces, et par tout la ou il vient est l'en liez de sa venue.
33. **in traueille:** en charitey et en trauail.

XV. CHALCEDONIUS.

p. 30, l. 1. **shall be well spekyng of gode:** est bien parlant et de bonne loquence.
    he speke: Not in P.
3. **hit kepeth hym his ryghte:** son droit luy garde dieu par la vertu de la pierre.
5. **he shall be wel . . . his synne:** est bien vertueulx se il par son pechie ne le pert.
7. **grace:** grand grace.
10. **þat drawen . . . gode werkys:** qui attraient a dieu les pecheurs par leurs sainctes parolles.

XVI. SARDONYX.

p. 30, l. 15. **be nyghte:** par nuyt sans songier trop.
    drechyng: Not in P.
17. **shamefast:** Not in P.
    (Not in B): Cy fenissent les pierres que dieu nomma a moyse le prophete et a saint Jehan l'euangeliste et ensuit le nom de plusieurs aultres pierres bonnes et excellentes pour toute creature humayne et premier du dyamant.

XVII. ADAMAS.

p. 30, l. 22. **named & deuised:** premierement nommee et deuisee en lapidaire.
28. **What man . . . of his riches:** Nul ne la peult amender de beautey ne pour polir ne pour aultre chose de teil maniere sunt neyz et trouuez.
32. **greuouse metynge & temptacions:** de griefz songes et de fantome.
p. 34, l. 4. **of value:** Not in P.

5.   and encreaseth hym . . . þat berith hit: Et se il ne croist en auoir tout-
effois il ne appetiche mye. Et sy n'est pas de legier temptes qui nettement le porte.

7.   a witles man: forceney.

10.   The boke: les liures.

13.   & hoole: Not in P.

holy he shal . . . in clennesse: proudomme doibt estre cely qui le
porte et qui vertueuse pierre porte.

XVIII. ALECTORIAS.

p. 31, l. 17.   iiij yere: troiz ans.

18.   a been: une petite feue.

20.   & yef he holde it: et se l'omme a grant soif et il la tienge.

22.   & brought hym-self ayein fro the chaces: elle ramaine les dechachiez.

24.   well spoken of: bien parlant.

25.   & to a woman: et qui.

26.   of her lord: de son mary. Et moult aide a auoir compaignie de femme
a homme qui est trop froit et qui veul est.

touchith hit: porte.

XIX. CHELIDONIUS.

p. 31, l. 34.   folisshe & witles long tyme: fol. Elle garist les forcenes et les enlangoures.

p. 32, l. 1.   wel spoken of: bien parlant.

2.   wel wounden: Not in P.

5.   grete thing: grans choses se l'omme les a encommenchiez.

6.   of Princes: d'autres gens.

7.   hoote: l'uyl.

8.   þat þe sacrement is in: taint en safren.

XX. GAGATES.

p. 32, l. 12.   Lytie: licie.

13.   ademaunde: gemme.

17.   in water: en eau est destaint en huille.

18.   in skyn & in flesche: entre cuir et chair.

20.   wasshed in a litel water . . . his kynde: mise en de l'eau, afferme les
dens a homme qui luy croulent.

21.   When a man brenneth . . . resteth: Et quant homme qui a goute
chaiue sent l'oudeur d'elle tantost y chiet.

24. **serpentes:** serpent et moult est contraire au deable.
25. **hem that taken crowes:** ceulx qui les corneilles tendent.
26. **& voideth:** Not in P.
27. **& also hit it disproueth maynden-hoode:** Not in P.

XXI. MAGNES.

p. 32, l. 31. **Magnete:** De la magnet qui en latin est nomee magnez.
    in a place: entre une gent.

32. **Tragodice . . . of Iren:** Tragodite. En ynde auxy eu treuue l'en. Elle a couleur de fer et tire le fer a soy.

33. **Deldour þe enchauntour . . . founden & knowen:** Les enchanteurs layment mout.

p. 33, l. 5. **bedde:** chief. (The English probably miswritten for *hedde*.)

7. **spouse-breker:** le contraire.
    she shall falle dounn . . . his hande: elle la boutera hors du lit auxy comme se elle la boutast de sa main.

9. **a fauour:** l'oudeur.

13. **fle for drede . . . fall vppon hem:** s'en fuiront auxy comme se la maison deust ardre.

17. **in oyle:** Not in P.

19. **to brenning:** a arsure et a eschaufeure se l'en la met dessus le mal.

XXII. CERAUNIUS.

p. 33, l. 21. **Teramus:** Theraunius.
    thondre: foidre ne tempeste.

23. **ne in fire . . . amonges men:** ou elle sera. La nef ou elle sera ne sera perillee ne par estourbillon ne par foidre.

XXIII. HELIOTROPIUM.

p. 33, l. 28. **ful of water:** Not in P.

29. **smered:** rouge.

31. **profite many things:** profecier plusieurs choses aduenir.

33. **filthe:** tricherie.

35. **as he wolde:** ou il voudroit sans que ja nul le veist.

p. 34, l. 1. **cyope:** ethiope.
    cypte: cipre.

XXIV. HEPHAESTITIS.

p. 34, l. 4. **aspites:** aspetites.

6. **She doth awey the briddes . . . sowe:** Not in P.

8.   **hoole**: seur.

10.   **Ryghte**: senestre.

XXV. ASBESTOS.

p. 34, l. 12.   **Egiftys**: Egestes.

is a ston: est trouuee.

archade: cartage.

13.   **þe femel**: la femelle come le masle.

Article on Celonitis in P omitted in B

XXVI. SAGDA.

XXVII. MEDUS.

p. 34, l. 24.   **in þe south landes**: en la terre de tire.

26.   **puttith to his eyen**: et la frotte a vne aspre . . . et la met ez yeulx.

27.   **sight ayein**: elle luy rend. mez la . . . doibt estre verte.

28.   **mylke that ne hath hade but oon lombe**: let de brebis qui n'ait eu que vng aignel masle.

30.   **heele þe lymmes of hym**: guerist l'en du mal des rains.

31.   **Men shulde stewe . . . slee hym**: L'en en doibt garder la destrempe en vaissel d'argent et au soir donner a boire au pacient avecquez vin. Qui la destremperoit en eaue et en laueroit ses yeulx il aueugleroit. et qui la beroit il vomiroit son poumon et mourroit.

XXVIII. HEXACONTALITHOS.

Not in P.

XXIX. PRASIUS.

Not in P.   First Prose Lapidary LVI (Studer & Evans, *op. cit.*, p. 111).

p. 35, l. 15.   **grene**: verte e avient en or.

17.   **figured white**: ad treis figures blanches.

XXX. GALACTITES.

p. 35, l. 19.   **Caladista**: P. calastida.

20.   **in oyle**: en eaue.

22.   **þat is white lombe**: Not in P.

26.   **& anoynte the thee with-inne & oute**: et l'en esrousoit l'enfant.

28.   **þe olde auncestres**: et ne deuient lettiere se dient les anciens.

29.   **hit shal auaile . . . his witte**: elle vault moult pour remettre son sang a raison a qui l'a troubley.

XXXI. ORITIS.

36, l. 2.   **Corynthe:** Corites.

3.   **euel beestis . . . & oþre:** beste.

4.   **russet:** rosat.

8.   **more preised:** la plus prisie.

sharpe & on þe oþre . . . iren grounden: auxy comme se elle fust plaine de cloux et de l'autre part auxy comme fer esmoulu.

10.   **not retche . . . for-lore:** na garde d'engroessir. Et s'elle est grosse et elle la porte, elle pert l'enfant tout maintenant.

XXXII. HYAENIA.

Not in P. This paragraph is taken from the First Prose Lapidary XXXIII (Studer & Evans, *op. cit.*, p. 107).

XXXIII. LIPAREA.

Not in P. First Prose Lapidary XXXIV.

36, l. 21.   **All hunting:** tute selvagine.

XXXIV. ENHYGROS.

Not in P. First Prose Lapidary XXV gives the first two sentences, but the rest comes from another source.

XXXV. ANDRODAMAS.

Not in P. First Prose Lapidary XXXVII.

XXXVI. CRYSTALLUS.

37, l. 2.   **harde:** P. endurchie par plusiers ennees.

thise olde Auncestres: les anciens.

4.   **þe colours:** la froideur.

5.   **& so many contraries . . . greete coldenes:** que plusieurs contrees sont ou il a sy grant froidure que nulle sy grande est comme il ont.

8.   **the olde Auncestres:** Aucuns.

9.   **norisces:** a femme pour estre plus lettiere.

XXXVII. CORNEOLUS.

Not in P. First Prose Lapidary XVIII (Studer & Evans, *op. cit.*, p. 103).

37, l. 13.   **colour of coralle:** culur de laveure de char.

L

XXXVIII. ALABANDICA.

Not in P. First Prose Lapidary L (*op. cit.*, p. 110).

p. 37, l. 18.   **alabrace**: alabandine.

XXXIX. ADAMAS II.

p. 37, l. 21.   **Athemaunde**: P. aymant.

24.   **& so may a man ... swiche wise**: et aussy doibt l'en esprouuer se l'aymant est vray. Et ja soit ce que on ne la puisse depichier par nul engin de fer.

P. ends: Cy fenist le lapidaire qui fut compose pour l'amour de Phelippe de France. a qui dieu pardonne. Amen. (*In another hand*): Se il est aucune precieuse pierre qui ait perdu ses vertus. sy soit liee en vng blanc drap aueuc cristal. Puis soit mise en vgne boiste en vne huche l'espace de quarante jours sy reprendra ses vertus.

THE NORTH MIDLAND LAPIDARY OF KING PHILIP

MS. C

P=Lapidaire du Roi Philippe, Bib. Nat. MS. français 2008.

. 38, l. 20. **kyng:** P. bon roy.

21. **is:** fut.

thys buke ... I-begynne: ce liure qui est appele le liure des pierrez.

23. **clerkes:** bons clers.

gederers of precyuous stones: perrierez.

24. **ladys:** sages deuins.

meysterys ... vertus: l'auctorite.

26. **for loue:** par l'acord.

27. **& schewed us:** Not in P.

28. **of tho yt ye byble spekes of:** ce que la bible en dit.

29. **god hymself spake of:** ce que dieu mesmes en dit. ce que moyse en dit.

30. **ye whyche knew ... & ye synn:** et ce que l'empereour eracles en dit. Moult ont fait de grans merueillez et encore feissent se ce ne fust la mescreance des gens et la non foy aueucquez les pechies. Et en maint lieu ont vallu ou mieres herbes ne rachines ne pouuoient ne valloir ne aidier.

p. 39, l. 3. **beleues noght:** ne croit on le desdic.

Ye buke: La bible.

7. **pames:** paulmes.

& yai suld: et commanda que elles fussent.

8. **commaunded:** commanda a moyse quil prenist oniches naturielz et y feist entaillier les douze ligniez par art de peirerie. Et commanda.

10. **& yes two chens ... aparial:** ou lez oniches fussent fichiez.

19. **Birrus:** Beril.

20. **hymself named:** nomma a moyse le prophete.

23. **huge:** en maniere de.

xj stones ye whyche saynte John named: xij pierres ez xij fondemens de la chitey du celestiel regne. Les noms des xij pierres que saint Jehan nomma sy nomma.

27. **Iagunce:** Jagonce, la douziesme oniche. Vous auez ouy les noms des douze pierres que dieu nommà.

28. **ʒe haue hard named:** See above.

34. **ye significacions yt yai signefye appon ye nek of Aaron:** Not in P.

35. **of paradyse:** du vray regne.

I. SARDIUS.

p. 40, l. 1. **grenes**: grenaus.

Alemandres: alemandines.

3. **ye fynest thyng of yis warld**: la plus fine.

4. **gentil & red**: vermeille.

5. **dwell & in trowth**: manoir en jouuente et en loiautey.

6. **enchauntement ne stangyng of wormes**: atouchement de venin ne de vermine.

8. **perlyous places**: eue perilleuse.

11. **as ye buk says . . . hed to**: come les vrais tesmoignent.

The rest of the article on Sard (see MS. B) is missing in C.

II. TOPAZIUM.

Except for this one sentence (not in P) the article on Topaz is missing.

III. SMARAGDUS.

p. 40, l. 14. **al grennes**: toutez les verdeurs de verdeur.

Ye buk: Lez liurez.

18. **appering**: empirer.

19. **be-hold**: esgarder.

Neyrons: P has the incorrect reading Aaron.

22. **& sal do a man spek in gud tempour**: et fait a homme parolle raisonnable.

23. **a sekenes yt is cald ennentesce**: goute.

24. **& a-gayns lyghthinge**: Not in P.

27. **gladly he sal ber hym-self fayr**: Not in P.

32. **ye gret grennes . . . wyll ber ane emeraud**: the order of the sentences in P is transposed in C.

p. 41, l. 1. **Saynt Iohn telles us**: Les lyures nous dient.

8. **Arimples**: Arompiles (i.e. Arimaspi).

9. **in yer heddes and yt is**: Not in P.

10. **watter**: fleuue de paradis.

14. **gud**: Not in P.

15. **wer so fynly gretly grennhed**: oulrent [la foi] sy grand et sy treffine-ment.

17. **as saynt Iohn says**: Not in P.

18. **Ihesu crist**: Jhesu crist pour ensuivre sa doctrine.

19. **yam yt seches ye emeraud**: les arompiles qui armes vont querre les esmeraudes et qui se combatent es griffons sont les bons crestiens qui sont bien fermes contre les temptacions du deable.

IV. CARBUNCULUS.

41, l. 22. **is worth:** vaint.
Ye buk: les liurez.

23. **red:** net.

24. **gemme of gemmes:** gemme des gemmes. Elle enlumine les euures par nuit et par jour et moult esprent et enlumine l'er cler et toutes choses cleres.

27. **honour:** grace et se iouissent de sa venue.
Ye buk: les liures.

31. **of yt ston:** que dieu y a mise.

32. **ye eyn:** Not in P.

p. 42, l. 1. **yt ben cleped grinonfez:** qui grigneurs d'elle sont.

2. **Ye buk of Moyses:** la bible.
god bad ye Ruby suld be ye fyrst: que le rubi fut mis premier.

3. **xij stones:** xij pierres sur la poitrine aaron.

4. **& for to alyghtyn yam . . . thynke on Ihesu criste:** Nulle clartey ne se prent a sa jentil et joieuse couleur. Les liures nous dient qu'elle senefie Jhesucrist qui est vraie lumiere qui vint en ce monde pour enluminer le peuple qui estoit en tenebres et en vmbre de mort. Toux cheulx qui la clartey du noble ruby esgardent doyuent esgarder par digne contemplacion a la vraie lumiere Jhesucrist.

V. SAPPHIRUS.

p. 42, l. 20. **holy and:** Not in P.
In ye lond of leby in ye reuer of ye oryent: Il en y a de trois manieres qui sont trouuees en libie en la grauelle du fleuue d'orient.

21. **I fynd:** Not in P.

22. **tho yt bes mor . . . fote of ye watter:** celuy qui plus est de gentil couleur le plus ynde semblable au pur chiel en la parfondesse du fleuue est trouuey. Les obscurs sont trouuez plus hault.

23. **I fynd:** Cy en retreuue.

25. **& al:** mes toux.
vertus & al of god . . . of his grace: vertueulx de dieu et plains de grace.

27. **Yes iiij:** Ces trois.

28. **lymme3:** membres enviemment.
it helpes . . . to dolyuer hym: Ils destournent homme d'emprisonner et se il l'est ilz luy aident a deliurer.

31. **belefe:** creance en dieu.

32. **The buk:** les liures.
saphyrs ar moche worth: moult est bon saphir auoir pour acorder gens ensemble et pour depechier sorcheries et moult vault.

34. **if a man … of yt ston:** quant elles sont de luy cernees.

if a man wesch ye saphyr in water: qui trible safir.

p. 43, l. 1.   **vertu yt sett in ye sapher:** la vertu que dieu a ottroye au safir.

& ye saphir sal … mans teth: et oste la douleur du chief. Cy garist de Jaunice et chache la chacie des yeulx.

5.   **hym yt wald … brek wychecraft:** cheluy qui nettement le porte et fait auoir bon sens. Moult se deburoit deduyre nettement qui sy vertueuse pierre porte.

9.   **Ye trew buke … saphir:** le noble saphir.

11.   **gud holy men:** bon homme.

12.   **Ihesu criste:** Jhesucrist plus forment en enquiert du roiaume du chiel. Et auxy come notre veue nous fait sauoir la veue du chiel auxy le regard de Jhesucrist par grace nous fait sentir de la glorieuse joie du chiel.

15.   **yerfore he was sett:** Et en reelle segnefiance fut mise.

VI. JASPIS

p. 43, l. 20.   **in welles in diuers parttes of ye warld:** es forennes parties du monde.

22.   **when he is sleked … precle:** quant il a goutes noires mains en vault.

24.   **shape of ye old shape:** entailliez.

26.   **venum:** vermine.

29.   **lukes on:** esgarde contre le jour.

30.   **mak hym myghty & halsom:** il le garde de fantosme et fait homme puissant et sain.

32.   **ydell thoghttes:** contraire.

33.   **ye buk:** Les vrais liures.

gud: Not in P.

of grace & of grennes: de grant verdeur.

34.   **syght:** foy.

ye whiche takes hed: qui sont de simple entendement et croient fermement.

p. 44, l. 1.   **awnswer no nother … betokenes Iaspe:** ilx ne sauroient respondre por ce quilx sont simple gent cy sont compareyz au jaspe.

2.   **Moses:** La bible nous dit que jaspe fut la tierche pierre de la segonde tire qui fut mise sur la poitrine aaron et dit Moise.

3.   **for yis ston betokenes … dewyll:** car la foy de la segonde loy c'est delabenoiste Trinitey destruit la fantosme au deable.

8.   **gud man … remembre hym:** proudomme qui jaspe porte. La premiere est appellee foy la seconde esperance la tierce charitey.

VII. LYNCURIUM.

p. 44, l. 13.   **hydes it within ye grauell dep:** garde et la muche dedens sa gueule bien en parfond.

14. **The buk**: Les liures.

16. **ensens**: enchens et teilx y a qui sont de telle maniere dont la verdeur jaunoie.

17. **of ye colour of lettur**: de couleur de letre.

18. **Thefatus**: Theophatus.

20. **Iountes**: jaunice.

21. **euyl vyces**: de faire son contraire.
    Ligur is gud to be born: elle est bonne.

23. **is gladnes**: appare et esleesce.

24. **malsen**: de meneson et de membres senglans.
    The buk: Les liures.

27. **yt a man has**: qui la met.

28. **any sor**: es yeulx.

32. **and yer within . . . ye lygur**: et se muche en plus parfont dedens la grauelle.

34. **yis stone**: ceste beste.

34. **of yis stone**: de elle (i.e. beste).

45, l. 5. **yt is londes . . . holy predicacon**: qui terre gaignent gardent et aerent par saincte predicacion ce sont les bons prescheurs.

7. **apon Aaron**: sur la poitrine de aaron.

8. **of Ihesu criste**: de saincte eglise.

VIII. ACHATES.

45, l. 9. **in a reuer cleped Acate**: en la terre d'Inde en vng fleuue mesmes qui est appelley achate.

10. **Yer ben som . . . whyt crosse**: Il en est de blancez chaintes de noyres chaintures et de telles ou il n'a que vne chainture.

13. **as yt wer resonneȝ**: comme de rames et comme de fieulez comme d'arbres comme de testes.

14. **as Iaspeȝ**: vertes comme jaspes.

15. **named of mony**: nommee dyotrople (i.e. heliotropium).

17. **as of gold**: aux riues.
    so says ye scriptur . . . of wex: Le scripture nous dit que celle ou il a couleur d'or de mierre d'enchens ou de coural goutee est la milleur. Aucunes en y a de couleur d'or et telle y a qui est de couleur de chire.

21. **he gyfues gud spech & cler**: fait homme bien parlant.

22. **in redyng**: Not in P.

23. **yt is cleped Cylyne**: essuyee.

24. **for ye strength of ye ston**: Not in P.

26. **gretly**: verte.

28. **strake**: raim.

31.   hytere3 ... frute euer-lastyng: sains hommes qui par bonnes œurez font fruict pardurable.

yes two significacouns: par ceste segnefiance.

32.   secund: Not in P.

IX. AMETHYSTUS.

p. 46, l. 2.   blod. Ye bukes of Mercur: sanc martirie. les liures.

3.   namly agayns: quant.

5.   yt wyl comon: Et dient que cheluy qui la porte est bien venu.

be-for a kyng & a prinse: deuant roys et deuant princes.

8.   haue on hym-self mynd ... gracyouse: se il requiert dieu il lui sera gracieulx.

14.   gret courte3 and gret festes: haute court.

Salamon: la diuine page.

15.   manteyn ye clothyng ... marters: ramentenoir la vesteure de pourpre que Jhesucrist vestit deuant sa mort que lez juifz luy vestirent par eschar. Et doibt ramentenoir la seigneurie des angelx et la mort dez martirs.

X. CHRYSOLITHUS.

p. 46, l. 19.   castes to ye egh: gette flambe.

20.   Ye buke: Les liures.

21.   a-gayns naturell stones: Not in P.

He yt beres ... courte3: qui nettement la porte n'est pas ort de pechie ne de mauvaistie. Cy peult doncquez en haulte court entrer.

23.   & ye scriptur: et sy nous deuise le lapidaire que qui crisollite percheroit et il mettroit une saie d'asne par my il pourroit aller entre les deables et cachier les seurement sans doubter. Et sy nous dit le liure.

30.   Ye glose of ye Apokalips: Et dit moyse le prophette que dieu nomma crisolite la xᵉ pierre pour segnefier les x commandements de la loy. Saint Jehan dit en l'appochalipse que il vit crisolite vijᵉ pierre en fondement du vray regne. Ce segnefie lez vij dons du saint esprit. La glose de l'appocalipse.

31.   predicacouns of ye myrakels: predicacions que font les bons prescheurs des miracles.

32.   coueres: tourne.

p. 47, l. 1.   forbydes ye pepyll: font au peuple.

Saynte John ... ye law. See above.

XI. ONYX.

p. 47, l. 8.   of Tyr: Not in P.

10.   a name: noir.

11.   **rybbeʒ:** coustures.

12.   **roget:** rougettes.

14.   **courtes:** courageux.

     & he sal haue . . . of gudes: et ly fait auoir plantey de saliue.

18.   **if it be nedfull:** de ce don le mort est besoigneux.

19.   **Ye glos:** Les gloses moyse.

21.   **and also ouercomes ye holy men . . . in his synn:** quer aussy comme l'ongle est plus dur de la molle chair aussy la vollentey que les sains homes ont a Jhesucrist qui est la ferme pierre est plus dure que leur chair. et par bonne affection sourmontent les molestes de la chair mes ilz ne parviennent pas a la durte de la pierre au deable comme le pecheur fait qui s'endurchist et endort en sa pechie.

25.   **natturel yt has on hym red & white; whit:** Not in P.

27.   **yt is ye fellow to Ihesu criste:** qui vient de la compaignie Jhesucrist.

XII. BERYLLUS.

p. 47, l. 32.   **an Egle:** eue.

34.   **ryall:** ront.

     Ye buke: les liures.

p. 48, l. 3.   **seke een:** yeux mallades.

5.   **roting:** l'eschaufoison du foie.

6.   **Ye holy wryte:** les liures.

8.   **& he be cutt:** et il nest entailly, il brulle qui le tient.

10.   **Ihesu criste:** Jhesucrist. ou le diable ne peult trouuer ne sa fourme ne sa fantosme.

12.   **baptym:** baptesme de Ihesucrist.

14.   **ye place yer ye vpryssyng sal ben:** le viij^e aage de la resurrection.

     ye autorite: le lapidaire.

17.   **yt semles . . . fyr of charyte:** qui se joignent et parollent es sains homes qui enflambes sont de la chaleur de charitey et de ces sains hommes mesmez espranent.

21.   **& ye xj . . . paradys:** entre lesquellez en ya huit de celles mesmement que saint Jehan l'euangeliste vit en fondement de la celestiel cytey cest paradis.

22.   **of ye viij . . . autorite says:** apres vous diron des aultres quatre pierres que saint Jehan nomma, les vertus et les segnefiances ainxy que promis le vous auion au commenchement de ceste œuure.

XIII. BALAS.

p. 48, l. 25.   **town:** isle.

26.   **sees:** mers qui a nom toracle. en ceste isle qui est ainxy appellee naist ceste pierre.

31.   **of Iagonce**: des pierres.
      ye Iagunce is a ruby: Jagonce ruby.
33.   **Centeryn**: citrin.
p. 49, l. 2.   **Ye buk**: les liures.
      yt ye balyes: que qui porte ballaiz qu'il.
5.   **it thynkes his enmy loth**: tart luy est.
7.   **a corner**: iiij cornetz.
9.   **worme**: vermine ne tempeste.
11.   **agayn fayr weder**: contre beau temps et contre le laid.
12.   **iiij wyse clerkes**: les tressages clers et les tressages mestres.
      moues & spekes: parollent et sermonnent.
      Iuez: gens.
13.   **to ye gud clerk & to ye Iewes**: es clers et es lays.
16.   **land**: isle.

XIV. CHRYSOPRASUS.

p. 49, l. 17.   **Ye buk**: les liures.
18.   **gren**: verdellette et ressemble a jus de poreaulx.

XV. CHALCEDONIUS.

p. 49, l. 24.   **God almyghty**: Damedieu.
28.   **dolyuer hym**: luy garde dieu par la vertu de la pierre.
30.   **grace**: grand grace.
31.   **gaderys**: chelent.
      Ye glos of ye Apokalips: Les gloses de l'appocalipse.
32.   **withdrawes gret speche**: attrait la parolle.
33.   **withdrawes ye synfull men to gude warkes**: attraient a dieu les pecheurs par leurs sainctes parolles.

XVI. SARDONYX.

p. 50, l. 1.   **red colour with a blake lyst**: rougette rougeur noirace.
5.   **Ye buke**: les gloses.
8.   **synfull men**: pecheurs. Cy fenissent les pierres que dieu nomma a moyse le prophete et a Saint Jehan l'euangeliste et ensuit le nom de plusieurs aultres pierres bonnes et excellentes pour toute creature humayne et premier du dyamant.

XVII. ADAMAS.

p. 50, l. 10.   **Ye dyamaunde yt comes of ynd**: Euax qui fut roy d'arabe dit que les dyamans qui viennent de ynde.
14.   **for he kerues . . . al oyer stones**: Not in P.

20.   **dremynge**: griefs songes.

24.   **chydynge**: tenchon.

27.   **chydyng**: temptes.

        Al yes vertus . . . Dyamaund: Not in P.

28.   **Dyamaund is a man defyneȝ**: Dyamant vault mout a forceney et est deffense.

29.   **He yt beres hym**: qui nettement le porte.

32.   **Ye buke . . . ston wyll ber**: Les liures nous dient que il doibt estre porte a senestre partie. Qui le veult esprouuer de ses vertus sy le doibt auoir de loial achat ou de don et de proudomme doibt estre cely qui le porte et qui vertueuse pierre porte.

p. 51, l. 3. **De lapidibus preciosis . . . vertus yai have**: This prologue is ultimately derived from the prologue to Marbode's Lapidary,[1] which is reproduced with variations in several of the Anglo-Norman lapidaries: the First French Version and other Verse adaptations, and two of the Anglo-Norman Prose Lapidaries.[2] It also appears in the French *Lapidaire de Berne*,[3] and that beginning 'Al qui aiment pierres de pris.'[4]

5.   **Emperour after Augustus**: This phrase does not occur in any of the lapidaries mentioned above.

XVIII. ALECTORIUS.

p. 51, l. 16. **yt myche is to prays**: Not in P; Marbode 76: cujus non ultima laus est.

17.   **efterward**: P. touz jours juquez a vij ans.

18.   **a ben**: une petite feue.

        lyk to: clere comme.

19.   **Old men . . . wyll haue vyctory**: elle donne victoire a homme qui la porte.

20.   **& yt he sal noght . . . Mylons of his enmys**: Not in P., which has 'et se l'omme a grant soif et il la tienge en sa bouche elle luy estanchera la soif.' We do not know of any source for the instructions in C.

        Mylons: Marbode 84: Nam Milo Crotonias pugiles hoc praeside vicit.

28.   **many oyer knyghtes**: P. plusieurs roys.

29.   **be vertu of yis ston**: par son aide.

        & he staunches . . . mouth: See above.

30.   **conqueres a man . . . in his mouthe**: Elle ramaine les dechachiez et acquiert a homme bons amis et fait homme bien parlant et estre bien amey. Elle vault moult a femme qui d'enfant trauaille et qui

---

[1] *Liber Lapidum, auctore Marbodo Episcopo Redonensi,* ed. Bourassé, in Migne, *Patrologia Latina,* vol. clxxi, 1854.

[2] See Studer & Evans, *op. cit.,* pp. 28, 71, 97, 139.

[3] Pannier, *op. cit.,* p. 109.

[4] *Ibid.,* p. 238.

veult estre aymee de son mary. Et moult aide a auoir compaignie de femme a homme qui est trop froit et qui veul est. Quant l'en la porte en sa bouche a donc a telles vertus.

XIX. CHELIDONIUS.

The account of this stone differs little in its meaning from that given in P, but does not appear to be directly derived from it. The version given in P is this: 'Celidoine est une pierre que l'en treuue en ventre de l'arondelle. Elle n'est mie belle non pour tant elle vault mieux et est plus proufitable que telle est plus belle. Il en est de deux manieres et de deux couleurs. L'une est noire et l'autre rouge. La rouge est bonne contre passion qui prent a homme par lunesons dont il chiet et dont il est fol. Elle garist les forcenes et les enlangoures. Cheluy qui la porte fait bien parlant et bien amey. L'en la doibt porter en ung linge drap pendue au senestre costey. La noyre se l'en la porte en telle maniere elle aide a faire grans choses se l'omme les a encommenchiez. Et aide encontre menesches de rois et d'autres gens. L'eaue ou elle est mise vault mout a l'uyl malade. Ceste pierre mesmes liee en ung drap taint en safren oste la fiebvre. Et trait mauvaises humeurs qui en corps naissent par maintes manieres.'

(Subsequent articles in P omitted in C.)

XX. MAGNES.

This account of Magnet differs in several details from that given in P; it is nearer to that in the Second Anglo-Norman Prose Lapidary (Studer & Evans, p. 128).

XXI. CORALIUM.

This account is in relation with that given in the First Anglo-Norman Prose Lapidary (Studer & Evans, p. 103).

p. 53, l. 13. **He gyffes in cerins gud forton**: ? *cerins* = wax, an allusion to its magical use as an inscribed gem (Damigeron x, Evans: *Magical Jewels*, p. 198).

XXII. CORNEOLUS.

XXIII. AETITES.

These two are also in relation with the First Anglo-Norman Prose Lapidary (*loc. cit.*).

XXIV. SELENITIS.

This account, which is in relation with Marbode XXVI, is fuller than that given in any of the Anglo-Norman Prose Lapidaries.

p. 54, l. 8. **& for to syk**: Marbode 397: Languentes etiam phitisicosque juvare putatur.

XXV. CERAUNIUS.

The account of this stone and those of the eight which follow (XXV-XXXIII) are fuller than those given in P or the Anglo-Norman Prose Lapidaries. They are ultimately derived from those of Marbode's Lapidary, probably by way of a Latin Prose Version.

XXVI. HELIOTROPIUM.

XXVII. HEPHAESTITIS.

5, l. 8.   **more precyous yan a ston yt is cleped Aram:** Marbode 459: pretiosior aero Corintho.

XXVIII. HAEMATITIS.

XXIX. GALACTITIS.

XXX. PANTHEROS.

XXXI. OPALUS.

XXXII. TECOLITHUS.

XXXIII. CHRYSELECTRUM.

XXXIV. CAPUDUASCUM.

We have not been able to identify this stone.

THE ASHMOLE LAPIDARY (MS. D)

I. OPALUS.

Based on Marbode XLIX.

p. 58, l. 11. **wrappyd yn a loryll leue**: Not in Marbode.

14. **Constantume hath þe same vertu**: We have not identified this stone, unless it be the Heliotrope or Bloodstone. (Marbode XXIX, l. 446.)

II. CHELONITIS.

Marbode XXXIX is considerably fuller.

III. TOPAZIUM.

Marbode XIII (besides much omitted here) states: 'Ferventes etiam compescere dicitur undas.'

IV. MEDUS.

This property is not attributed to Medus in Marbode. But cf. Hieracitis (XXX, 451):

> 'Quem prius abluto si quis gustaverit ore
> Dicere mox poterit quid de se cogitet alter.'

V. ALECTORIUS.

VI. CHELIDONIUS.

These two differ from Marbode III. We have not identified their source.

RICHARDOUNE'S VERSES (MS. E)

L. 16. ALABANSTRE: This stone is rarely mentioned in lapidaries, but it occurs in the Anglo-Norman Alphabetical Lapidary VI (Studer & Evans, p. 208).

ALLECTORY: A.L. IV.

AURIPIGMENT: Not in A.L.

L. 17. ASTERON: A.L. IX.

ADAMAS: A.L. I.

L. 18. AMATISTES: XI in MS. M of the Alphabetical Lapidary.

ASTERITES: A.L. VIII.

L. 30. BERILLE: A.L. XIV.

CELIDONE: A.L. XXII.

CHARBUNCLE: Not in A.L.

L. 31. CIPRES: ? Caprates (Capnitis) A.L. XIX.

CERSOPAS: A.L., MS. M, IX.

L. 32. CORAL: A.L. XVIII.

L. 33. SAPHIR: A.L. LXXVI.

L. 36. SMARAGDUS: A.L., MS. M, III.

L. 38. SERENICE: A.L. LXXV.

L. 39. SARDIUS: A.L., MS. M, V.

THE PETERBOROUGH LAPIDARY
(MS. F)

Isidore = *Isidori Hispalensis episcopi Etymologiarum sive Originum libri xx.* Ed. W. M. Lindsay, Oxford [1911].

Marbode = *Marbodi liber lapidum seu de gemmis,* Ed. Beckmann, Göttingen, 1799.

B.A.   = Bartholomaeus [Anglicus]. De proprietatibus rerum. (English translation by John of Trevisa.) London, 1535.

B.A.Lat. = *ibid.* (Latin text.) Strasbourg, 1491.

A.M.   = Albertus Magnus. *Liber Mineralium.* Oppenheim, 1518.

T.C.   = Thomas Cantimpratensis. *De lapidibus preciosis,* in Evans: *Magical Jewels,* Appendix D.

P.M.   = Le Lapidaire en francoys composé par Messire Jehan de Mandeville, chevalier. Lyons [*c.* 1520].

P.   = The Lapidary of King Philip. (French.) See notes to MS. B.

B.   = The London Lapidary of King Philip. (See p. 17.)

V.A.   = The First Anglo-Norman Verse Adaptation of the First French Version. (Studer & Evans, p. 70.)

A.L.   = The Alphabetical Lapidary, *ibid.,* p. 204.

P.L. 1 = The First Anglo-Norman Prose Lapidary, *ibid.,* p. 97.

P.L. 2 = The Second Anglo-Norman Prose Lapidary, *ibid.,* p. 118.

p. 63, l. 29. **Evax·** Marbode: Evax rex Arabum.

tyberi: Marbode (and most of the lapidaries derived therefrom) gives *Nero;* but Damigeron, following some inferior MSS. of Pliny, gives *Tiberius* (Evans: *Magical Jewels,* p. 195; Studer & Evans, *op. cit.,* p. 297). The Third Anglo-Norman Prose Lapidary also gives *Tybere l'empereur (ibid.,* p. 297).

33.   **also he seythe . . . her vertues:** P.L. 2, Prologue B.

p. 64, l. 5. **takeþ stones for a precius tresowur:** P.L. 2: fit un des greignurs tresors des peres, et lur duna greingnur vertu et greygnur pusaunce ke as herbes. Mut dyyssum estre luy reddevables des vertus k'il mist pur mus et tuz nus abaundona.

7.   **by the A. b. C.:** The A.L. was the first lapidary to attempt an alphabetical arrangement; it was followed by T.C., A.M. and B.A.

10.   **Auycene:** Albertus Magnus quotes him as an authority (e.g. *De rebus metallicis,* I, 4), & so does Bartholomaeus Anglicus, *passim.*

Ysodor: Isidore; his *Etymologiae* XVI is used as a source by Bartholomew.

11.   **Plynius:** There is no evidence to shew that the writer consulted Pliny (Nat. Hist., Bk. XXXVII) direct, though he is one of the sources for Isidore's treatise and is quoted by Bartholomew.

bartholomus: Bartholomaeus Anglicus, *De proprietatibus rerum*.

Richard rufus: Richard Rufus, a man of Cornish origin, who entered the Franciscan order about 1270. We have not been able to trace a lapidary by him, but Bartholomaeus Anglicus quotes him as a source.

I. APSYCTOS.

This is a double version, presumably derived from two sources, of Isidore XVI, xi, 2: 'Apsyctos nigra et ponderosa, distincta venis rubentibus. Haec excalefacta igni septem diebus calorem tenet.'

II. ACHATES.

A free version, with some rearrangement, of P.L. 2, X, followed by excerpts from B. VIII and from the V.A., with additions from B.A. XVI, xi.

p. 64, l. 22. **and some seyþ . . . secyl**: Not in P.L. 2. Isidore XVI, xi, 1: 'Achates reperta primum in Sicilia.'

25. **And such þer bene þat haue branchis . . . old men**: B. VIII.

27. **þat kynde haþe put to**: P.L. 2: ke nature i ad mises.

34. **gret poynctes**: P.L. 2: gutes.

p. 65, l. 5. **he holpeþ . . . þe wordell**: P.L. 2: le rent pleysaunt a Deu e al munde.

6. **and he seiþe that ther is . . . of gret valewe**: V.A., V, 173-84.

12. **Also bartholomewe . . . achatem**: Not in B.A. Lat. XVI, xi.

17. **Also we fynd . . . brist of Arone**: B. VIII.

23. **Also þer is . . . if it be nye, as Dias seiþe**: B.A., XVI, xi.

III. ANDRODAMAS I.

Isidore XVI, xv, 8: Androdamas argenti nitorem habet et pene adamans, quadrata semper tesseris. Magi putant nomen impositum ab eo quod animorum impetus vel iracundias domare et refrenare dicatur, si credimus.

IV. AETITES I.

This closely follows P.L. 2, XXIII.

p. 66, l. 14. **helpe & doþe awaye þe fowle euell**: le tent en saunte, et tout a homme gute chaive.

15. **of yuel**: ke li voile mal fere.

16. **& he schall mow . . . done awaye**: e se cil est copables vers luy, ja n'en purra manger taunt cum la pere seit ilokes; et taunt tost cum ele serra ouste, il mangera.

18. **round**: ruisse.

& it is good . . . egle nest: Not in P.L. 2. Isidore XVI, iv, 22: 'Aetites lapides reperiuntur in nidis aquilarum.' T.C., p. 229: 'facit victorem.'

M

V. ASSIUS LAPÏS.
An abbreviation of A.L., V.

VI. ADAMAS I.
p. 66, l. 31. **Adamant is a ston . . . ouercome in bataile:** B. XXXIX or a parallel text.

p. 67, l. 10. **Also a man . . . lefte honde:** P.L. 1, I: Ele deit estre close en or u en argent: si la deit l'um porter el senestre bras.

11. **& while þu berist . . . many mo:** Not in B.

VII. ACHATES II.
Abbreviated from A.L. II & III.

p. 67, l. 29. **Tiberius:** Apparently a reminiscence of the preface, or borrowed from A.L. VIII, 164.

VIII. ALECTORIUS.
For the most part abbreviated from A.L. IV.

p. 68, l. 3. **Also dias seiþ . . . fayr speker:** Not in A.L. IV.

6. **And yf he . . . be hole:** Not in A.L. IV.

8. **croantis:** A.L. IV, 108: Crotoniates.

9. **Some men . . . master:** Translated, with a few omissions, from P.L. 2, XVI.

15. **Also this stone . . . mete:** Not in P.L. 2.

16. **makeþ a woman to be delyuerd [of] child:** Cf. V.A. VIII, l. 234.

18. **Also many kynges . . . mowthe:** Based on a text having some connection with P.L. 1, XII.

IX. ALABASTRON.
Abbreviated from A.L. VI.

p. 68, l. 25. **eysel:** aisil.

26. **all maner sore in þe fote or in þe knee:** Del mal del piz senes guarra li d'un' altre enferte, si l'ad.

X. ALABANDICA I.
p. 68, l. 29. **Ysodre seyþ:** This reference is not justified by fact; it is drawn from Marbode XXI; B.A. XVI.

XI. ALABANDICA II.
Closely based on B. XXXVIII.

XII. HEPHAESTITIS I.
Almost identical with B. XXIV.

XIII. ASBESTOS.

9, l. 8. **Albestus ... lieʒt of him:** P.L. 2, XXVII.

12. **Ðat stone ... de gemmis:** Isidore XVI, iv, 4: 'De quo lapide mechanicum aliquid ars humana molita est, quod gentiles capti sacrilegio, mirarentur. Denique in templo quodam fuisse Veneris fanum, ibique candelabrum et in eo lucernam sub divo sic ardentem ut eam nulla tempestas nullus imber extingueret.' See also B.A. XVI.

XIV. ARISTINCTUS.

This is based on A.L. VII, Amistunte, a stone not found in other lapidaries but connected with the pyrites described in Isidore XVI, iv, 5.

l. 21. **it schal hele þe brennyng:** Not in A.L. or Isidore.

XV. AMETHYSTUS.

The first part closely follows B. IX.

l. 24. **or red rose in color:** Not in B. Isidore XVI, ix, 1: 'quasi rosae nitor.'

27. **boþe to body ... gode voys:** Not in B.

o, l. 1. **Also whoso bereþ ... trenche:** Not in B. Probably based on some text in relation with the Latin Lapidary in Bodleian Digby MS. 13, fol. 17v: 'Ametistus valet ad febres, et calidum malum et ad fantasma et ad pavorem dormiendo, et ad mala sompnia et ad inimicos, et tradicionem et ad diaboli nocumenta, et insidias, et ad equi infuturam et ad sortelure et ad trencescuns et ad farchi et strangelum' (Evans, *Magical Jewels*, Appendix C).

10. **Also isodre ... and writhe:** Isidore XVI, ix, 1: 'Amethystus purpureus est permixto violacio colore; et quasi rosae nitor, et leniter quasdam flammulas fundens. Alterum eius genus descendit ad iacinthos. Causum hominis eius afferunt quia sit quiddam in purpura illius non ex toto igneum, sed vini colorem habens. Est autem sculpturis facilis: genera eius quinque.' B.A. XVI, x, is very near our text.

21. **Of þis color ... courtes:** B. IX.

XVI. ANANCITIS.

Abbreviated from A.L. XIII.

l. 23. **lik to oþer ... by a:** de mole manere.

XVII. ANDRODAMAS II.

Marbode XLVIII.

XVIII. HEXACONTALITHOS I.

Closely follows B XXVIII.

XIX. ANTHRACITIS.

Abbreviated from A.L. X.

XX. AKAMANDA.

We have not identified this stone.

XXI. ASTERITES.

A confused version of A.L. VIII, with additions from B.A.

p. 71, l. 16. **Asterides & . . . togeder:** Not in A.L.

18. **no s[o]ne so trobel:** Ja n'ert soleil ensi troble.

19. **All þe vertues . . . þis:** Asez ad en li de vertuz.

20. **Asterides is wyȝth . . . lyȝt:** Isidore XVI, x 3, probably by way of B.A. XVI, xviii.

XXII. ASTRION.

p. 71, l. 23. **Astrion is . . . colour:** A.L. IX.

25. **Also þer is . . . as it is befor seyd:** i.e. XIX, Anthracitis.

27. **Ðis stone . . . de cristall:** Isidore XVI, xiii 7; B.A. XVII, xvi.

XXIII. ARGYRITES.

Isidore XVI, xv, 8; B.A. XVI, xv.

XXIV. ANDRODAMAS III.

Isidore XVI, xv, 8.

XXV. BERYLLUS.

Chiefly based on B. XII.

p. 72, l. 8. **& it is myche worþe:** Not in B.

9. **& also myche lyk cristall . . . some lese:** Not in B. Cf. P.L. 3 XI.

18. **The boke of dyuynyte:** Some of B omitted here.

25. **also þei þat taken . . . vertu of þe stone:** A.L. XIV, 229-32.

28. **Ised seyþ:** Isidore XVI, vii, 6: 'Chrysoberyllus dictus eo quod pallida eius viriditas in aurem colorem resplendeat. Et hunc India mittit.' B.A. XVI, xxi.

l. 28. **x maners kynd:** Isidore XVI, vii 5, mentions nine kinds, but Bartholomaeus gives ten.

30. **Dias seyþe . . . matremonye:** B.A. XVI, xxi.

p. 73, l. 2. **And he holdeþ . . . splene:** We have not found a source for this.

3. **Berellus is a stone . . . be hole:** Abbreviated from A.L. XV.

10. **Also it is seyd . . . ynde:** Based on P.L. 2, XXII (Beryllus & Iris).

XXVI. HERILLICUS.

A confused abbreviation of A.L. XVI.

p. 73, l. 13. **he is like water:** Not in A.L.

XXVII. BELI OCULUS.

Based on A.L. XVII.

p. 73, l. 17. **like to berell:** Not in A.L.

20. **no egge tole:** nule rien.

XXVIII. SAGDA.

B. XXVI.

XXIX. ASBESTOS II.

p. 73, l. 27. **Betumques:** ? a confusion with bitumen. Cf. Sloane Lapidary XXII. The rest of the account comes from P.L. 2, XXVII.

XXX. BALAS.

For the most part taken from B. XIII, but following the version of P more closely than does that text.

XXXI. CHRYSOLITHUS.

B. X, with small variations and omissions.

p. 74, l. 18. **& of schrewdnes:** Not in B.

19. **cowrtes:** Not in B.

26. **ethiopie:** B. cyop.

29. **the bible seyþ . . . aarone:** Not in B, but in P.

30. **Also Ised seyþe . . . a lyȝe:** Isidore XVI, xv, 3: 'Chryselectrus similis auro, sed in colorem electri vergens, matutino tantum aspectu iucundus, rapacissimus ignium, et, si iuxta fuerit, celerrime ardescens.' B.A. XVI, xxix.

XXXII. CHALCEDONIUS.

B. XV, or rather another version of P with additions.

p. 75, l. 1. **Of white pale coler:** Not in B. P.L. 2, IX: 'blauns de truble blanchur.' P.M.: 'blanche ou bleue de couleur pale.'

2. **and it is lik to cristal:** Not in B. A.L. 656: 'de cristal manere ad colur.'

10. **and if a man . . . clen:** Not in B. Marbode VI, 132.

12. **Also Isod seyþe . . . þe mone:** B.A. XVI, xxviii.

14. **and he is not founde but of iij colours:** Marbode 133; B.A. XVI, xxviii.

15. **all kynde þer-of . . . Ised seyþe:** B.A. XVI, xxviii.

XXXIII. CHRYSOPRASUS I.

B. XIV, with additions.

p. 75, l. 25.   **This crisopas . . . gold:** P.L. 2, XXIV.

          And som men . . . gold: Isidore XVI, vii 7.

27.   **and he þat bereþ . . . women:** We have not found the source of this.

28.   **And some men . . . nyȝt:** B.A. XVI, xxvii.

XXXIV. CYLINDRUS.

Cf. Isidore XX, xiv, 9: 'Cylindrus lapis est teretis in modum columnae qui a volubilitate nomen accepit.'

XXXV. CORANUS.

Cf. Isidore XVI, iv, 31: 'Coranus albus est duriorque Pario.'

XXXVI. CINAEDIA I.

Cf. Digby 13, fol. 19ᵛ: 'Chimedia lapis qui solet inveniri in capite piscis et valet ad tempestates et ad omnia mala.'

XXXVII. CAMAEUS.

Cf. A.L. XXIX.

XXXVIII. CALLAICA.

Cf. Isidore XVI, vii, 10: 'Callaica colore viridi, sed pallens et nimis crassa.'

XXXIX. CRYSTALLUS.

p. 76, l. 5.   **Cristallus is . . . sone beem:** P.L. 1, XXX: 'Iceste piere conceit bien le fu el rai del soleil.' B. XXXVI: 'This stone conceaueth wele the fire atte the sonne beem.'

6.   **Also make pouder . . . vertu of cristall:** P.L. 2: 'Fetes de cristal pudre deliee, si la dunet a beivere a nurices, si multipliera lur leit. Tuchez le cristal a la pere dunt vos dutet k'ele eit sa vertu perdue par peche et cil seit confes ki la porte.'

12.   **Som men seyn . . . cristall:** P.L. 1, XXX: Cristal est glace enduree par mulz aunz.

13.   **Also he kepeth a man chast:** P.L. 2, XXXI: Il refreide home.

14.   **& maketh . . . araby:** We have not found the source of this.

15.   **and old anceters . . . coldnes:** B. XXXVI.

18.   **Also Ised . . . may suffre:** Isidore XVI, xiii, 1; B.A., XVI, xxi.

27.   **Also dias . . . colica passio:** Abbreviated from B.A., XVI, xxi.

31.   **Hunc et tritum . . . latte:** Marbode XLI.

32.   **partibus:** Marbode: matribus.

XL. CHELIDONIUS I.
B. XIX, though not verbally identical.

p. 77, l. 12. And if it be . . . sor yene: Not in B.

XLI. CORALIUM.
P.L. 2, XX, with a few variations from P.L. 1, XVII, and additions from A.L., XXVI.

p. 77, l. 14. in þe red see: en la mer.
15. þat is gren: P.L. 1: si est verte la u ele creist.
17. louely: P.L. 2: sauvable.
18. ȝerastos, Methodorus & þe gode autour phytonas: Not in P.L. 2. P.L. 1 has 'Zoraster et Metrodorus.'
23. & stancheþ blod . . . redische: This appears to be taken from an account of cornelian, e.g. P.L. 1, XVIII. The virtue of staunching blood is, however, also given to Coral in A.L., XXVI.
25. Also whoso bereth . . . cramp: Not in any of the other sources.
29. Also ysodre seyþe . . . whirlewyndes: Isidore XVI, viii, 1; B.A., XVI, xxiii.

p. 78, l. 6. If a man . . . powder of þis ston: A.L., XXVI.

XLII. CINAEDIA II.
A.L., XXVIII.
& a wiȝt: Not in A.L.

XLIII. AMBRA.
Abbreviated from A.L., XXVII.

p. 78, l. 20. & þat fyssh men clepen ȝele: A.L. balaine.
22. neuer be gret scleper: ja nuls hom ne enveillera.

XLIV. COLLYRIA.
Abbreviated from A.L. XXXI.

XLV. CAPNITES.
A confused abbreviation from A.L. XIX.

p. 78, l. 32. & if a man . . . be hole:

> Ke, si hom est ydropicus—
> Iço est un mal que hom ad,
> Cum il plus beit et plus sei ad—
> E al senestre braz la lit,
> Senes garra.

XLVI. ORITIS I.

B. XXXI.

p. 79, l. 4.   **haue with corenthe:** haue with hym þe corinthe þat tourneth in-to grenehede.

7.   **a woman þat . . . here wombe:** A woman þat berith hit uppon her, she thar not retche with whom she goo with childe, for yef she bere hit uppon her she shal be for-lore.

XLVII. CRAPODINUS I.

We have not found a source for this. It is mentioned in the index to one manuscript of P.L. 2, but is not described; a fuller text may have been the source of this description. (See Studer & Evans, *op. cit.*, p. 323.) The version of P.L. 2 in the Sloane Lapidary gives an account of the stone (XXXII) that is in relation with this article.

XLVIII. CHALCOPHANOS.

Apparently paraphrased from P.L. 2, XXXIV.

XLIX. GALACTITES I.

B. XXX, with the last sentence omitted.

L. CORNEOLUS.

A version of P.L. 1, XVIII, parallel with B. XXXVII.

p. 80, l. 10.   **blake flessh:** B: coralle; P.L. 1: laveure de char.

LI. CHELONITIS.

p. 80, l. 13.   **Calonite it is . . . feyr:** P.L. 2, XXVIII; 'de vaire' and 'sor le limaz' omitted.

23.   **And some seyne . . . persce:** A confusion with Silenitis.

LII. TECOLITHUS.

A free version of P.L. 1, XLII.

LIII. CERAUNIUS I.

p. 80, l. 28.   **Ceramus is a stone . . . araby:** We have not found a source for this statement.

and who þat bereþ . . . .: A.L. 432-438.

31.   **And some seyn . . . founde in:** Perhaps a misunderstanding of Isidore XVI, xiii, 5: 'Dicta autem ceraunia quoniam alibi non inveniatur quam in loco fulmine ictu proximo: Graece enim fulmen κεραυνὸς dicitur.'

33.   **and þis ston . . . to a man:** A.L. 441-444.

1, l. 4. **And some seyne . . . heuen:** Isidore XVI, xiii, 5: Cerauniorum duo genera sunt. Unum, quod Germania mittit, crystallini simile, splendet tamen caeruleo, et si sub divo positum fuerit, fulgorem rapit siderum. Ceraunium alterum Hispania in Lusitanis litoribus gignit, cui color e pyropo rubenti, et qualitas ut ignis. Haec adversus vim fulgurum opitulari fertur, si credimus.

LIV. CATARICUS.

We have not identified this stone.

LV. CERAUNIUS II.

We have not discovered a source for this stone.

LVI. CHELIDONIUS II.

An abbreviation of A.L., XXII.

LVII. CARBUNCULUS I.

A translation of Isidore XVI, xiv, 1, probably by way of B.A., XVI, xxvi.

2, l. 14. **starida sirus:** Sandasirus.

20. **þe name of smellynge of lanternys:** Lychni . . . a lucernarum flagrantia.

21. **is clepid remissus carbuncels:** Quidam eam remissiorem carbunculum esse dixerunt.

23. **of red sylk:** quasi cocci rubore. B.A.: of redde sylke.

28. **Amonge þe maner . . . þe to:** B.A., XVI, xxvi.

LVIII. CHRYSOPRASUS II.

B.A., XVI, xxvii.

83, l. 6. **lapidary of bartholomewe:** B.A.: in Lapidario.

LIX. ADAMAS II.

B. XVII, with some additions.

3, l. 11. **resonable . . . cristall:** Not in B.

13. **No man may amend . . . noþþyng:** Not in B.

15. **bore in gold:** P.L. 1, I: ele deit estre close en or.
Þe lapidare . . . clenly ber it: A version of P.L. 2, 1.

27. **A diamaund is myche worthe . . . clennesse:** B. XVII.

36. **Also þis . . . gote buke:** P.L. 1, 1.

LX. DIADOCHOS I.

An abbreviation of A.L., XXXII.

LXI. DIONYSIAS I.
Based on A.L. XXXIV.

LXII. ANDRODAMAS IV.
A shortened version of B. XXXV.

LXIII. LIPAREA I.
A version of B. XXXIII.

LXIV. DIADOCHOS II.
An abbreviation of A.L. XXXII. Cf. LX above.

LXV. DAPHNEION.
Based on A.L. XXXIII.

p. 85. l. 1. like berell . . . palyssh: Not in A.L.

LXVI. DIONYSIAS II.
A.L. XXXIV.

LXVII. DRACONTITES.
A version of A.L. XXXV.

LXVIII. SMARAGDUS I.
B. III, with some small omissions and variations in order and phrasing, in some cases nearer P.

p. 85, l. 18. tyre: B: syre.

LXIX. HELIOTROPIUM.
p. 86, l. 10. Elitropia is a stone . . . as it were blody: B. XXIII.
19. Þys ston is gode . . . seynctes: P.L. 2, XIX.
30. Somme men seyne . . . many mo vertues: A.L. XXXVII.
p. 87, l. 4. Also Ised seyþe . . . befor seyd: Isidore XVI, vii, 12; B.A. XVI, xii, a little shortened.
14. nam si . . . gerentem: Marbode 439-448.

LXX. AETITES II.
p. 87, l. 17. Etite, de egle . . . riche & kynde: V.A. XI.
22. Also som men seyn . . . without payne: we have not found a source for this.
31. Also dias seyþ . . . as Ised seyþe: an abbreviation of Marbode XXV, taken from B.A. XVI, xxix.

LXXI. HEPHAESTITIS II.

A rather confused version of P.L. 1, XXV, or possibly of its ultimate source, Marbode XXXI.

p. 88, l. 7. **Also he makeþ . . . sikernes:** Not in P.L. 1. Marbode 470: 'Et tutum servat dubia sub sorte gerentem.'

LXXII. HEXACONTALITHOS II.

A version of Marbode XXXVIII, with one line ('Dum tot gemmarum fert gemmula sola colores') omitted.

LXXIII. ASBESTOS III.

A version of P; cf. B. XXV.

LXXIV. ENHYGROS.

p. 88, l. 19. **Enydros . . . reynbowe:** A version of P; cf. B. XXXIV.

24. **Enydros, þat ston . . . abowte þe ston:** B.A. XVI, xlii.

LXXV. EXEBENUS.

A version of A.L. XXXIX.

LXXVI. HEPHAESTITIS III.

An abbreviation, with some omissions, of A.L. XXXVIII.

LXXVII. HEXACONTALITHOS III.

A confused version of Marbode XXXVIII.

p. 89, l. 14. **fowrty:** sexaginta.

LXXVIII. PHRYGIUS LAPIS.

A.L. XLI.

LXXIX. MEMNONIUS

A.L. XLI.

p. 89, l. 21. **fimionis:** A.L. fumonius.

LXXX. MEDUS I.

An abbreviation of A.L. XLIV, which also has Fedus.

LXXXI. PHOENICITIS.

A.L. XLII.

p. 90, l. 6. **Fensites:** A.L. Fenicites.

LXXXII. PYRITES I.

Marbode LVI, with additions.

p. 90, l. 12.   **arthetica:** Not in Marbode.

LXXXIII. GAGATES.

p. 90, l. 15.   **Gagatis . . . grace of gode:** A version of P; cf. B. XX.

33.   **Also yf a man . . . meve:** We have not found a source for this.

p. 91, l. 8.   **Also the fumusite . . . child:** Abbreviated from A.L. XLVII.

12.   **Ised seyþ . . . þing:** Isidore XVI iv, 3; B.A. XVI, xlix.

LXXXIV. HIERACITIS I.

Based on Marbode XXX, which gives the name Gerachiten.

p. 91, l. 21.   **genardus:** We have not found this reading elsewhere; P.L. 2 has *genatide.*

LXXXV. GAGATROMAEUS.

P.L. 2, XXVI.

LXXXVI. GALACTITES II.

p. 91, l. 26.   **Galactida . . . childberynge:** Abbreviated from P.L. 2, XXXII.

30.   **Ðis ston . . . a-ferryd:** Abbreviated from A.L. XLVI.

p. 92, l. 4.   **And if þe child:** berbiz.

10.   **This galaxide . . . :** Isidore XVI, iv, 20; B.A. XVI, xlix.

12.   **This stone iclowsid . . . wyt:** Marbode XLII 584: Sed turbat mentem si clausus in ore liquescat; B.A. XVI, xlix.

13.   **and yef hit be bore . . . yessy byrth:** Marbode XLII; B.A., XVI, l.

LXXXVII. PRASIUS I.

p. 92, l. 19.   **Garsius . . . figuryd whit:** B. XXIX.

22.   **Isid saiþe . . . fyre:** Not in Isidore or Marbode or B.A.

LXXXVIII. CHALAZIAS.

A.L. XLVIII.

LXXXIX. HYAENIA.

p. 92, l. 30.   **Hieme . . . strengeþ:** B. XXXII.

34.   **Also yf . . . askeþ him:** A.L. XLIX.

XC. MACEDONIUS.

A.L. LXIV.

XCI. HERINACEUS LAPIS.
A.L. L.

p. 93, l. 7.   **hawke:** ostur.

XCII. HISPANNEN.
We have not identified this stone. It may possibly be in relation with the Specularis of P.M., 'croissant en terre d'espagne,' or with the Iscustos of A.M. II, ii, VIII.

XCIII. JASPIS.

p. 93, l. 11.   **Đer bene . . . Jaspe:** B VI.
xvij: B: nyne. A.L. LI has 'seze.'

17.   **Đes jaspes ben founde . . . vertues:** Not in B.

18.   **Iaspes is good . . . clene life:** A version of P rather nearer to it than B.

28.   **Đe bok . . . Jaspe:** Abbreviated from P.

31.   **Đe grenest . . . olyvetre:** A.L. LI.

p. 94, l. 3.   **& his vertu is gret . . . gold:** P.L. 2 IV or V.A. XVI.

4.   **also þer is . . . fantome:** We have not found a source for this.

7.   **Also Ised seyþ . . . smaragdus:** Not in Isidore but in B.A. XVI, liii.

XCIV. HYACINTHUS I.

p. 94, l. 13.   **Iagunce . . . many maners:** All the accounts we have studied describe three kinds.
Đe gret iacunce . . . in golde: P.L. 2, XII.

22.   **Some men seyne . . . pleyn:** A.L. LII.

24.   **and þey comforteþ . . . heuynes:** V.A. XX, 368, or Marbode XIV, 222.

25.   **& he is . . . wher he wolle:** Marbode XIV.

27.   **And some seyn . . . þe mor:** V.A. XX, 378.

28.   **Also he is gode for medesyns:** V.A. XX, 366.

29.   **Al þes iagunce . . . harme:** Abbreviated from A.L. LII.

p. 95, l. 2.   **Đe ryȝt colour . . . knowe:** Marbode XIV, 225.

XCV. CHELIDONIUS III.

p. 95, l. 7.   **iij maners:** All the accounts we have studied give only two kinds.

8.   **celidonus . . . albertus:** Not in A.M. II, ii, II.

11.   **Đat ston . . . profitable:** We have not found a source for this.

XCVI. HYACINTHUS II.

p. 95, l. 18.   **Iacincte . . . gold:** Slightly abbreviated from V.A. XX.

25.   **Đis iacincet . . . colour:** A.L. LIII.

28.   **Ised seyþ . . . as Ised seyþe:** Isidore XVI ix, 3; B.A. XVI, liv.

XCVII. PANTHEROS I.
An abbreviation of P.L. 2 XXXIII.

XCVIII. HYACINTHIZON.
A.L. LIV.

XCIX. IREN.
Apparently the same stone as Pseudo-Mandeville's *quirin:* 'Quirin est pierre trouvee au nid de la huppe. Elle est dessellement de secretz, car se on la met sur la poictrine d'une personne dormant elle luy fera dire tous ses secretz et le esmeut les fievres et amoneste fantasies et amaine de nuyt moult de perilz a celluy qui la porte et se le dormant reclame les diables tantost il lappera a luy.' Cf. B.A. XVI, lxxxiii.

C. INDRES.
Probably the same stone as P.M. *Euandros:* 'Euandros est pierre trouuee au voulteur qui la porte sur luy. Il est fortune de venatione d'oiseaux par faucons et autres oyseaux de proye," and B.A. *Quandros,* XVI, lxxxiv.

CI. IPACON.
Apparently *Liparea.* Cf. LXIII, CVI.

CII. HIERACITIS II.

CIII. MELAS.
A confused abbreviation of A.L. LXIII.

CIV. LYNCURIUM I.
p. 97, l. 30.   **Ligurie is . . . brest of arone:** A slightly confused version of P parallel with B VII.

p. 98, l. 24.   **Also it helpeth . . . man hole:** A.L. LVIII or P.L. 2 XXXV.

27.   **Also Ised seyþ . . . to himself:** Marbode XXIV; B.A. XVI.

CV. GLOSSOPETRA.
Lange was included in a version of P.L. 2 now lost (Studer & Evans, p. 6), which may possibly have been the original of this. Their actual use against poison is well attested. (See Evans, *Magical Jewels,* pp. 114-16.) The account of *Lange de Serpent* given in P.M. is not the source of this, but Sloane Lapidary XXXIII is in close relation with it.

CVI. LIPAREA II.
p. 99, l. 4.   **Laparie . . . huntyng:** P.L. 1, XXXIV.

7.   **Ised seyþe . . . laparia:** Marbode XLV, by way of B.A. XVI, lxi.

CVII. MAGNES.

,l. 13.   **Magnes is ... wife:** A version of P.L. 1, XVI.

20.   **in þe verses:** ? An allusion to Marbode XIX or to V.A. II.

21.   **Also yf ... brenyng:** P.L. 1, XVI.

26.   **Also whoso bereþ ... fal downe:** A.L. LXII.

33.   **Ðis stone is fonden ... rynge azure:** We have not found a source for this.

34.   **Also Isodre seyþ ... more better it is:** Isidore XVI, iv, 1; B.A. XVI, lxxx.

ɔo, l. 1.   **in Iudea among the trogodytes:** Not in Isidore, but in B.A.

13.   **Also diascorides ... heere:** B.A. XVI, lxxx.

26.   **fallyng of heere:** B.A.: faylynge of the harte.

CVIII. SAPPHIRUS.

ɔ, l. 27.   **Saphyr is ... ierusalem:** A version of P parallel with B V, with some abbreviation.

ɪ, l. 20.   **Also þe saphir ... palesye:** V.A. XXIII, 443-9.

23.   **Ðe best saphirs ... & godly:** B.A. XVI, lxxxvi, with a few omissions.

CIX. SMARAGDUS II.

ɔ3, l. 3.   **Smaraddus ... all þes seyþ Ised:** Isidore XVI, vii, 1, by way of B.A. XVI, lxxxviii.

28.   **And þis ston ... in bokes:** Marbode VII, by way of B.A. XVI, lxxxviii.

ɔ4, l. 9.   **Also whoso bereþ ... disestes:** Cf. T.C., p. 233: 'Si caste portetur fugat morbum caducum. ... Visum refocillat. Purgat oculos. ... Reddit hominem gratum in verbis. Auget opes. Auxiliatur eis qui scrutantur abdita. Avertit tempestates. Compescit lasciuos motus.'

CX. SARDIUS.

ɔ4, l. 15.   **Sardis ... enchanthementes & fro wyche crafte:** B.A. XVI, lxxix.

31.   **Also þe lapidarie ... kyngdome:** A parallel version to B I.

CXI. SARDONYX.

ɔ5, l. 14.   **Ðis stone ... chast:** Isidore XVI, viii, 4; B.A. XVI, lxxxx.

22.   **Ðe lapidarie ... graciose:** B. XVI.

CXII. PANTHEROS II.

V.A. XV.

ɔ5, l. 34.   **and also ... venym:** Not in V.A.

CXIII. TOPAZIUM.

p. 105, l. 35. **Topaces is . . . strenþe:** B. İI with a few omissions.

p. 106, l. 17. **Also þis topacie . . . set in gold:** An abbreviation from P.L. 2, VI.

21. **Also Ised . . . grete of precios stones:** Isidore XVI, vii, 9; B.A. XVI, xcvi.

p. 107, l. 1. **Plinius wrote . . . lengþe:** T.C., p. 234: 'Plinius dicit tante magnitudinis fuisse repertum topazium ut pholoneus philadelphus statuam exinde faceret quatuor cubitorum.' B.A. XVI, xcvi.

3. **Also in þe glose . . . holowȝ myrror:** B.A. XVI, xcvi.

CXIV. MARGARITA.

B.A. XVI, lxii, a little abbreviated.

CXV. MEDUS II.

p. 108, l. 19. **Medus is . . . Diascorides seyþe:** B.A. XVI, lxxvii.

19. **And som sey . . . & lyfe:** B XXVI.

22. **Ðe vertu . . . of þe stomak:** B.A. XVI, lxxvii.

30. **Ðis ston is blak . . . þey noyene:** Marbode XXXVI.

32. **Som men seyn . . . hole:** A parallel version with B XXVI.

CXVI. ONICHINUS.

B.A. XVI, lxxii.

CXVII. OBSIANUS.

A.L. LXVIII.

CXVIII. ONYX I.

An abbreviation of A.L. LXIX.

CXIX. ENYSUS.

We have not identified this stone.

CXX. MELICHROS.

Isidore XVI, vii, 15; he does not describe the sweetness of the stone, which is added in B.A. XVI, lxiii.

CXXI. MYRRHITES.

Isidore XVI, vii, 14; B.A., XVI, lxvi.

CXXII. CARBUNCULUS II.

p. 110, l. 6.   **Rubie is a red ... of þe xij stones:** a version parallel with B. IV.

21.   **Also þis stone ... fyne gold:** P.L. 2 XV.

24.   **Also he makeþ ... emperour:** V.A. XXX.

CXXIII. LYCHNITES.

An abbreviation of A.L. LVI.

CXXIV. LYNCURIUM II.

A.L. LVII.

CXXV. LYNCURIUM III.

A.L. LVIII.

CXXVI. LITHARGYRUM.

A.L. LIX. The virtue of healing burns and wounds is omitted.

CXXVII. LUPI DENS (ODONTELICIUS).

A.L. LX.

CXXVIII. LAPIS LAZULI.

A.L. LXI.

CXXIX. MOLOCHITIS.

l. 111, l. 16.   **Molochit.ʒ ... yuelys & happes:** B.A. XVI, lxviii.

21.   **& whoso ... greue him:** We have not found a source for this; possibly it is a mistranslation of T.C., p. 232: 'protigit a sinistris casibus.'

CXXX. MARMOR.

A version of Isidore XVI, v, with some abbreviations and omissions, by way of B.A. XVI, lxix.

l. 111, l. 34.   **purpurices:** Isidore: Porphyrites.

p. 112, l. 1.   **alabastrum:** alabastrites.

3.   **coralicitum:** coralliticus.

6.   **telaicum:** Thebaicus.

12.   **charistium:** Caristeum.

13.   **of aspeton:** ab aspectu.

15.   **virundicum:** Numidicum.

20.   **In þe veynes ... small stones:** Not in Isidore but in B.A.

N

CXXXI. CRAPODINUS II.

B.A. XVI, lxxi.

CXXXII. HIERACITIS III.

An abbreviation of A.L. LXV.

CXXXIII. VITRUM.

p. 113, l. 16.   Ysed seyþe . . . as Ised seyþe: A description not of *vitrum* but of *nitrum* from Isidore XVI, ii, 7; B.A. XVI, lxx (Nitrum).

27.   And Platea seith . . . thyrd degre: B.A. XVI, lxx.

p. 114, l. 7.   and it laxeth . . . as Ised seyþe: Isidore XVI ii 6, & B.A.

8   Also glas as auycen . . . is hidde: B.A. XVI, c.

13.   Al maner licor . . . & to contrefet, as Ised seyþ: Isidore XVI, xvi, 1-5; B.A. XVI, c.

p. 115, l. 7.   But ther was . . . gold, as Ised seyþ: Isidore XVI, xvi 6; B.A. XVI, c.

CXXXIV. ORITIS II.

P.L. 2, XXX.

CXXXV. ONYX II.

p. 115, l. 32.   Onicle is a stone . . . trauel: A version, with some additions, of P.L. 2, vii.

37.   he doeþ away . . . loke þerone: Not in P.L. 2; apparently a misunderstanding of V.A. XXIV.

p. 116, l. 7.   Ðe bible seyþe: Cf. B XI.

CXXXVI. OPALUS.

B.A. XVI, lxxiii.

CXXXVII. ORITIS III.

An abbreviation from A.L. LXVI.

CXXXVIII. PYRITES II.

Marbode LVI.

CXXXIX. PAEANITIS I.

A version of Marbode XXXIV.

CXL. PRASIUS II.

p. 117, l. 10.   Prassio is . . . aȝens wraþ: A repetition of the foregoing article.

15.   Ðis stone . . . mych gold: Marbode XL.

CXLI. PANTHEROS III.

117, l. 20.   **Panteros ... yuel ney3bores:** A.L. LXXI.

22.   **Ðis ston ... dyuers bokes:** Marbode LI, by way of B.A. XVI, lxxx.

CXLII. DROSOLITHUS.

A.L. LXXIV.

CXLIII. PARIUS.

117, l. 30.   **Parius ... oynementes:** Isidore XVI v. 8.

33.   **passeþ lances & ...:** Isidore has 'lances craterasque non excedat.'

. 118, l. 1.   **Also Ised ... chastite:** Not in Isidore.

CXLIV. PAEANITIS II.

B.A. XVI, lxxix.

CXLV. PERIOT.

Probably the peridot (chrysolite) and apparently the same as the *peridon* of the Second Lapidary of Engraved Gems XLIV (Studer & Evans, p. 294, and see note).

THE SLOANE LAPIDARY (MS. G)

ALL but two of the sections of the Sloane Lapidary are rather freely translated from the Second Anglo-Norman Prose Lapidary (Studer & Evans, *op. cit.*, p. 119). This is referred to as P.L. 2. Only differences of sense are here noted; mere verbal modifications are omitted.

I. ADAMAS.

P.L. 2, I.

p. 119, l. 22.	**Inde:** Inde la maiur.
24.	**appon light shininge:** semblable de culur a oylle.
27.	**Iron or steele:** le fer et l'ascer et les peres.
	taking no harme: Elle est aydable as enchaunteurs.
29.	**from wroth & chiding:** de gref sunge et de fantasme et de tuz venims. Ele tout ires et tençuns.
30.	**It sendeth & helpeth men to great worth:** et sane les forcenez.
p. 120, l. 1.	**it comforte . . . of ritches:** de sens, de pris, de valurs, de richessce; s'il ne crest, il n'apetice mie.
3.	**a cart or a wale:** de chival, ne de mur, ne de charette.
4.	**it doth away:** Sa greinur vertu est dunee plus ke achatee, si de leal aver n'est achatee. Ele tout. . . .
6.	**so yt he feare god:** kar il eime Dampnedeu. E garde semence de homme dedenz le ventre de sa femme, ke li emfes net oue tuz ses membres.

II. SAPPHIRUS.

P.L. 2 II.

p. 120, l. 13.	**bythen:** Libie apres les Sirtes.
	kings, queenes, & great lords: a reys et a cuntes.
14.	**& other coulors:** parmi utre.
15.	**The best Saphir commeth from the red sea:** Une autre manere de saphirs sunt ki venent de la parfunde Turkie.
16.	**but some of more vertue then other:** Une autre manere de saphirs sunt ke l'em trove pres de un puy, ke l'em tent a meyns vaylaunt; mes tuit sunt del tresor Dampnedeu. Tutes ces treys maneres de saphirs sunt, et mut unt greygnure vertu li un ke li autre.
20.	**ye bliss & ye lykning of hert:** al celestien regne.
21.	**keeps man from poyson:** veint boydies et envies.
23.	**irons:** quatre aungles.
29.	**hedach & sore eyes:** la suyllure des oilz et la dolur del chef, et est bon al mal de la launge.

30. **It geueth good cownsell . . . be chast:** Et Dampnedeu conseile volunters celuy ky le porte et le rend seur. Et cil ki le vout espruver de tutes ses vertuz, deit estre chastes.

32. **and bore on the right side of a man:** Not in P.L. 2.

III. SMARAGDUS.

P.L. 2 III.

1, l. 3. **Sirie:** Sithie.

Those of Siria are ye best: Celes de Sithie sunt li meȝdres et de plus gentil culur et poet l'em ver sa culur de utre en utre. Et une gent ki unt a nun Arsmiples [= Arimaspi] les vont querre tut arme et les tuelent as griffuns par bataẏlle. Mult est bone pleine esmeraude a esgarder et a mirer. Nerun en ot un mirur u il esgardoit et savoit par la force de ceste pere ço ke il voleit enquerre.

5. **of word and fortune wyse:** Ele fet a homme parole acceptable. Quant l'em la porte a sun col pendue, [elle le garde de malvaise fevre qui aucun homme atrait a mort].

9. **and without euell:** et penser de sa alme.

10. **& bore on ye right side of a man:** Not in P.L. 2.

IV. MAGNES.

P.L. 2, XVIII.

?, l. 13. **It droweth . . . many one:** Deu luy dona de ses vertuz ausi cum il fit as autres. Ele tret fer a soy.

17. **stir as a beast:** tresaudra.

18. **and cry . . . vngodly sight:** kar avis li serra k'ele sente trop grant pour par la vertu de la pere. E auncienement soleient li enchaunteurs mettre charbuns ardaunz en quatre parties de la meysun u il venoyent, et par desus les charbuns rere de ceste pere; et les genz ky veoyent ices charbuns ardaunz guerpisoyent l'oustel ausi cum enfantasme.

?, l. 20. **Marchants know . . . of wether:** Et par ceste pere et par sa grant vertu cunuysent li marinens les venz.

22. **It is good for ye dropsy:** e mult vault a homme ky en use oue leit a garir de ydropesie.

23. **& woman:** Not in P.L. 2.

24. **in great power & strengh:** le rend ben emparle, et le met en grant poer.

And whoso putteth . . . for euer: Ky la ret sur char arse moylee de vin, si garist de l'arsun.

V. JASPIS.

P.L. 2, IV.

p. 121, l. 30. **of more greatness:** de plus grasse verdur.

32. **it hath red dropps:** et ele ad gutes vermeyles, ele est de haute vertu.

p. 122, l. 1. **co[n]tertaking & fiting:** de cuntraire ky la porte, et fet homme estre ame et puissant.

VI. CHRYSOLITHUS.

P.L. 2, V.

p. 122, l. 8. **He that bereth it . . . of all people:** Ele est bone a porter sur soy encuntre naturels pours. Homme ky la porte n'est pas suspechiez de mauvestie; et mut eyde homme a entrer la u li plet, et mut est gracius et amiables.

11. **thred of silk:** soye de asne.

13. **erly & late:** Not in P.L. 2.

VII. TOPAZIUM.

P.L. 2, VI.

p. 122, l. 17. **fleme of the East Contry:** d'Arabe del flum de orient.

18. **gold in ye sea:** or esmere.

20. **that cometh sodenly to a man:** Not in P.L. 2.

23. **It kepes a man from sinne:** Ele refreidit homme.

VIII. ONYX.

P.L. 2, VII.

p. 122, l. 28. **be drawing:** sunt concriees.

29. **stronge:** corajus et irrus.

31. **his frend . . . of one coulor:** a sun ami mort de nuit, il luy parole en dormaunt; et al matin luy sovent de ço dunt li mort est busuingnus. E a celuy ky le porte rend salu et acrest beaute. Onicles est neyrs. [E ad sa vertu en or e dehors.]

IX. HYACINTHUS.

P.L. 2, XII.

p. 123, l. 2. **It is red of kind . . . & couler:** Jagunces sunt de deus maneres. Jagunce grenax est vermeil de gentil colur.

7. **without dred . . . or water:** saunz pour; e si n'ad l'em garde de entusche; et de ses hostes serra l'em honurre, ne ja de ço ke l'em requert resunablement ne serra l'em escundit.

11. **for it is his kind:** Not in P.L. 2.

X. BALAS.

123, l. 14. **Counche:** Corinthe.

16. **the fore halffe:** as quatre parties.

18. **contention & strifes ... to hurt him:** medlees, e ki la mustre a sun enemi meyntenaunt li est tard k'il soyt acorde a luy. Si l'em la porte entre ses enemis, returner s'en purra saus ses membres.

XI. AMETHYSTUS.

P.L. 2, XIV.

123, l. 22. **& it is shining:** et retret a sanc martyre.

24. **And if any wild beast ... missgouernd:** seurement poet chacer ki l'ad, kar ele est de si grant vertu ke les bestes sauvages venent a celuy ky la porte. Mult est de grant confort cuntre iveresce.

XII. CARBUNCULUS.

P.L. 2, XV.

123, l. 29. **mervealous:** vermeyles.

p. 124, l. 5. **It driueth away all taches & ill conditions:** Et li desconfortez ky esgarde ceste pere, se conforte par la vertu ke Deus i ad mise et ublye sun contraire. Ele pest les oils e conforte le cors.

XIII. ALECTORIUS.

P.L. 2 XVI.

p. 124. l. 8. **It waxeth ... of strengh:** Alectorie est une pere ke crest en le ventre d'un chapun puys ke il est treys aunz chapun, et crest tutjurs taunt k'yl ad set aunz.

12. **It maketh enemies friends:** Plusurs unt vencu lur batailles par le alectorie. Ele remanauntist les deschoys e conquert a homme bons amys.

15. **they ought not ... that bereth it:** mes cil ky la porte.est luxurius.

XIV. CHELIDONIUS.

P.L. 2, XVII.

p. 124, l. 20. **But it is of much bewty in him-selfe:** nepurquant ele veint les beles de bunte.

21. **blew:** neyre.

22. **It is good:** La russe est bone.

25. **It helpeth:** La neyre kaunt l'em la porte en sa aumenere, ele le ayde.

26. **& ladies:** Not in P.L. 2.

31. **greene:** jaune.

XV. HELIOTROPIUM.
P.L. 2, XIX.

p. 125, l. 4.   **and then it is bright & of his owen coulor:** et ke ele mue sa culur e k'ele fet en petit tens l'ewe boyllir u ele est enz.

6.   **purchaser & happi to gett goods:** de grant purchaz.

7.   **& of great verchue and power:** et le fet estre de bone renumee.

8.   **venome wormes:** boydie.

9.   **greas:** l'erbe.

     Solsicle: Solsequium.

11.   **without any dred:** la u il voudra, kar la gent averunt ayliurs k'a li lur esgard.

12.   **Ethiope and Africk:** d'Ethiope ed de Cypre et de Aufrike.

XVI. CORALIUM.
P.L. 2, XX.

p. 125, l. 17.   **And as old maistres:** Ele est mut sauvable a celi ki la porte; kar si cum dient nostre auncien mestre.

19.   **tempest of wether:** tempeste en les lius u ele est.

20.   **or garden . . . from tempest:** u en sun gardin e pres de semence ke l'em vut garder e sauver de foudre, de tempeste e de tuit mals orez.

21.   **faintness:** fanteme.

22.   **what contry yt he taketh:** a cil ki la porte.

XVII. BERYLLUS.
P.L. 2, XXII.

p. 125, l. 25.   **hires:** eris (i.e. Iris).

27.   **a faire coulor . . . ye sonne:** feu encontre le soleil. Li eris costus furme l'arc del cel cuntre le soleil de la clarte de soy en une paroye.

28.   **and woman:** et femme et fet celuy honurer ky le porte.

XVIII. AETITES.
P.L. 2, XXIII.

p. 126, l. 1.   **Achilles:** Echites (i.e. Aetites).

2.   **This stone the egles:** Echites est numbre entre les bones peres. L'egle.

5.   **nor no member of it:** Not in P.L. 2.

6.   **kepeth them in age . . . & estate:** Ele defend homme ki·la porte de veillece et le rent amesure.

9.   **it causeth a good witt:** et vencur le fet. Et fet enfaunt garder sun senz et le tent en saunte.

11.   **thy tooth that thow dost eate with . . . toward him:** l'esquele u il devera manger; e se cil est copables vers luy.

p. 126, l. 14.   **rownd:** ruisse.

15.   **great sea:** la grant mer ke envirune tut le mund. Saunz le ne cove l'aigle.

XIX. CHRYSOPRASUS.
P.L. 2, XXIV.

126, l. 18.   **frute of a Appull:** jus de purret.

20.   **of all yt know ... woman:** de tute genz et conjois.

XX. SELENITIS.
P.L. 2, XXV.

126, l. 21.   **Silentes:** Silenites.

22.   **of a greene coulour:** vert de crasse verdur.

25.   **dissese:** tisikes.

26.   **it helpeth men yt be outlawed, wrongfully indited:** Not in P.L. 2.

XXI. GAGATROMAEUS.
P.L. 2, XXVI.

126, l. 28.   **Gaganturels:** Gagatroene.

29.   **a man:** prince.

31.   **of all ye host:** Not in P.L. 2.

    For sir hercules ... battaile: Not in P.L. 2.

XXII. ASBESTOS.
P.L. 2, XXVII.

127, l. 1.   **Berumques:** Abestos. Perhaps a confusion with Bitumen; cf. Peterborough Lapidary XXVIII.

XXIII. CHELONITIS.
P.L. 2, XXVIII.

127, l. 6.   **Colonite:** Celonite.

7.   **Fore:** fee.

8.   **black:** vaire. (Some MSS. of P.L. 2 have *neyre*.)

    in the land of ynde: sor le limaz en la tere d'inde.

9.   **in his mouth:** en sa buche, suz sa langue.

13.   **& it will never fade:** Ceste ne crient nul fu.

XXIV. HIERACITIS.
P.L. 2, XXIX.

127, l. 14.   **Genatides:** Genatides (i.e. Hieracitis).

15.   **It is of such a kind:** Genatides est neyres; si est de tel nature.

22.   **& frett him to the death in soth:** Not in P.L. 2.

XXV. ORITIS.
P.L. 2, XXX.

p. 127, l. 24.   **Orides:** Orites.

28.   **desert & every-whear ells:** hermitages entre bestes sauvages: ja a luy ne tucherunt.

29.   **He is greene:** Un autre en i ad ki est verz.

34.   **for euer:** Not in P.L. 2.

XXVI. CRYSTALLUS.
P.L. 2, XXXI.

p. 128, l. 5.   **through ye sine . . . ye Christall stone:** si la recuvera, s'ele l'eit perdue par peche et cil seit confes ki la porte.

XXVII. GALACTITES.
P.L. 2, XXXII.

p. 128, l. 9.   **Alectorie:** Galactide.

12.   **& after meate . . . thred of woll:** et apres bains et pendre a sun col oue fil de leyne de owaille enprins.

16.   **among shepe:** al toit de berbiz.

17.   **they shall beare ye smaller woll:** les berbiz en sunt meuz leiteres.

18.   **It hath a coulor:** Si dient li auncien ke ki ceste pere porte, k'ele li dune tuz bens; ky la frote a la keuz, si ad culur.

XXVIII. PANTHEROS.
P.L. 2, XXXIII.

p. 128, l. 21.   **Iaspes:** Jaspe paunter.

22.   **of many coulors:** de mutes colurs et de meinte maneres en i ad.

23.   **him behoueth to know:** il la deit esgarder.

25.   **hardy in fight:** hardi. Ele rent a homme grant plente de tuz bens.

XXIX. CHALCEDONIUS.
P.L. 2, IX.

p. 128, l. 29.   **If a man haue it vppon him in his plea:** Il rent celuy ky le porte ben parlaunt et plein de grant eloquence; et si il ad a pleider.

31.   **to ouercome them:** sa cause veintre. Et ky porte l'onicle et le sardoine et le caucedoine ensemble, mut rendent homme ben enteche.

XXX. ACHATES.
P.L. 2, X.

p. 129, l. 1.   **Acate:** Achate.

4.   **white lynes:** blaunches veines; s'en i ad de celes u il i ad blaunche croiz, et de celes u il i ad plusurs figures come de rois, come de bestes, come de foiles, come de roges taches, come de veines aurines ke nature i ad mises.

comforteth men of age ... be invisible: confortent veil homme et sa
veue.

10. It warnes a man ... god & man: Ele garnist home, si luy acrest sa
force, et le fet ben enparler et agreiable et de bone culur, et luy dune
bon conseil, et le fet estre ben cru, et le rent pleysaunt a Deu e al
munde.

XXXI. CORNEOLUS.
P.L. 2, XI.

9, l. 14. lump: laveure.
16. man or woman: les dames.
17. and to recover ... all men: E sur tutes peres deivent les dames ceste
amer, kar mult les conforte de lur maladies et les rent pleysauntes et
amees.

XXXII. CRAPODINUS.
An account probably derived from a lost manuscript of P.L. 2 that
included the toadstone. (See Studer & Evans, p. 323.) An account
in many respects parallel is given in the Peterborough Lapidary
(XLVI).

XXXIII. LANGUES DE SERPENT (Glossopetra).
Lange was included in a version of P.L. 2, now lost (Studer & Evans,
p. 6), which was probably the source of this. It is in close relation
with Peterborough Lapidary CIV.

XXXIV. GAGATES.
P.L. 2, XXI.

0, l. 11. Lince: Geet.
12. from Lince: de une cuntree ki ad nun Lice.
14. black and a playne stone: neyre e legere et pleine.
17. for fleame ... if he smelleth to it: fleume entre quir et char, cum
homme enfundu. La pudre de geet afferme les denz ki lochent.
Desuz estreint a femme sa nature. Quant l'em l'art, si hom ky ad gute
chaive sent l'odur, taunt tost chet.
25. against euell spirits and euells: as diables. Mult vaut a ceus ky unt
les ventres turnez et a ceus ky les corneilles tendent. Ele defent
sorceries et charmes.
28. iij draughts: treis jurs.

XXXV. SARDONYX.
P.L. 2, VIII.

0, l. 33. bore on him ... complexion and chast: et rent homme simple et
chaste et vercundeus. [E estaunche ben saunc; e gard la femme de
peril a sun enfaunter.]

LIST OF STONES IN THEIR MS. ORDER

MS. A

I.	Hyacinthus	geaspis	XII. Carbunculus	carbunculus
II.	Sapphirus	saphyrus	XIII. Adamas	adamans
III.	Chalcedonius	calcedonius	XIV. Magnes	magneten
IV.	Smaragdus	smaragdus	XV. Asbestos	abestus
V.	Sardonyx	sardonix	XVI. Pyrites	piriten
VI.	Onyx	onichinus	XVII. Selenitis	seleten
VII.	Sardius	sardius	XVIII. Alectorius	alexandrius
VIII.	Beryllus	berillus	XIX. Syrtitis	stircites
IX.	Chrysoprasus	crisoprassus	XX. Catochitis	cathotices
X.	[Omitted]		XXI.	mocritum
XI.	Topazium	topazius	XXII. Achates	[acates]

MS. B

I.	Sardius	Sardes	XXI. Magnes	magnete
II.	Topazium	Topace	XXII. Ceraunius	teramus
III.	Smaragdus	emeraude	XXIII. Helitropium	elyotrope
IV.	Carbunculus	rubie	XXIV. Hephaestitis	aspites
V.	Sapphirus	safire	XXV. Asbestos	egiftes
VI.	Jaspis	iaspes	XXVI. Sagda	hadda
VII.	Lyncurium	ligure	XXVII. Medus [thos	medus
VIII.	Achates	accate	XXVIII. Hexacontali-	aracontalides
IX.	Amethystus	amatist	XXIX. Prasius	carcius
X.	Chrysolithus	crisolide	XXX. Galactites	caladista
XI.	Onyx	onicles	XXXI. Oritis	corynthe
XII.	Beryllus	berille	XXXII. Hyaenia	hyeme
XIII.	Balas	baleys	XXXIII. Liparea	dipparea
XIV.	Chrysoprasus	crisophas	XXXIV. Enhygros	onidros
XV.	Chalcedonius	calcedoyne	XXXV. Androdamas	diadama
XVI.	Sardonyx	sardoynes	XXXVI. Crystallus	cristalle
XVII.	Adamas (i)	diamaunde	XXXVII. Corneolus	corneal
XVIII.	Alectorius	allectories	XXXVIII. Alabandica	alemandine
XIX.	Chelidonius	celidoyne	XXXIX. Adamas (ii)	athemaunde
XX.	Gagates	ieet		

MS. C

I.	Sardius	sardes	V. Sapphirus	saphir
II.	Topazium	thopace	VI. Jaspis	iaspes
III.	Smaragdus	emeraud	VII. Lyncurium	lygur
IV.	Carbunculus	ruby	VIII. Achates	acate

MS. C—*continued*

ix.	Amethystus	amatistes	xxii.	Corneolus	cornellyn
x.	Chrysolithus	crisolyte	xxiii.	Aetites	etrayte
xi.	Onyx	onycles	xxiv.	Selenitis	selinete
xii.	Beryllus	berels	xxv.	Ceraunius	saramoyd
xiii.	Balas	baleys	xxvi.	Heliotropium	elyscrope
xiv.	Chrysoprasus	crisopas	xxvii.	Hephaestitis	espetyt
xv.	Chalcedonius	calcydoyn	xxviii.	Haematitis	ematite
xvi.	Sardonyx	sardoyn	xxix.	Galactites	galatite
xvii.	Adamas	dyamaunde	xxx.	Pantheros	panter
xviii.	Alectorius	electoyr	xxxi.	Opalus	apthalme
xix.	Chelidonius	celidoyn	xxxii.	Tecolithus	thegolite
xx.	Magnes	magnete	xxxiii.	Chryselectrum	griseletre
xxi.	Coralium	corayle	xxxiv.		capuduascum

MS. D

i.	Opalüs	ovtalmus	iv.	Medus	medas
ii.	Chelonitis	silonicus	v.	Alectorius	alectorius
iii.	Topazium	thophasion	vi.	Chelidonius	celidonius

MS. E

i.	Alabastron	alabanstre	x.	Carbunculus	charbuncle
ii.	Alectorius	allectory	xi.?	Capnitis	cipres
iii.	Auripigmen-	auripigment	xii.	Chrysoprasus	cersopas
iv.	Astrion [tum	astrion	xiii.	Coralium	coral
v.	Adamas	adamas	xiv.	Sapphirus	saphir
vi.	Amethystus	amatistes	xv.	Smaragdus	smaragdus
vii.	Asterites	asterites	xvi.	Selenitis	serenice
viii.	Beryllus	berille	xvii.	Sardius	sardius
ix.	Chelidonius	celidone			

MS. F

i.	Apsyctos	absittus	xiv.		aristinctus
ii.	Achates (i)	achate	xv.	Amethystus	amatitus
iii.	Androdamas (i)	andromada	xvi.	Anancitis	anittida
iv.	Aetites (i)	achites	xvii.	Androdamas (ii)	adredamian
v.	Assius lapis	adamas *or* asius	xviii.	Hexacontalithos	aracontalides
vi.	Adamas (i)	adamant	xix.	Anthracitis [(i)	aricheces
vii.	Achates (ii)	agatten	xx.		akamanda
viii.	Alectorius	alistores	xxi.	Asterites	asterides
ix.	Alabastron	alabastre	xxii.	Astrion	astrion
x.	Alabandica (i)	alabanda	xxiii.	Argyrites	argirites
xi.	Alabandica (ii)	alemandyne	xxiv.	Androdamas	andromia
xii.	Hephaestitis(i)	alpitistes	xxv.	Beryllus [(iii)	berel
xiii.	Asbestos (i)	albestus	xxvi.	Herillicus	bericia

MS. F—continued

xxvii.	Beli oculus	belloculyis	
xxviii.	Sagda	badda	
xxix.	Asbestos (ii)	betumques	
xxx.	Balas	baleis	
xxxi.	Chrysolithus	crisolide	
xxxii.	Chalcedonius	calcidonice	
xxxiii.	Chrysoprasus(i)	crisopas	
xxxiv.	Cylindrus	chilindris	
xxxv.	Coranus	coramis	
xxxvi.	Cinaedia (i)	cemedia	
xxxvii.	Camaeus	cemieus	
xxxviii.	Callaica	calluca	
xxxix.	Crystallus	cristallus	
xl.	Chelidonius (i)	celidonie	
xli.	Coralium	coral	
xlii.	Cinaedia (ii)	cymydia	
xliii.	Ambra	cymbria	
xliv.	Collyria	collorus	
xlv.	Capnitis	capnices	
xlvi.	Oritis (i)	corinthe	
xlvii.	Crapodinus (i)	crapadoune	
xlviii.	Chalcophonos	caltophono	
xlix.	Galactites (i)	caladista	
l.	Corneolus	corneole	
li.	Chelonitis	calonite	
lii.	Tecolithus	cecolite	
liii.	Ceraunius (i)	ceramus	
liv.		cataricus	
lv.	Ceraunius (ii)	coparius	
lvi.	Chelidonius (ii)	cleridonius	
lvii.	Carbunculus (i)	carbuncculus	
lviii.	Chrysoprasus	crisopassus	
lix.	Adamas(ii) [(ii)	diamand	
lx.	Diadochos (i)	diadose	
lxi.	Dionysias (i)	dionisa	
lxii.	Androdamas(iv)	diodoma	
lxiii.	Liparea (i)	disparea	
lxiv.	Diadochos (ii)	deadotes	
lxv.	Daphneion	diaffinian	
lxvi.	Dionysias (ii)	dianya	
lxvii.	Dracontites	draconitidis	
lxviii.	Smaragdus (i)	esmeraude	
lxix.	Heliotropium	elitropia	
lxx.	Aetites (ii)	etite	
lxxi.	Hephaestitis(ii)	epistidio	
lxxii.	Hexacontalithos	exacontalito	
lxxiii.	Asbestos(iii) [(ii)	egestes	
lxxiv.	Enhygros	enydros	
lxxv.	Exebenus	exebenius	
lxxvi.	Hephaestitis (iii)	epetites	
lxxvii.	Hexacontalithos (iii)	excoleritos	
lxxviii.	Phrygius lapis	firigins	
lxxix.	Memnonius	fimionis	
lxxx.	Medus (i)	fedus	
lxxxi.	Phoenicitis	fensites	
lxxxii.	Pyrites (i)	florendanius	
lxxxiii.	Gagates	gete	
lxxxiv.	Hieracitis (i)	gerastie	
lxxxv.	Gagatromaeus	gagantruels	
lxxxvi.	Galactites (ii)	galactida	
lxxxvii.	Prasius (i)	garsius	
lxxxviii.	Chalazias	galcido	
lxxxix.	Hyaenia	hieme	
xc.	Macedonius	macedone	
xci.	Herinacius lapis	herimacius	
xcii.		hispannen	
xciii.	Jaspis	iaspes	
xciv.	Hyacinthus (i)	iagunce	
xcv.	Chelidonius (iii)	irunde	
xcvi.	Hyacinthus (ii)	iacincte	
xcvii.	Pantheros (i)	iapectes	
xcviii.	Hyacinthizon	iacinctornicta	
xcix.		iren	
c.		indres	
ci.		ipacon	
cii.	Hieracitis (ii)	irachie	
ciii.	Melas	molas	
civ.	Lyncurium (i)	ligurie	
cv.	Glossopetra	lange serpent	
cvi.	Liparea (ii)	laparie	
cvii.	Magnes	magnes	
cviii.	Sapphirus	saphyr	
cix.	Smaragdus (ii)	smaraddus	
cx.	Sardius	sardis	
cxi.	Sardonyx	sardonix	
cxii.	Pantheros (ii)	serpentyne	
cxiii.	Topazium	topaces	
cxiv.	Margarita	margarita	

MS. F—*continued*

cxv.	Medus (ii)	medus	cxxxi.	Crapodinus (ii)noset
cxvi.	Onichinus	onychinus		crapendien
cxvii.	Obsianus	obxianus	cxxxii.	Hieracitis (iii) niger
cxviii.	Onyx (i)	oblyx	cxxxiii.	Vitrum glas
cxix.		enysus	cxxxiv.	Oritis (ii) orides
cxx.	Melichros	melotes	cxxxv.	Onyx (ii) onicle
cxxi.	Myrrhites	merites	cxxxvi.	Opalus optalio
cxxii.	Carbunculus	rubie	cxxxvii.	Oritis (iii) orites
cxxiii.	Lychnites [(ii)	letates	cxxxviii.	Pyrites (ii) pirite
cxxiv.	Lyncurium (ii)	litugures	cxxxix.	Paeanitis (i) piante
cxxv.	Lyncurium(iii)	lincis	cxl.	Prasius (ii) prassio
cxxvi.	Lithargyrum	litigerus	cxli.	Pantheros (iii) panteros
cxxvii.	Lupi dens	lontucerius	cxlii.	Drosolithus prosultes
cxxviii.	Lapis lazuli	lasulus	cxliii.	Parius parius
cxxix.	Molochitis	molochites	cxliv.	Paeanitis (ii) proinces
cxxx.	Marmor	marble	cxlv.	Periot periot

MS. G

i.	Adamas	diamonde	xix.	Chrysoprasus crisopas
ii.	Sapphirus	saphir	xx.	Selenitis silentes
iii.	Smaragdus	emeraude	xxi.	Gagatromaeus gaganturels
iv.	Magnes	adamand	xxii.	Asbestos berumques
v.	Jaspis	iaspes	xxiii.	Chelonitis colonite
vi.	Chrysolithus	crisolite	xxiv.	Hieracitis genatides
vii.	Topazium	topase	xxv.	Oritis orides
viii.	Onyx	onicle	xxvi.	Crystallus christall
ix.	Hyacinthus	iagnuces	xxvii.	Galactites alectorie
x.	Balas	baleyes	xxviii.	Pantheros iaspes
xi.	Amethystus	amatistes	xxix.	Chalcedonius cansidoyne
xii.	Carbunculus	rubie	xxx.	Achates acate
xiii.	Alectorius	alectorie	xxxi.	Corneolus carnelyne
xiv.	Chelidonius	celidoyne	xxxii.	Crapodinus crapaudines
xv.	Heliotropium	elitrope	xxxiii.	Glossopetra tongs of adders
xvi.	Coralium	corale	xxxiv.	Gagates lince
xvii.	Beryllus	berrelle	xxxv.	Sardonyx sardonyes
xviii.	Aetites	achilles		

INDEX OF STONES

For the sake of uniformity the ·stones are indexed under their Latin names as given by Pliny, or failing him, by Isidore. Where such equivalent has not been found, the name given in the MS. is printed in italics.

o

Lithargyrum: *litigerus* F cxxvi.

Lupi dens: *lontucerius* F cxxxvii.

Lychnites: *letates* F cxxiii.

Lyncurium: *ligure* B vii; *lygur* C vii; *ligurie* F civ; *litugures* F cxxiv; *lincis* F cxxv.

Macedonius: *macedone* F xc.

Magnes: *magneten* A xiv; *magnete* B xxi: C xxi; *magnete* B xxi; C xxi; *magnes* F cvii; *adamand* G iv.

Margarita: *margarita* F cxiv.

Marmor: *marble* F cxxx.

Medus: *medus* B xxvii; *medas* D iv; *fedus* F lxxx; *medus* F cxv.

Melas: *molas* F ciii.

Melichros: *melotes* F cxx.

Memnonius: *fimionis* F lxxix.

Mocritum: A xxi.

Molochitis: *molochites* F cxxix.

Myrrhites: *merites* F cxxi.

Obsianus: *obxianus* F cxvii.

Onichinus: *onychinus* F cxvi.

Onyx: *onichinus* A vi; *onicles* B xi; *onycles* C xi; *oblyx* F cxviii; *onicle* F cxxxv; G viii.

Opalus (Ophthalmius): *apthalme* C xxxi; *ovtalmus* D i; *optalio* F cxxxvi.

Oritis: *corynthe* B xxxi; *corinthe* F xlvi; *orides* F cxxxiv; *orites* F cxxxvii; *orides* G xxv.

Paeanitis: *piante* F cxxxix; *proinces* F cxliv.

Pantheros: *panter* cxxx; *iapectes* F xcvii; *serpentyne* F cxii; *panteros* F cxli; *iaspes* G xxviii.

Parius: *parius* F cxliii.

Periot: F cxlv.

Phoenicitis: *fensites* F lxxxi.

Phrygius lapis: *firigins* F lxxviii.

Prasius: *carcius* B xxix; *garsius* F lxxxvii; *prassio* F cxl.

Pyrites: *piriten* A xvi; *florendanius* F lxxxii; *pirite* F cxxxviii.

Sagda: *hadda* B xxvi; *badda* F xxviii.

Sapphirus: *saphyrus* A ii; *safire* B v; *saphir* C v; E xiv; *saphyr* F cviii; *saphir* G ii.

Sardius: *sardius* A vii; *sardes* B i; C i; *sardius* E xvii; *sardis* F cx.

Sardonyx: *sardonix* A v; *sardoynes* B xvi; *sardoyn* C xvi; *sardonix* F cxi; *sardonyes* G xxxv.

Selenitis: *seleten* A xvii; *selinete* C xxiv; *serenice* E xvi; *silentes* G xx.

Smaragdus: *smaragdus* A iv; *emeraude* B iii; *emeraud* C iii; *smaragdus* E xv; *esmeraude* F lxviii; *smaraddus* F cix; *emeraude* G iii.

Syrtitis: *stircites* A xix.

Tecolithus: *thegolite* C xxxii; *cecolite* F lii.

Topazium: *topazius* A xi; *topace* B ii; *thopace* C ii; *thophasion* D iii; *topaces* F cxiii; *topase* G vii.

Vitrum: *uytrum*, *glas* F cxxxiii.

TABLE OF STONES

		A	B	C	D	E	F	G
1.	Achates	22	8	8			2, 7	30
2.	Adamas	13	17, 39	17		5	6, 59	1
3.	Aetites			23			4, 70	18
4.	*Akamanda*						20	
5.	Alabandica		38				10, 11	
6.	Alabastron					1	9	
7.	Alectorius	18	18	18	5	2	8	13
8.	Ambra						43	
9.	Amethystus		9	9		6	15	11
10.	Anancitis						16	
11.	Androdamas		35				3, 17, 24, 62	
12.	Anthracitis						19	
13.	Apsyctos						1	
14.	Argyrites						23	
15.	*Aristinctus*						14	
16.	Asbestos	15	25				13, 29, 73	22
17.	Assius lapis						5	
18.	Asterites					7	21	
19.	Astrion					4	22	
20.	Auripigmentum					3		
21.	Balas		13	13			30	10
22.	Beli oculus						27	
23.	Beryllus	8	12	12		8	25	17
24.	Callaica						38	
25.	Camaeus						37	
26.	Capnitis					11	45	
27.	*Capuduascum*			34				
28.	Carbunculus	12	4	4		10	57, 122	12
29.	*Cataricus*						54	
30.	Catochitis	20						
31.	Ceraunius		22	25			53, 55	
32.	Chalazias						87	
33.	Chalcedonius	3	15	15			32	29
34.	Chalcophonos						48	
35.	Chelidonius		19	19	6	9	40, 56, 95	14
36.	Chelonitis				2		51	23
37.	Chryselectrum			33				
38.	Chrysolithus		10	10			31	6
39.	Chrysoprasus	9	14	14		12	33, 58	19
40.	Cinaedia						36, 42	

TABLE OF STONES—*continued*

		A	B	C	D	E	F	G
41.	Collyria						44	
42.	Coralium			21		13	41	16
43.	Coranus						35	
44.	Corneolus		37	22			50	31
45.	Crapodinus						47, 131	32
46.	Crystallus		36				39	26
47.	Cylindrus						34	
48.	Daphneion						65	
49.	Diadochos						60, 64	
50.	Dionysias						61, 66	
51.	Dracontites						67	
52.	Drosolithus						142	
53.	Enhygros		34				74	
54.	*Enysus*						119	
55.	Exebenus						75	
56.	Gagates		20				83	34
57.	Gagatromaeus						85	21
58.	Galactites		30	29			49, 86	27
59.	Glossopetra						105	33
60.	Haematitis			28				
61.	Helitropium		23	26			69	15
62.	Hephaestitis		24	27			12, 71, 76	
63.	Herillicus						26	
64.	Herinacius lapis						91	
65.	Hexacontalithos		28				18, 72, 77	
66.	Hieracitis						84, 102, 132	24
67.	*Hispannen*						92	
68.	Hyacinthizon						98	
69.	Hyacinthus	1					94, 96	9
70.	Hyaenia		32				89	
71.	*Indres*						100	
72.	*Ipacon*						101	
73.	*Iren*						99	
74.	Jaspis		6	6			93	5
75.	Lapis lazuli						128	
76.	Liparea		33				63, 106	
77.	Lithargyrum						126	
78.	Lupi dens						127	
79.	Lychnites						123	
80.	Lyncurium		7	7			104, 124, 125	
81.	Macedonius						90	
82.	Magnes	14	21	21			107	4

TABLE OF STONES—*continued*

		A	B	C	D	E	F	G
83.	Margarita						94	
84.	Marmor						130	
85.	Medus		27		4		80, 115	
86.	Melas						103	
87.	Melichros						120	
88.	Memnonius						79	
89.	*Mocritum*	21						
90.	Molochitis						129	
91.	Myrrhites						121	
92.	Obsianus						117	
93.	Onichinus						116	
94.	Onyx	6	11	11			118, 135	8
95.	Opalus			31	1		136	
96.	Oritis		31				46, 134, 137	25
97.	Paeanitis						139, 144	
98.	Pantheros			30			97, 112, 141	28
99.	Parius						143	
100.	*Periot*						145	
101.	Phoenicitis						81	
102.	Phrygius lapis						78	
103.	Prasius		29				87, 140	
104.	Pyrites	16					82, 138	
105.	Sagda		26				28	
106.	Sapphirus	2	5	5		14	108	2
107.	Sardius	7	1	1		17	110	
108.	Sardonyx	5	16	16			111	35
109.	Selenitis	17		24		16		20
110.	Smaragdus	4	3	3		15	68, 109	3
111.	Syrtitis	19						
112.	Tecolithus			32			52	
113.	Topazium	11	2	2	3		113	7
114.	Vitrum						133	

GLOSSARY

REFERENCES TO MSS.

A = Cott. Tiberius A III (The Old English Lapidary).

B = Bodl. Douce 291 (The London Lapidary of King Philip).

C = Bodl. Add. A 106 (The North Midland Lapidary).

D = Bodl. Ashmole 1447 (The Ashmole Lapidary).

E = B.M. Add. 34360 (Richardoune's Verses).

F = Peterborough Cathedral 33 (The Peterborough Lapidary).

G = B.M. Sloane 2628 (The Sloane Lapidary).

amenused, v. pp. diminished, B xvii. [A.-Fr. *amenuser*, O.Fr. *amenuisier;* from *à* and Low Lat. **minūtiāre*, fr. Lat. *minūt-us*, lessened.]

amonestyng, n. admonishing, B x. [O.Fr. *amonester*, fr. L. Lat. *admonestāre*, variant of Lat. *admonēre*, to admonish.]

anfeld, n. anvil, B xxxix. [O.E. *anfilte*; cf. O.H.G. *anafalz*.]

ange, n. affliction, F cviii. [In O.E.D. cited only from Orm. Cf. O.N. *öngur* (pl. of **anga*); O.N. *angr*, trouble, whence *anger*.]

apeired, v. p.p. injured, F vi; **apperyng**, pres. p. C iii. [O.Fr. *empeirer*, fr· *em-* and Lat. *pēiōrāre*, to cause to become worse, deteriorate.]

apparacion, n. appearance, F ii. [Apparently formally from Lat. *apparātiōnem*, preparation. The V.A. has *apercevaunce* (one MS. *apurteynaunce*.)]

apropred, v. p.p. assigned, attributed, F lxix. [O.Fr. *aproprier*, fr. L. Lat. *adpropriāre*.]

arthetica, n. arthritis, F lxxxii. [O.Fr. *artetique*, adj., Lat. *arthrīticus*, fr. Gk., fr. ἄρθρον, a joint.]

attercop, n. spider, F cxxiii; **attorcope**, F cviii. [O.E. *attorcoppa*, fr. *attor*, poison, and *coppa*, spider; the etymology of the second element is doubtful.]

awnges, n. anguish, C iv. [O.Fr. *anguisse*, fr. Lat. *angustia*, narrowness, straitness.]

berstill, n. bristle, B x. [S.E. form, dimin. of O.E. *byrst*, bristle; cf. Dutch *borstel*.]

bile, n. boil, B v. [O.E. *bȳl*; cf. M.H.G. *biule*.]

blacerne, n. lamp, lantern, A f. 101v. [O.E. *blāc*, bright, shining; *ern*, place.]

blaces, adj. blackish, F I. [-es apparently = -ish.]

bleders, n. pl. boils, blisters, F xli. [O.E. *blǣdre, blēdre,* bladder, blister; cf. O.N. *blǎðra,* O.H.G. *blātara.*]

bolkyng, n. eructation, F xxv. [Cf. Germ. *bolken,* to roar; cognate with *belch.*]

bolnynges, n. pl. swellings, F cviii. [M.E. *bolnen,* to swell; O.N. *bolgna,* Dan. *bolne;* cognate with O.E. *belgan,* to swell.]

boystous, adj. rough, coarse, violent, F cxxix. [M.E.; etymology doubtful.]

brede, n. breadth, B f. 121v. [O.E. *brǣdu;* cf. *brād,* broad.]

bredis, n. pl. birds, F lxxi. [O.E. *briddas.*]

caduce, adj. epileptic, F xcv. [O.Fr. *caduc,* fr. Lat. *cadūcus,* falling; epileptic.]

cardeacle, n. palpitation of the heart, F cviii; **cordiacle,** F cxiv. [O.Fr. *cardiaque,* fr. Lat. *cardiaca,* 'cardiac passion,' fr. adj., fr. Gk. καρδιακός fr. καρδία, heart.]

castrons, n. pl. bezel, B f. 121v. [O.Fr. *chaston;* etymology doubtful.]

cebled, v. p.p. ? spotted, striped, F lxix. [?]

cedyng, n. boiling, seething, F xii. [O.E. *sēoðan,* to boil; cf. O.H.G. *siodan.*]

cendre, adj. ash-coloured, F ix. [O.Fr. *cendre,* ash; *cendré,* ash-coloured, fr. Lat. *cinerem,* ash, cinder.]

cerins, n. wax, C xxi. [Lat. *cēra.*]

cherkyng, n. a grating noise made with the teeth, F xxv. [O.E. *čearcian.*]

chynnes, n. pl. clefts, fissures, F cix. [O.E. *činu;* cf. M.Dutch *kēne.*]

clowce, n. small nail, F cxxxvii. [A.L. has *cloez,* pl. of *cloet,* dimin. of *clou,* fr. Lat. *clāvus,* nail.]

clypsse, n. eclipse, F lxix. [From *eclipse,* fr. O.Fr., fr. Lat., fr. Gk. εκλείπσις.]

codidiane adj. daily, quotidian, F lvi. [O.Fr. *cotidian,* fr. Lat. *cotīdiānus.*]

colours, n. pl. cholers, B vi. [O.Fr. *col(e)re,* fr. Lat., fr. Gk. χολέρα.]

conable, adj. suitable, F cxiv; **connable,** G xviii; **conabil,** C v. [Earlier *covenable,* fr. O.Fr. variant of *convenable,* fr. *co(n)venir,* to suit, agree, fr. Lat. *convenīre.*]

contrarious(e)te, n. adversity, B i, iv.   [A.-Fr. *contrariousete*, fr. Med. Lat., fr. Lat. *contrāriōsus*, adj.]

cordiacle see cardiacle.

corue, v. p.p. cut, B ii. [O.E. *ċeorfan*, p.p. *corfen*.]

contertaking, v. p.p. opposition, G v. [? counter- & take.]

courageful, adj. abounding in courage, B xi. [M.E. *courage* and *-ful*.]

creable, adj. credible, F ii. [O.Fr. *creable*, fr. Lat. *crēābilis*.]

defyneჳ, n. defence, C xvii. [O.Fr. *defens*.]

dipped, v. p.p. dyed, F ii. [O.E. *dyppan*, to dip, dye.]

disteyned, v. p.p. stained, coloured, F lxxvii. [O.Fr. *destreindre*, fr. *des-*, fr. Lat. *dis-*, and *tingere*, to dye, colour.]

diuinable, adj. capable of divining, prophesying, B xxxii. [M.E. *devine, divine*, fr. O.Fr. *deviner*, fr. Lat. *dīvīnāre*, and *-able*. Not in this sense in O.E.D.]

diuinitees, n. pl. writers on divinity, B ii. [O.Fr. *devinite*, fr. Lat. *dīvīnitātem*. Not in this sense in O.E.D.]

drechyng, n. trouble, annoyance, B xvi. [O.E. *dreċċan*, to trouble, harass.]

dropped, v. p. p. spotted, dotted, F xciii; droped, B vi, viii; droppid, F ii. [O.E. *drop(p)ian*, to drop, etc.; cf. O.H.G. *tropfōn*.]

drynkenchipe, n. drunkenness, C ix. [M.E. *drunkenship*, influenced by *drink*.]

dyscordabyll, adj. in disagreement, discordant, C xxxiv. [O.Fr. *descordable*, fr. Lat. *discordābilis*, fr. *discordāre*, to disagree.]

elyng(e)nese, n. misery, F xcvi, cxvi. [O.E. *ǣlenge*, tedious, miserable; connected with *long*.]

emitritene, n. semi-tertian fever, F cix; ennentesce, C iii. [From Low Lat. *hēmitritaeus*, fr. Gk. ἡμιτριταῖος, fr. ἡμι-, half, and τριταῖος, on the third day.]

enfourmynges, n. pl. teachings, B xii. [*inform* and *-ing*.]

ennentesce see emitritene.

enpleted, v. p.p. impleaded B xv. [*implead*.]

entached, v. p. p. provided with (good or bad) qualities, C xv; entatched, B xv; enttached, F xxxii. [O.Fr. *entachier*, fr. *en-* and *tache*, spot, mark, trait.]

entermeteþ (of), v. 3s. pres. occupies himself with, is engaged in, F xv; entermeth, B ix, C ix. [O.Fr. *entremetre*, fr. Lat. *intrōmittere*.]

eryen, v. pl. pres. plough, till, B viii. [O.E. *erian;* cf. O.H.G. *erran.*]

ey(e)rne, n. pl. eggs, F c; **yren,** F xcix. [O.E. *ǣġ(ru)*, egg(s); cf. O.H.G. *ei.*]

eysel, n. vinegar, F ix. [O.Fr. *aisil*, fr. Low Lat. *acētillum, dimin. of Lat. *acētum.*]

flawmy, v. inf. to burn, blaze, flame, F xiv. [O.Fr. *flammer, flamber*, fr. *flamme*, flame, Lat. *flamma.*]

fleame, n. phlegm, G xxxiv. [O.Fr. *fleume*, fr. Late Lat. fr. Gk. φλεγμα.]

fleme, n. river, G vii, xii; **flemme,** G xxvii; **fleume,** G xxx. [Apparently a variant of O.Fr. *flum*, fr. Lat. *flūmen.*]

flitten, v. inf. to pass away, depart, B iii. [M.E. *flitten*, fr. O.N. *flytja.*]

flume, n. river, F liii; **flom,** B iii; C iii; F ii; **flome,** F cxxii. [O.Fr. *flum*, fr. Lat. *flūmen.*]

fordoth, v. 3s. pres. destroys, B xxiv, xxxv, xxxvii. [O.E. *fordōn*, fr. *for-* and *dōn*, to do.]

fret, v. imp. s. rub, F cxxxviii. [Etymology doubtful.]

frot, v. imp. s. rub, F v; **frotith,** 3s. pres. B xxxv; **froted,** p.p. F cxxx. [O.Fr. *froter.*]

frotynge, n. rubbing, B xx. [See frot.]

gasteneȝ, n. terror, dread, C xvii. [From M.E. *gast*, afraid, fr. p.p. of O.E. *gǣstan*, to terrify, and *-ness.*]

glyme, adj. rheumy, F cxxxiii. [M.E. *gleim*, slime, rheum; etymology doubtful.]

gold, n. marigold, F ii; **goulde,** B viii. [Probably fr. *gold* (the metal).]

goldy, adj. golden, F lviii. [*gold* and *-y*].

gomes, n. pl. gums, Bv; **goomes,** Fcviii. [O.E. *gōma;* cf. O.H.G. *guomo.*]

goulde see **gold.**

goute fallyng, n. epilepsy, B xx. [Cf. Med. Lat. *gutta cadūca.*]

grenehed(e), n. greenness, B iii, F lxviii [*green* and *-head*].

grenes, n. greenness, Biii, xiv; **grennesses,** pl., Biii. [O.E. *grēnnes; green* and *-ness.*]

grifon, n. griffin, C iii; pl., **grifons** C iii; **gryffons,** B iii; **gryffonnes,** F lxviii. [O.Fr. *grifoun*, fr. Lat. *grȳphus, grȳps*, fr. Gk. γρῡψ.]

ȝexyng, n. hiccuping, F xxv; **yixing,** B xii. [O.E. *ġiscung, ġicsung*, n., fr. *ġiscian*, v.; cf. O.H.G. *geskōn.*]

harbourgh, v. inf. to entertain, harbour, B 1; **harbarowჳ,** F cx. [O.E. **herebeorgian* (cf. O.N. *herebergja,* to lodge), from *here,* army, and *beorgian,* to shelter.]

hele, v. inf. to conceal, C 1. [O.E. *helan;* cf. O.H.G. *helan.*]

herbarowჳ see **harbourgh.**

herdes, herdis, n. pl. coarse flax, F xiv. [O.E. (pl.) *heordan;* cf. Fris. *heedſ* early Mod. Dutch *herde.*]

hytereჳ, C viii [?]

iountes, n. jaundice, C vii. [O.Fr. *jaunice,* fr. *jaune,* yellow, fr. Lat. *galbinum.*]

kele, v. inf. to cool, F cviii; **kell,** C v; **kel** C xiii; 3s. pres. **kelles,** C vii. O.E. *celan,* to cool, fr. *col,* cool.]

kyndelich, adj. natural, B f. 121; **kyndely** Bx. [O.E. *cyndelic,* fr. (*ge*)*cynd,* kind, nature.]

kyndely, adv. by nature, B xi. [O.E. *cyndelice;* see **kyndelich.**]

la(m)pwynch, n. lapwing, F xcix. [O.E. *hleapewince,* fr. *hleap-an,* to run, leap, and a base **winc-,* to totter, cognate with O.H.G. *wincan,* to waver.]

laton, n. latten, C xxxiii. [O.Fr. *laton,* etymology doubtful.]

leemes, n. pl. flames, F lvii. [O.E. *leoma;* cf. O.N. *liomi.*]

lefe, adj. precious, B xxix. [O.E. *leof;* cf. O.H.G. *liob.*]

lettur, n. electrum, C vii. [O.Fr. *electre;* Lat. *electrum,* Gk. ἠλεκτρον.]

liure, n. liver, B xii. [O.E. *lifer;* cf. O.H.G. *libara.*]

loos, n. praise, B xxiii. [O.Fr. *los, loz;* Lat. *laudes.*]

lunatix, n. lunacy, F xl. [From M.E. adj. *lunatik;* fr. O.Fr., fr. L. Lat. *lunaticus.*]

lyჳe, n. flame, F xxxi. [O.E. *leg;* cf. O.H.G. *loug.*]

lyk, n. leek, F lviii. [O.E. *leac;* cf. O.H.G. *louch.*]

lyst, n. stripe, C xvi. [O.E. *liste,* border, edge; cf. O.H.G. *lista.*]

lyterg, n. litharge, F liv. [O.Fr. *litarge,* fr. Lat., fr. Gk. λιθάργυρος.]

lytted, v. p. p. dyed, stained, C x. [O.N. *lita,* to colour; cf. O.N. *litr,* colour, face.]

malsen, n. dysentery, C vi, vii. [? A mistake for *menison;* perhaps by confusion with *malison*, curse, plague.]

malues, n. pl. mallows, F cxxix. [O.F. *malve*, Lat. *malva*.]

medelynge, n. fighting, B xxiv; **medlynges**, pl., F xii. [O.Fr. *mesler*, *mesdler*, *medler*, fr. Low Lat. **misculāre*, fr. Lat *miscēre*, to mix.]

menyson, n. dysentery, B vi, vii. [O.Fr. *menison*, fr. L. Lat. *mānātiōnem*, a flowing.]

mervailes, adj. marvellous, F f. i. [O.Fr. *merveillos*, fr. n. *mervaille*, fr. Lat. *mīrābilia*.]

metynge, n. dream, B vi, xi, xvii; **metynges**, pl., B xxii; F lix. [O.E. *mǣtan*, to dream.]

moce, n. hiding-place, niche; setting, B xi; **moos**, B f. 121, 121v; **mouce**, B iv. [O.Fr. *muce*, *muche*, *mouce*, hiding-place.] The meaning may be influenced by that of *morse*, 'clasp of a cope,' though this is not recorded in English till 1404.

mysbeyng, n. misadventure, B i. [*mis-* and *being*.]

nunpower, n. powerlessness, impotence, E 8. [O.Fr. *nonpooir*; *non-* and *power*.]

opostome, n. imposthume, F viii; **postom**, F cviii; **postome**, F cxxxiii; **postomes**, pl., F cviii. [O.Fr. *aposteme*, *-tume;* Gk. ἀπόστημα.]

pardurable, adj. everlasting, B viii; **pardurabill** C xii. [O.Fr., fr. L. Lat. *perdūrābilis*.]

parsched , v. p.p. destroyed, imperilled, C xxv. [M.E. *perischen*, O.Fr. *periss-*, stem of *perir*, Lat. *perīre*, to perish.]

parscour, adj. blue, B xi. [A form of, or a mistake for, M.E. *perse*, *perske;* O.Fr. *pers*, blue, bluish-grey; Med. Lat. *persus*, *persicus*, fr. Lat. *Persia*, *Persicus*.]

peckled, v. p. p. speckled, G xxi. [Variant of *speckled;* quoted fr. 1570 in O.E.D.]

perrere, n. jeweller, B f. 121v. [O.Fr. *perrere*, fr. *pierre*, stone.]

pirnell, n. pupil (i.e. of the eye), F. xxvii. [O.Fr. *prunel*, dimin. of *prune*, Lat. *prūnum*.]

ploncket, adj. lead-coloured, B xi. [M.E. *plonket*, *plunket*, from O.Fr. *plunkié*, p. p. of *plunkier*, to cover with lead, fr. Lat. *plumbicāre*.]

post(e), n. power. **post**, F xviii; **pouste**, B xxix. [M.E. *poust(ey);* O.Fr. *pouste*, *poeste*, fr. Lat. *potestātem*.]

postom see **opostome**.

potagre, n. gout, B xxvii; F v, cvx; as adj., F lxxx. [M.E. *pot-*, *podagre*, Lat. *podager*, fr. Gk. ποδαγρός.]

prames, n. pl. prasius, F lxviii. [O.Fr. *pra(s)me*, *proesme*.]

precle, adj. dotted, freckled, C vi. [O.E. *pricel*, n. prick, point; M.E. *prikel;* from *prīcian*, to prick; cf. L. Germ. *prickel*, a sting.]

primeth, v. 3 s. pres. (of the moon) appears new, enters on its first phase, F li. [See **pryme**.]

pryme, adj. (of the moon) entering its first phase, F li. [M.E. *prime*, first, new, fr. O.Fr. *prime*, Lat. *prīmus*.]

puson, n. poison, B xiii. [M.E. *poisun, puison, puson;* O.Fr. *puison*, Lat. *pōtiōnem*, drink; poisonous drink.]

pyce, n. breast, C iii, v, viii, xi; **pyse**, C f. 45. [O.Fr. *piz, peiz*, Lat. *pectus*.]

quarre, adj. square, B f. 121v, xxxv. [O.Fr. *quarré;* Lat. *quadrātus*, square.]

qwiter, qwyter, n. pus, suppurating sore, F cxxxiii. [M.E. *quiture, qwetor;* etymology doubtful.]

resaue, v. inf. to receive, C i. [A.-Fr. *receivre*, Lat. *recipere*.]

resonneȝ, n. pl. branches, C viii. [Apparently a mistake for *rames;* see note.]

roget, adj. red, C xi. [O.Fr. *rouget*, dimin. of *rouge*, fr. Lat. *rūbeus*, red.]

roset, adj. distilled from roses: **oyle roset**, F xlvi; **oyle russeth**, B xxxi. [Late Lat. *(oleum) rosātum*.]

russetes, adj. red, reddish-brown, B xi. [O.Fr. *rousset*, dimin. of *rous*, red, Lat. *rūssum*.]

sauen, n. savin, F xxv, xxviii. [M.E., O.Fr. *savine*, Lat. *(herba) Sabīna*.]

scoymes, adj. repulsed by, squeamish of, F lx. [M.E. *squaimous, scoymous*, A.-Fr. *escoymous;* etymology doubtful.]

semblen, v. pl. pres. resemble, B v. [O.Fr. *sembler*, Lat. *simulāre*.]

sendrine, adj. ash-coloured, B xxx. [From O.Fr. *cendre*, fr. Lat. *cinerem*, ash.]

seyinctes, n. pl. bands, F lxix. [M.E. *seint*, etc., a girdle; O.Fr. *ceint;* Low Lat. *cinctum*, Lat. *cinctus*, fr. *cingere*, to gird.]

shadde, v. p. p. shed, B i. [O.E. *scēadan*, to divide, separate, shed; cf. O.Fris. *skēda*, Goth. *skaidan*.]

shewith see sueþ.

sigh, v. 3 s p. saw, B f. 121, ii, etc. [O.E. *seah*.]

sleked, v. p. p. polished, C vi. [M.E. *sleken*, variant of *sliken;* apparently cognate with O.N. *slikja*, to make sleek.]

smeke, n. fumes, F cviii. [M.E. *smek(e)*, Nthn. variant of *smech*, smoke, fumes, O.E. *smēĕ;* cf. O.E. *smēocan*, M.Dutch *smieken*, to smoke.]

smyche, n. smoke, C xx. [M.E., O.E. *smīĕ*, variant of *smec* (unexplained); see **smeke.**]

solle, n. soul, B iii. [M.E. *sowl*, O.E. *sāwol.*]

sompnes, n. pl. dreams, G i. [O.Fr. *somne*, Lat. *somnium.*]

sonderes, v. 3 s. pres. ? grows, C xxvii. [?]

sprekled, v. p. p. speckled, C viii. [M.E.; cf. Germ. (dial.) *gespreckelt.*]

sprekleȝ, n. pl. speckles, C viii. [M.E.; cf. M.H.T. *spreckel.*]

squynacye, n. quinsy, F xcv. [M.E. *squinsy*, *squina(n)cy*, Med. Lat. *squinantia.*]

stangyng, n. stinging, C i, xxviii. [O.N. *stanga,* to sting; cognate with *sting.*]

stencelettes, n. pl. sparks, F lxi. [O.Fr. *estencelette*, dimin. of *estencele*, fr. Lat. *scintilla*, spark.]

stoope, v. inf. to steep, G ii. [? Error for *steepe.*]

sueþ, v. 3s. pres. follows, F ii; **shewith,** B viii. [A.-Fr. *suer;* Low Lat. **sequere*, to follow, Lat. *sequi.*]

swendes, n. pl. dreams, F vi. [M.E. *sweven*, *swene;* O.E. *swefn*, dream; cf. O.N. *svefn.*]

tacchis, n. pl. stains, blemishes, F v; **taches** F xii; **tatches,** B ii, xvi. [O.Fr. *teche*, *tache*, mark, blemish.]

thar, v. 3 s. pres. need, must needs, B xxxi; C xii; *thare* B xiii, xxxi, xxxix. [M.E. variant of *tharf*, O.E. *þearf;* cf. O.S. *tharf*, Goth. *þarf.*]

tollen, v. inf. to draw, allure, F cvi. [M.E. *tollen*, *tullen*, etymology doubtful.]

trenche, n. colic, F xv. [O.Fr. *trencescun.*]

troubles, adj. turbid, B xv. [O.Fr. *troubleus; trouble* and *-ous.*]

ventosite, n. windiness, flatulence, F cviii. [O.Fr. fr. Lat. *ventositātem.*]

vnhilled, v. p. p. revealed, uncovered, F cix. [M.E., fr. O.E. *un-* and *hyllan*, to cover; cf. Goth. *huljan.*]

yesse, n. ice, F xxxix. [O.E. *īs.*]

yixing see **ȝexyng.**

ynde, adj. violet, B v, C iv. [O.Fr., fr. *Inde*, India.]

yren, see **ey(e)rne.**

yrene, n. spider, F cxxiii. [O.Fr. *araigne*, *iraigne*, etc.; Lat. *arāneus.*]

Early English Text Society

OFFICERS AND COUNCIL

Honorary Director
PROFESSOR NORMAN DAVIS, M.B.E.
Merton College, Oxford

J. A. W. BENNETT
PROFESSOR BRUCE DICKINS, F.B.A.
PROFESSOR P. HODGSON
MISS P. M. KEAN
N. R. KER, F.B.A.

C. T. ONIONS, C.B.E., F.B.A.
PROFESSOR J. R. R. TOLKIEN
PROFESSOR D. WHITELOCK, F.B.A.
PROFESSOR R. M. WILSON
PROFESSOR C. L. WRENN

Honorary Secretary
R. W. BURCHFIELD
40 Walton Crescent, Oxford

Bankers
THE NATIONAL PROVINCIAL BANK LTD.
Cornmarket Street, Oxford

THE Subscription to the Society, which constitutes full membership, is
£2. 2s. a year for the annual publications, from 1921 onwards, due in
advance on the 1st of JANUARY, and should be paid by Cheque, Postal
Order, or Money Order crossed 'National Provincial Bank Limited', to
the Hon. Secretary, R. W. Burchfield, 40 Walton Crescent, Oxford.
Individual members of the Society are allowed, after consultation with
the Secretary, to select other volumes of the Society's publications
instead of those for the current year. The Society's Texts can also be
purchased separately from the Publisher, Oxford University Press,
through a bookseller, at the prices put after them in the List, or through
the Secretary, by members only, for their own use, at a discount of
2d. in the shilling.

The Early English Text Society was founded in 1864 by Frederick
James Furnivall, with the help of Richard Morris, Walter Skeat, and
others, to bring the mass of unprinted Early English literature within

the reach of students and provide sound texts from which the New English Dictionary could quote. In 1867 an Extra Series was started of texts already printed but not in satisfactory or readily obtainable editions. At a cost of nearly £35,000, 159 volumes were issued in the Original Series and 126 in the Extra Series before 1921. In that year the title *Extra Series* was dropped, and all the publications of 1921 and subsequent years have since been listed and numbered as part of the Original Series. Since 1921 some eighty volumes have been issued. In this prospectus the Original Series and Extra Series for the years 1867–1920 are amalgamated, so as to show all the publications of the Society in a single list. In 1955 the prices of all volumes issued for the years up to 1936 and still available, were increased by one-fifth.

LIST OF PUBLICATIONS
Original Series, 1864–1959. Extra Series, 1867–1920
(One guinea per annum for each series separately up to 1920, two guineas from 1921)

O.S. 1. **Early English Alliterative Poems,** ed. R. Morris. 20*s.* 1864
2. **Arthur,** ed. F. J. Furnivall. 5*s.* „
3. **Lauder on the Dewtie of Kyngis, &c.,** 1556, ed. F. Hall. 5*s.* „
4. **Sir Gawayne and the Green Knight,** ed. R. Morris. (*Out of print, see* O.S. 210.) „
5. **Hume's Orthographie and Congruitie of the Britan Tongue,** ed. H. B. Wheatley. 5*s.* 1865
6. **Lancelot of the Laik,** ed. W. W. Skeat. (*Out of print.*) „
7. **Genesis & Exodus,** ed. R. Morris. (*Out of print.*) „
8. **Morte Arthure,** ed. E. Brock. 8*s. 6d.* „
9. **Thynne on Speght's ed. of Chaucer,** A.D. 1599, ed. G. Kingsley and F. J. Furnivall. 12*s.* „
10. **Merlin,** Part I, ed. H. B. Wheatley. (*Out of print.*) „
11. **Lyndesay's Monarche, &c.,** ed. J. Small. Part I. (*Out of print.*) „
12. **The Wright's Chaste Wife,** ed. F. J. Furnivall. (*Out of print.*) „
13. **Seinte Marherete,** ed. O. Cockayne. (*Out of print, see* O.S. 193.) 1866
14. **Kyng Horn, Floris and Blancheflour, &c.,** ed. J. R. Lumby, re-ed. G. H. McKnight. (*Out of print.*) „
15. **Political, Religious, and Love Poems,** ed. F. J. Furnivall. 9*s.* „
16. **The Book of Quinte Essence,** ed. F. J. Furnivall. (*Out of print.*) „
17. **Parallel Extracts from 45 MSS. of Piers the Plowman,** ed. W. W. Skeat. (*Out of print.*) „
18. **Hali Meidenhad,** ed. O. Cockayne, re-ed. F. J. Furnivall. (*Out of print.*) „
19. **Lyndesay's Monarche, &c.,** ed. J. Small. Part II. (*Out of print.*) „
20. **Richard Rolle de Hampole, English Prose Treatises of,** ed. G. G. Perry. (*Reprinted* 1920.) 7*s.* „
21. **Merlin,** ed. H. B. Wheatley. Part II. (*Out of print.*) „
22. **Partenay or Lusignen,** ed. W. W. Skeat. 7*s. 6d.* „
23. **Dan Michel's Ayenbite of Inwyt,** ed. R. Morris. (*Out of print.*) „
24. **Hymns to the Virgin and Christ; The Parliament of Devils, &c.,** ed. F. J. Furnivall. (*Out of print.*) 1867
25. **The Stacions of Rome, the Pilgrims' Sea-voyage, with Clene Maydenhod,** ed. F. J: Furnivall. (*Out of print.*) „
26. **Religious Pieces in Prose and Verse,** from R. Thornton's MS., ed. G. G. Perry. 6*s.* (*See under* 1913.) „
27. **Levins' Manipulus Vocabulorum,** a rhyming Dictionary, ed. H. B. Wheatley. 14*s.* „
28. **William's Vision of Piers the Plowman,** ed. W. W. Skeat. A–Text. (*Reprinted* 1956.) 20*s.* „
29. **Old English Homilies** (1220–30), ed. R. Morris. Series I, Part I. 8*s. 6d.* „
30. **Pierce the Ploughmans Crede,** ed. W. W. Skeat. (*Out of print.*) „
E.S. 1. **William of Palerne or William and the Werwolf,** re-ed. W. W. Skeat. (*Out of print.*) „
2. **Early English Pronunciation,** by A. J. Ellis. Part I. 12*s.* „
O.S. 31. **Myrc's Duties of a Parish Priest,** in Verse, ed. E. Peacock. (*Out of print.*) 1868
32. **Early English Meals and Manners: the Boke of Norture of John Russell, the Bokes of Keruynge, Curtasye, and Demeanor, the Babees Book, Urbanitatis, &c.,** ed. F. J. Furnivall. (*Out of print.*) „
33. **The Book of the Knight of La Tour-Landry,** ed. T. Wright. (*Out of print.*) „
34. **Old English Homilies** (before 1300), ed. R. Morris. Series I, Part II. (*Out of print.*) „
35. **Lyndesay's Works,** Part III: The Historie and Testament of Squyer Meldrum, ed. F. Hall. 2s. 6*d.* „
E.S. 3. **Caxton's Book of Curtesye,** in Three Versions, ed. F. J. Furnivall. 6*s.* „
4. **Havelok the Dane,** re-ed. W. W. Skeat. (*Out of print.*) „

2

3

The Original and Extra Series of the 'Early English Text Society'

4

E.S. 58. Caxton's Blanchardyn and Eglantine, c. 1489, ed. L. Kellner. (*Out of print.*) 1890
O.S. 96. The Old-English Version of Bede's Ecclesiastical History, re-ed. T. Miller. Part I, 2. (*Reprinted* 1959.) 30s. 1891
    97. The Earliest English Prose Psalter, ed. K. D. Buelbring. Part I. 18s. „
E.S. 59. Guy of Warwick, 2 texts (Auchinleck and Caius MSS.), ed. J.Zupitza. Part III. (*Out of print.*) „
    60. Lydgate's Temple of Glas, re-ed. J. Schick. 18s. „
O.S. 98. Minor Poems of the Vernon MS., ed. C. Horstmann. Part I. 24s. 1892
    99. Cursor Mundi. Preface, Notes, and Glossary, Part VI, ed. R. Morris. 12s. „
E.S. 61. Hoccleve's Minor Poems, I, from the Phillipps and Durham MSS., ed. F. J. Furnivall. 18s. „
    62. The Chester Plays, re-ed. H. Deimling. Part I. (*Reprinted* 1959.) 25s. „
O.S. 100. Capgrave's Life of St. Katharine, ed. C. Horstmann, with Forewords by F. J. Furnivall. 24s. 1893
    101. Cursor Mundi. Essay on the MSS., their Dialects, &c., by H. Hupe. Part VII. 12s. „
E.S. 63. Thomas à Kempis's De Imitatione Christi, ed. J. K. Ingram. (*Out of print.*) „
    64. Caxton's Godeffroy of Boloyne, or The Siege and Conqueste of Jerusalem, 1481, ed. Mary N. Colvin. 18s. „
O.S. 102. Lanfranc's Science of Cirurgie, ed. R. von Fleischhacker. Part I. 24s. 1894
    103. The Legend of the Cross, &c., ed. A. S. Napier. 15s. „
E.S. 65. Sir Beves of Hamtoun, ed. E. Kölbing. Part III. (*Out of print.*) „
    66. Lydgate's and Burgh's Secrees of Philisoffres ('Governance of Kings and Princes'), ed. R. Steele. (*Out of print.*) „
O.S. 104. The Exeter Book (Anglo-Saxon Poems), re-ed. I. Gollancz. Part I. (*Reprinted* 1958.) 30s. 1895
    105. The Prymer or Lay Folks' Prayer Book, Camb. Univ. MS., ed. H. Littlehales. Part I. 12s. „
E.S. 67. The Three Kings' Sons, a Romance, ed. F. J. Furnivall. Part I, the Text. (*Out of print.*) „
    68. Melusine, the prose Romance, ed. A. K. Donald. Part I, the Text. (*Out of print.*) „
O.S. 106. R. Misyn's Fire of Love and Mending of Life (Hampole), ed. R. Harvey. 18s. 1896
    107. The English Conquest of Ireland, A.D. 1166–1185, 2 Texts, ed. F. J. Furnivall. Part I. 18s. „
E.S. 69. Lydgate's Assembly of the Gods, ed. O. L. Triggs. (*Reprinted* 1957.) 25s. „
    70. The Digby Plays, ed. F. J. Furnivall. (*Out of print.*) „
O.S. 108. Child-Marriages and -Divorces, Trothplights, &c. Chester Depositions, 1561–6, ed. F. J. Furnivall. 18s. 1897
    109. The Prymer or Lay Folks' Prayer Book, ed. H. Littlehales. Part II. 12s. „
E.S. 71. The Towneley Plays, ed. G. England and A. W. Pollard. (*Re-issued* 1952.) 24s. „
    72. Hoccleve's Regement of Princes, and 14 Poems, ed. F. J. Furnivall. (*Out of print.*) „
    73. Hoccleve's Minor Poems, II, from the Ashburnham MS., ed. I. Gollancz. (*Out of print.*) „
O.S. 110. The Old-English Version of Bede's Ecclesiastical History, ed. T. Miller. Part II, 1. 18s. 1898
    111. The Old-English Version of Bede's Ecclesiastical History, ed. T. Miller. Part II, 2. 18s. „
E.S. 74. Secreta Secretorum, 3 prose Englishings, one by Jas. Yonge, 1428, ed. R. Steele. Part I. 24s. „
    75. Speculum Guidonis de Warwyk, ed. G. L. Morrill. 12s. „
O.S. 112. Merlin. Part IV. Outlines of the Legend of Merlin, by W. E. Mead. 18s. 1899
    113. Queen Elizabeth's Englishings of Boethius, Plutarch, &c., ed. C. Pemberton. 18s. „
E.S. 76. George Ashby's Poems, &c., ed. Mary Bateson. 18s. „
    77. Lydgate's DeGuilleville's Pilgrimage of the Life of Man, ed. F. J. Furnivall. Part I. (*Out of print.*) „
    78. The Life and Death of Mary Magdalene, by T. Robinson, c. 1620, ed. H. O. Sommer. 6s. „
O.S. 114. Ælfric's Metrical Lives of Saints, ed. W. W. Skeat. Part IV and last. 30s. 1900
    115. Jacob's Well, ed. A. Brandeis. Part I. 12s. „
    116. An Old-English Martyrology, re-ed. G. Herzfeld. 20s. „
E.S. 79. Caxton's Dialogues, English and French, ed. H. Bradley. 12s. „
    80. Lydgate's Two Nightingale Poems, ed. O. Glauning. 6s. „
    81. The English Works of John Gower, ed. G. C. Macaulay. Part I. (*Reprinted* 1957.) 40s. „
O.S. 117. Minor Poems of the Vernon MS., ed. F. J. Furnivall. Part II. 18s. 1901
    118. The Lay Folks' Catechism, ed. T. F. Simmons and H. E. Nolloth. 6s. „
    119. Robert of Brunne's Handlyng Synne, and its French original, re-ed. F. J. Furnivall. Part I. (*Out of print.*) „
E.S. 82. The English Works of John Gower, ed. G. C. Macaulay. Part II. (*Reprinted* 1957.) 40s. „
    83. Lydgate's DeGuilleville's Pilgrimage of the Life of Man, ed. F. J. Furnivall. Part II. (*Out of print.*) „
    84. Lydgate's Reason and Sensuality, ed. E. Sieper. Part I. (*Out of print.*) „
O.S. 120. The Rule of St. Benet in Northern Prose and Verse, and Caxton's Summary, ed. E. A. Kock. 18s. 1902
    121. The Laud MS. Troy-Book, ed. J. E. Wülfing. Part I. 18s. „
E.S. 85. Alexander Scott's Poems, 1568, ed. A. K. Donald. (*Out of print.*) „
    86. William of Shoreham's Poems, re-ed. M. Konrath. Part I. (*Out of print.*) „
    87. Two Coventry Corpus Christi Plays, re-ed. H. Craig. 15s. (*See under* 1952.) „
O.S. 122. The Laud MS. Troy-Book, ed. by J. E. Wülfing. Part II. 24s. 1903
    123. Robert of Brunne's Handlyng Synne, and its French original, re-ed. F. J. Furnivall. Part II. (*Out of print.*) „
E.S. 88. Le Morte Arthur, re-ed. J. D. Bruce. (*Reprinted* 1959.) 30s. „
    89. Lydgate's Reason and Sensuality, ed. E. Sieper. Part II. 18s. „
    90. English Fragments from Latin Medieval Service-Books, ed. H. Littlehales. (*Out of print.*) „
O.S. 124. Twenty-six Political and other Poems from Digby MS. 102, &c., ed. J. Kail. Part I. 12s. 1904
O.S. 125. Medieval Records of a London City Church, ed. H. Littlehales. Part I. 12s. 1904
    126. An Alphabet of Tales, in Northern English, from the Latin, ed. M. M. Banks. Part I. 12s. „
E.S. 91. The Macro Plays, ed. F. J. Furnivall and A. W. Pollard. (*Out of print.*) „
    92. Lydgate's DeGuilleville's Pilgrimage of the Life of Man, ed. Katherine B. Locock. Part III. (*Out of print.*) „
    93. Lovelich's Romance of Merlin, from the unique MS., ed. E. A. Kock. Part I. 12s. „

The Original and Extra Series of the 'Early English Text Society'

The following is a select list of forthcoming volumes. Other texts are under consideration:

April 1960

Publisher

OXFORD UNIVERSITY PRESS

The manufacturer's authorised representative in the EU for product
safety is Oxford University Press España S.A. of El Parque Empresarial
San Fernando de Henares, Avenida de Castilla, 2 - 28830 Madrid
(www.oup.es/en or product.safety@oup.com). OUP España S.A. also acts
as importer into Spain of products made by the manufacturer.
Printed and bound by CPI Group (UK) Ltd, Croydon, CR0 4YY

27/04/2026

02097696-0001